REDEEMED

through Christ

A Study of the Bible's Teachings on Redemption

By Leland M. Haines

June 2001

Bro. Petterson,
My prayer is that the Lord will bless your Bible study and preaching.
God bless,
Leland M Haines

Biblical Viewpoints Publications
16416 Sutters Lane Court
Northville, MI 48167

REDEMPTION REALIZED *through Christ*

Originally entitled *The Unfolding Plan of Redemption*

Revised edition:
Copyright 1996 by Leland M. Haines
Northville, MI 48167
All rights reserved

First edition:
Copyright 1982 by Christian Light Publications, Inc.

All Scripture quotations in this book, except those noted otherwise, are from the *King James Version* of the Bible.

Library of Congress Catalog Card Number: 96-95344

Cataloging Data:

Haines, Leland M.
   Redemption realized through Christ : a study of the Bible's teachings on redemption / Leland M. Haines
   Includes bibliography and index.
   ISBN: 1-890133-03-5
   1. Redemption   2. Bible, O. T.   3. Bible, N. T   4. Mennonites
   I. Haines, Leland   II. Title.
   BT777.H37   1996
   291.22–Dc21
                                             96–95344
                                                  CIP

This book is printed on acid-free paper.

Printed in the United States of America

                ISBN:1-890133-03-5 Paper
                      1-890133-33-7 Hardcover

Contents

Introduction	5
Preface	7
The Need for Redemption	9
Preparation for the Coming Redeemer	16
The Appearance of the Redeemer	38
Redemption Interpreted	83
Redemption Appropriated	107
Redemption Clarified	139
The Completion of Redemption	180
Bibliography	238
Index	240

Introduction

Redemption Realized through Christ

This book gives keen insights into the subject angels like to look into—REDEMPTION. Christians frequently express the idea that we will spend eternity marveling over our redemption through Jesus Christ. While that is in our future, this book is a unique arrangement of Scripture that lays before the reader the wondrous plan of redemption that is available now. It clearly shows God's plan for saving people from their sins in this life and the completion of redemption in the future. This volume reflects the author's extensive search of the Scriptures for truth that develops this crucial theme. The copious Scripture references are helpfully illuminated by objective comments and explanations. The frequent brief explanations of biblical history are presented in a manner that makes them meaningful to us. Above all, the book focuses on the need of redemption, the coming of the Redeemer, the price of redemption, and, finally, the consummation of redemption when Christ's redeemed will be with Him forever.

Every Christian should have a grasp of the past and a hopeful expectation of the future. *Redemption Realized through Christ* is an excellent study of Scripture that will help the reader to obtain this grasp on history and have a positive outlook on the future

Since the redeemed anticipate rejoicing in Christ's redemption throughout eternity, it is appropriate that special attention be given to the subject in this present life. This will enhance the glorious expectation of joining the redeemed to honor the Redeemer—the King of kings and Lord of lords.

The entrance of sin into the world robbed man of his pure fellowship with God. This book highlights God's plan to redeem the lost back to Himself. Angels cannot partake of redemption; yet they have an interest in the subject. We humans have the privilege of being able to be redeemed and restored to intimate fellowship with God. I challenge you to carefully read this excellent work and drink freely from this subject that is offered, not to angels, but to you.

I recommend it!
Simon Schrock

Preface

In our age of fast technological advances, made possible by increased knowledge of the laws that govern God's physical universe, it is tragic that so many people do not understand their spiritual relationship to God. They are essentially ignorant of the redemption brought by Jesus Christ and how to receive it. It is important to learn from Christ about His teachings on repentance, faith, the new birth, discipleship, and the Holy Spirit. Only then will we understand how to obtain salvation.

The purpose of this book is to tell what the Word of God reveals about the redemption that can be realized through Christ. To do this, we begin with the creation and the fall of man and then proceed to the call of Abraham and of Israel; to the life, death, and resurrection of Jesus Christ; to the New Testament interpretation and explanation of the redemption; and finally to the prophecies to be fulfilled in the last days. Central to this study is Christ's teaching that men must abide in Him and be faithful disciples of Him. Discipleship is a necessary part of the Christian faith (John 15:6).

To allow the Bible to tell its own story, this book contains extensive Bible quotations and references. What J. C. Wenger stated in the preface of the first book of this series equally applies to this book.

> A particular aspect of the book struck me favorably and forcibly. It is this: Quoting Scripture freely attests not only to the high view of the Bible held by the author, even more, it gives the Lord an opportunity to use His powerful Word to enable Christians to grow in their understanding of the adequacy of God's grace and in their perception of His ability to transform them into the spiritual image of His Son, the Lord Jesus.

The extensive use of Scripture in this volume is not intended to be a substitute for personal Bible study. Since the Bible is the source of the redemption message, it is hoped this book will increase interest in Bible study and serve as a guide for a study of redemption.

This volume is a major reversion of the author's book, *The Unfolding Plan of Redemption*. I wish to thank Richard Polcyn for his wealth of theological input and editing, and Lloyd Hartzler, Delbert Strubhar, and Clay Zimmerman for their proof reading and suggestions. I thank also the other brethren who reviewed this book and made suggestions for improving it.

I pray this book will help fill the vacuum in man's understanding of the Bible's message of redemption through Jesus Christ, and that it will increase interest in Bible study.
Soli Deo Gloria!

Leland M. Haines

Chapter 1

The Need for Redemption

God Created Man in His Image

"God created man in his own image, in the image of God created he him; male and female created he them" (Genesis 1:27). This sweeping statement of the creation of man is both profound and perplexing. In part it answers the question of why man is unique in all creation. But it raises questions concerning the ways man and God are similar. As he was originally created, man was as close to being like God as humanly possible. Yet at the same time man was sufficiently different to make him dependent on his Creator for knowledge and guidance.

When God created man in His own image, He gave him a distinctive nature and place in creation (Genesis 5:3; 9:6; I Corinthians 15:39; James 3:9). Man "is the image and glory of God" (I Corinthians 11:7), "made a little lower than the angels, and [God] hast crowned him with glory and honour" (Psalm 8:5; cf. Hebrews 2:9). As sovereign among the creatures, man had dominion over everything on earth (Genesis 1:26, 28).

After God created man out of the elements of the earth, He "breathed into his nostrils the breath of life; and man became a living soul" (Genesis 2:7). As a result of this divine action, man has both a material and a spiritual nature. The spiritual nature of man reflects his being created in God's image. Man was given intellect, which means he could think and reason. As a rational being, man was unique in creation and clearly distinct from the animals. The image of God in man means he was "created in righteousness and true holiness" (Ephesians 4:24; cf. Colossians 3:10). Man therefore would have had a natural tendency to do what is right. In his moral perfection, man had free and open communion and fellowship with his Maker. Man walked and talked with God.

Adam and Sin

Man was not created to be a puppet but was given the ability to choose whether he would follow his Maker's will. For his freedom to choose to be meaningful, man needed to exercise it. God provided him with the opportunity to do so. "God took the man, and put him into the garden of Eden to dress it and to keep it. And the Lord God commanded the man, saying, Of every tree of the garden thou mayest freely eat: But of the tree of the knowledge of good and evil, thou shalt not eat of it: for in the day that thou eatest thereof thou shalt surely die" (Genesis 2:15-17). At the beginning of man's existence, God revealed His will to Adam in a simple command. Now man would be able to exercise his freedom of choice. The test was simple. Adam was not forced to act either way. Choosing to obey God, however, would mean passing the test, and choosing to disobey would mean failure.

Adam and Eve were created in a perfect environment. They knew nothing of the evil that now surrounds us. Their only understanding of evil and death came by simple faith in God's Word. An angel who fell because of pride, called the devil and Satan (Isaiah 14:12-15; Ezekiel 28:15-17; I Timothy 3:6), came to Eve in the form of a serpent (II Corinthians 11:3; Revelation 12:9; 20:2). The serpent challenged Eve to rethink her acceptance of God's command to Adam. Satan lied about God's Word and said, "Ye shall not surely die: For God doth know that in the day ye eat thereof, then your eyes shall be opened, and ye shall be as gods, knowing good and evil" (Genesis 3:4, 5). Eve listened to Satan and gazed at the tree. When she "saw that the tree was good for food, and that it was pleasant to the eyes, and a tree to be desired to make one wise, she took of the fruit thereof, and did eat, and gave also unto her husband with her; and he did eat" (v. 6).

When Adam and Eve disobeyed God, they knew it. After they had disobeyed His Word, they experienced guilt and fear and then tried to hide from God. But God knew where they were and what they had done. He asked them, "Hast thou eaten of the tree, whereof I commanded thee that thou shouldest not eat?" (Genesis 3:11). Adam, in fear and despair, attempted to avoid admitting his sin by blaming

Eve. "The woman whom thou gavest to be with me, she gave me of the tree, and I did eat" (v. 12). Eve, too, tried to excuse herself: "The serpent beguiled me, and I did eat" (v. 13).

At the time of the Fall, God began to reveal man's need for redemption. The first step involved condemning the serpent, Satan's instrument, for his actions: "Because thou hast done this, thou art cursed above all cattle, and above every beast of the field; upon thy belly shalt thou go, and dust shalt thou eat all the days of thy life: And I will put enmity between thee and the woman, and between thy seed and her seed; it shall bruise thy head, and thou shalt bruise his heel" (Genesis 3:14, 15). The latter part of verse 15 is a prophecy of the redemption of man from the consequences of his sin.

Adam and Eve also were affected by God's pronouncement against sin. Despite their efforts to shift the blame, they were guilty. They had not believed and obeyed God's Word and were personally responsible for their actions. For Eve and all women since then, God's sentence has been: "I will greatly multiply thy sorrow and thy conception; in sorrow thou shalt bring forth children; and thy desire shall be to thy husband, and he shall rule over thee" (Genesis 3:16). For Adam and all men since then, God said they would have to toil and sweat for "bread, till thou return unto the ground; for out of it wast thou taken: for dust thou art, and unto dust shalt thou return" (v. 19). Paradise was lost, and man had experienced good and evil. God "sent him forth from the garden of Eden, to till the ground" (v. 23).

Because God is holy and righteous, He cannot tolerate sin in any form. Sin is an act or attitude of "missing the mark," that is, of falling short of God's standard.

The first mention of *sin* involved Cain's fruit offering, which the Lord rejected. "If thou doest well, shalt thou not be accepted? and if thou doest not well, sin lieth at the door. And unto thee shall be his desire, and thou shalt rule over him" (Genesis 4:7). Failure to please God is sin; and when sin is given the opportunity, it rules over a person. Sin creates a barrier between God and man. "Your iniquities have separated between you and your God, and your sins have hid his face from you" (Isaiah 59:2). This barrier does not leave man unaccountable for his sin. God is just and must punish disobedience. "He that doeth wrong shall receive for the wrong which he hath done" (Colossians 3:25; cf. Matthew 16:27; 25:46; John 5:29; Romans 2:6; II Corinthians 5:10; I Peter 1:17). Therefore, man was driven out of the Garden of Eden into a world that increasingly became dominated by evil. Man was now alienated from his Maker (Genesis 3:23, 24).

All Men Have Sinned

All men stand under condemnation because of Adam's disobedience. Because of his sin, all men are born with a sin nature. Adam's sin soon showed up in his son Cain and spread to all of his natural-born descendants. "God saw that the wickedness of man was great in the earth, and that every imagination of the thoughts of his heart was only evil continually.... The earth also was corrupt before God, and the earth was filled with violence. And God looked upon the earth, and, behold, it was corrupt; for all flesh had corrupted his way upon the earth" (Genesis 6:5, 11, 12; cf. 6:13).

The New Testament reveals that through Eve and Adam's actions, "sin entered into the world, and death by sin; and so death passed upon all men, for that all have sinned" (Romans 5:12). Also, "by one man's disobedience many were made sinners" (v. 19); "by man came death ... in Adam all die" (I Corinthians 15:21, 22). Because of Adam's sin, men are "by nature the children of wrath" (Ephesians 2:3), "alienated and enemies in [their] mind by wicked works" (Colossians 1:21). Every man is born with a sin nature that not only makes it possible for him to sin but insures he will. Thus men are not guilty of Adam's sin but of their own wicked works.

When Adam sinned, he blamed Eve. Part of Adam's sin was to surrender to Satan's influence through Eve. Since then natural man is described as a son of the wicked one (Matthew 13:38), with the devil as a father (John 8:44). The natural man follows Satan and is ruled by him (John:12:31; Acts 26:18; Ephesians 2:2). Satan's rule is described as "the power of darkness" (Colossians 1:13). He has "blinded the minds of them which believe not" (II Corinthians 4:4). To this day, whoever commits sin is of the devil (I John 3:8).

Satan's influence did not stop with Adam and Eve. He has continued to influence every son and daughter of Adam since. "There is no man that sinneth not" (I Kings 8:46; cf. Romans 3:9). "For there is not a just man upon earth, that doeth good, and sinneth not" (Ecclesiastes 7:20). "All we like sheep have gone astray; we have turned every one to his own way" (Isaiah 53:6).

All men "have sinned, and come short of the glory of God" (Romans 3:23). The biblical description of fallen man is appalling:

> There is none righteous, no, not one: There is none that understandeth, there is none that seeketh after God. They are all gone out of the way, they are together become unprofitable; there is none that doeth good, no, not one. Their throat is an open sepulchre; with their tongues they have used deceit; the poison of asps is under their lips: Whose mouth is full of cursing and bitterness: Their feet are swift to shed blood: Destruction and misery are in their ways: And the way of peace have they not known: There is no fear of God before their eyes. Romans 3:10-18

Romans 1:18-32 portrays an even bleaker picture of the degeneracy of man. Paul, in Galatians 5:19-21, lists more of the natural man's "works of the flesh." Those who practice such things are not a part of the kingdom of God.

The Consequence of Sin

Because natural man has "sinned, and come[s] short of the glory of God" (Romans 3:23), he must suffer the consequences of his sin. Man's sin provokes the wrath of God (1:18). Natural man is judged and punished according to his works (Matthew 16:27; John 5:29; Romans 2:8, 9; Colossians 3:25; Revelation 20:12-15). The Lord will take "vengeance on them that know not God, and that obey not the gospel of our Lord Jesus Christ: Who shall be punished with everlasting destruction from the presence of the Lord, and from the glory of his power" (II Thessalonians 1:8, 9).

The ultimate result of sin is death. God told Adam, "In the day that thou eatest thereof thou shalt surely die" (Genesis 2:17). God told our first parents after their disobedience, "for dust thou art, and unto dust shalt thou return" (3:19). The curse upon them brought physical death. Death was not limited to our first parents. Paul wrote that although "by one man sin entered into the world, and death by sin; and so death passed upon all men, for that all have sinned" (Romans 5:12; cf. v. 19). The general principle is that "the wages of sin is death" (6:23). This death is not only physical or biological, it is also spiritual, bringing eternal separation from God. But men must not despair because, as the reader will see in this book, God has acted to make it possible for men to have eternal life through His Son.

Sin Is Revealed by the Law

The Scriptures picture sin as man's disobedience to the living, personal God. Man has failed to live up to God's commandments and ideals. There are many specific scriptural principles to guide man through life. These should be thought of as expressions of God's will rather than impersonal laws.

If sin is disobedience to God's will, then man, to be chargeable or accountable for his sin, must be able to understand God's will. God reveals His will by His Word, nature, and man's conscience.

The Bible is God's most precise revelation of His will for man. Paul states this several times: "By the law is the knowledge of sin" (Romans 3:20). In Romans 7 he describes in detail the function of the law in his life. "What shall we say then? Is the law sin? God forbid. Nay, I had not known sin, but by the law: for I had not known lust, except the law had said, Thou shalt not covet" (v. 7). The law, an expression of God's will, reveals sin, for "sin is the transgression of the law" (I John 3:4).

Since the Scriptures are God's clearest revelation, those who are not acquainted with them have only a partial knowledge of God's will. "For the invisible things of him from the creation of the world are clearly seen, being understood by the things that are made, even his eternal power and Godhead; so that they are without excuse" (Romans 1:20). All men can have a knowledge of God—however imperfect—from the natural world. Yet they generally ignore this and choose to worship God's creatures rather than the Creator. God also makes His will known through man's conscience.

> When the Gentiles, which have not the law, do by nature the things contained in the law, these having not the law, are a law unto themselves: Which shew the work of the law written in their hearts, their conscience also bearing witness, and their thoughts the mean while accusing or else excusing one another. Romans 2:14, 15

The Bible teaches that there are degrees of punishment depending upon one's knowledge of God's will. Jesus, for example, noted a difference between Chorazin and Bethsaida and Tyre and Sidon: "It shall be more tolerable for Tyre and Sidon at the day of judgment, than for you" (Matthew 11:21, 22). Jesus spoke these words to the Jews who knew more about God's plan of redemption than the

Gentiles. Jesus did "mighty works" in Chorazin and Bethsaida, yet they would not repent. Their punishment therefore will be much greater than that of Tyre and Sidon, which were centers of sin. The citizens of Tyre and Sidon had opposed God's people and had blasphemously exalted themselves to the point of saying, "I am a God" (Ezekiel 28:2; see also chapters 26-28). Yet their knowledge of God's will was less than that of the people of Chorazin and Bethsaida, and this will be taken into account at the judgment. Jesus, the final Revealer and Redeemeer, stated "that [the] servant, which knew his lord's will, and prepared not himself, neither did according to his will, shall be beaten with many stripes . . . . he that knew not, and did commit things worthy of stripes, shall be beaten with few stripes" (Luke 12:47, 48).

Promise of a Hope

The ultimate consequence of sin—unless there is repentance—is depicted as strong expressions of punishment, such as wailing and weeping, gnashing of teeth, being cast into outer darkness, and enduring eternal fire (Matthew 8:l2; Luke 13:28; Matthew 22:13; 13:42, 50; 24:51, et al.). God, however, has not left man without any hope of escape. Following man's first sin, God promised that the Seed of the woman would crush Satan's power, making it possible for man's relationship with God to be restored (Genesis 3:15).

Chapter 2

Preparation for the Coming Redeemer

The Holiness and Love of God Bring Action

Holiness and love are frequently mentioned attributes of God. Other attributes are His faithfulness, forgiveness, goodness, justice, mercy, righteousness, and truthfulness. We can only know how these terms reflect and describe the nature of God by studying the Bible. This revelation expresses His personality with words that are commonly used of humans. We can only partly comprehend the meaning of these terms. We must be careful in using them not to over-simplify God's nature.

God's holiness is central to the Bible's message. God said, "I am the Lord your God: ye shall therefore sanctify yourselves, and ye shall be holy; for I am holy" (Leviticus 11:44; cf. 19:2). The Scriptures declare, "The Lord is righteous in all his ways, and holy in all his works" (Psalm 145:17). "Exalt the Lord our God, and worship at his holy hill; for the Lord our God is holy" (Psalm 99:9). "But as he which hath called you is holy, so be ye holy in all manner of conversation; because it is written, Be ye holy; for I am holy" (I Peter 1:15, 16). Jesus Christ addressed God as "Holy Father" (John 17:11) and taught His disciples to reverence God (Matthew 6:9). God's holiness is why He is separate from and hates sin (Psalms 5:5; 11:5; 45:7; Proverbs 15:9; Isaiah 59:1, 2; Habakkuk 1:12, 13).

A correct understanding of God's holiness and love is essential to rightly appreciate the plan of salvation. First, if it had not been for His holiness, God would not have had to separate Himself from sin. A plan of salvation would not have been necessary. His love could have overlooked man's weakness and disobedience. However, since

God is holy, His justice will not allow His love to overlook man's sin without the demands of His holy character being satisfied.

Second, God deals with man according to His love. God's love is His fatherly concern for mankind, and the word describes His beneficent attitude and kindness toward man. When God gave the law of Moses, He revealed Himself as "The LORD, The LORD God, merciful and gracious, longsuffering [slow to anger], and abundant in goodness and truth, Keeping mercy for thousands, forgiving iniquity and transgression and sin" (Exodus 34:6, 7; cf. Numbers 14:18; Nehemiah 9:17; Psalm 103:8; Jeremiah 32:18; Jonah 4:2). Moses told the Israelites that God "will love thee, and bless thee" (Deuteronomy 7:13; cf. 23:5; 33:3; I Kings 10:9; II Chronicles 2:11; 9:8; Psalms 97:10; 147:8; Isaiah 48:14).

In the New Testament the apostle John wrote "God is love" (I John 4:8; cf. 4:16). God's love moved Him to initiate His plan of salvation. "In this was manifested the love of God toward us, because that God sent his only begotten Son into the world, that we might live through him" (I John 4:9). "For God so loved the world, that he gave his only begotten Son, that whosoever believeth in him should not perish, but have everlasting life" (John 3:16). "God, who is rich in mercy, for his great love wherewith he loved us, even when we were dead in sins, hath quickened us together with Christ" (Ephesians 2:4, 5; see also Romans 5:6-8; 8:32). God desired to save man from sin because He loved him.

God's holiness and love worked together to bring redemption to mankind. Because God is *holy*, man separated himself from God by his sin. Because God is *love*, He promised to send a Redeemer to deliver man from sin.

God Prepares to Bless Man Through Abraham

Before the foundation of the world, God had planned for man's salvation. Christ's sacrifice "was foreordained before the foundation of the world, but was manifest in these last times for you" (I Peter 1:20). It was "promised before the world began" (Titus 1:2). "[God] hath saved us, and called us with an holy calling ... according to his own purpose and grace, which was given us in Christ Jesus before the world began" (II Timothy 1:9). Consequently, when man sinned against God in the Garden of Eden, God was ready to begin revealing His plan of redemption.

At the same time that God told man of the consequences of his sin, He told the serpent that He would "put enmity between thee and the woman, and between thy seed and her seed" (Genesis 3:15). This mention of the "seed" of the woman is the first prophecy referring to Christ. The full mystery behind Jesus Christ "was kept secret since the world began, but now is made manifest, and by the scriptures of the prophets, according to the commandment of the everlasting God, made known to all nations for the obedience of faith" (Romans 16:25, 26). This mystery unfolded progressively in the Old Testament and was completly revealed and became a reality in the New Testament.

The first step in preparing man for salvation and in bringing it to him was God's call to Abram. God spoke in a straightforward manner to him: "Get thee out of thy country, and from thy kindred, and from thy father's house, unto a land that I will shew thee: And I will make of thee a great nation, and I will bless thee, and make thy name great; and thou shalt be a blessing . . . in thee shall all families of the earth be blessed" (Genesis 12:1-3). God's call to Abram consisted of a command to go and a promise of blessings.

Abram believed God and "departed, as the Lord had spoken unto him" (Genesis 12:4). God led him "into the land of Canaan. . . . The Canaanite was then in the land. And the Lord appeared unto Abram, and said, Unto thy seed will I give this land" (vv. 5-8). God again made a promise to Abram who again believed and "builded an altar unto the Lord, and called upon the name of the Lord" (v. 8).

God's promise to Abram was threefold. It included a seed, a land, and a blessing. Abram was to become the father of a chosen people. They would receive a land where they could live separate from others and be used by God to be a blessing to all people. God repeated these promises several times to Abram (Genesis 13:16; 15:5, 7, 18). Each time Abram "believed in the Lord; and he [God] counted it to him for righteousness" (15:6).

When Abram was ninety-nine years old and still childless, God

> appeared to Abram, and said unto him, I am the Almighty God; walk before me, and be thou perfect. And I will make my covenant between me and thee, and will multiply thee exceedingly. . . . Behold, my covenant is with thee, and thou shalt be a father of many nations. Neither shall thy name any more be called Abram, but thy name shall be Abraham; for a

father of many nations have I made thee. And I will make thee exceeding fruitful, and I will make nations of thee, and kings shall come out of thee. And I will establish my covenant between me and thee and thy seed after thee in their generations for an everlasting covenant, to be a God unto thee, and thy seed after thee. . . . And God said unto Abraham, Thou shalt keep my covenant therefore, thou, and thy seed after thee in their generations. This is my covenant, which ye shall keep, between me and you and thy seed after thee; Every man child among you shall be circumcised . . . it shall be a token of the covenant betwixt me and you. Genesis 17:1-11

Circumcision was a sign to remind Abraham's descendants of their special relationship to God.

At that time God also said to Abraham,

As for Sarai thy wife, thou shalt not call her name Sarai, but Sarah shall her name be. And I will bless her, and give thee a son also of her; yea, I will bless her, and she shall be a mother of nations; kings of people shall be of her. Then Abraham fell upon his face, and laughed, and said in his heart, Shall a child be born unto him that is an hundred years old? and shall Sarah, that is ninety years old, bear? Genesis 17:15-17

Although it was difficult for Abraham to understand how God's promise could be fulfilled, he believed God, and God was faithful.

The Lord visited Sarah as he had said, and the Lord did unto Sarah as he had spoken. For Sarah conceived, and bare Abraham a son in his old age, at the set time of which God had spoken to him. And Abraham called the name of his son that was born unto him, whom Sarah bare to him, Isaac. And Abraham circumcised his son Isaac being eight days old, as God had commanded him. And Abraham was an hundred years old, when his son Isaac was born unto him. And Sarah said, God hath made me to laugh, so that all that hear will laugh with me. And she said, Who would have said unto Abraham, that Sarah should have given children suck? for I have born him a son in his old age. Genesis 21:1-7

This son was the beginning of the fulfillment of God's promise to Abraham. His faith was not disappointed; God was faithful.

Abraham's faith in God was then tested beyond any of his past experiences. He had believed God and had obeyed when called from Ur. He had believed the Lord that his descendants would be as numerous as the stars. Then God told him, "Take now thy son, thine only son Isaac, whom thou lovest, and get thee into the land of Moriah; and offer him there for a burnt offering" (Genesis 22:2). This child, through whom God's promise would be fullfilled, was to be offered. Abraham had no other son of the promise, and at his age he had little hope of having another. Abraham again trusted God and went to the mountain to offer Isaac. Abraham bound him and laid him on the altar. Just as Abraham took the knife to slay his son, the angel of the Lord appeared and said, "Lay not thine hand upon the lad neither do thou any thing unto him: for now I know that thou fearest God, seeing thou hast not withheld thy son, thine only son from me" (v. 12).

God then provided a ram, which was caught in the thickets, and Abraham offered it as "a burnt offering in the stead of his son" (Genesis 22:13). After Abraham demonstrated his faith by being willing to follow God's command unconditionally, God reconfirmed the promises He had made earlier: "In thy seed shall all the nations of the earth be blessed; because thou hast obeyed my voice" (v. 18).

God's promise to Abraham was repeated to Isaac, his son (Genesis 26:3, 4), who became the father of the twins, Esau and Jacob. Before they were born, the Lord told Rebekah their mother, "Two nations are in thy womb, and two manner of people shall be separated from thy bowels; and the one people shall be stronger than the other people; and the elder shall serve the younger" (v. 23).

God chose Jacob to receive the promise made to Abraham. Esau, the older twin, should have inherited the promise. It was his "birthright." But Jacob possessed the spirituality and leadership qualities needed to fulfill the promise. Eventually Jacob bought the birthright from Esau for some pottage (Genesis 25:29-34).

Even though he had obtained the birthright from his brother, Jacob still needed the blessing of his father, Isaac. Following the custom of the day, Isaac wished to bestow his blessing on his oldest son, Esau. He asked Esau to bring him food from the field, "that I may eat, and bless thee before the LORD before my death" (Genesis 27:7). When Jacob learned of this, he obtained the blessing with his mother's help, through deceit.

Because Jacob obtained the birthright and blessing, Esau sought to kill him. Jacob feared Esau. Upon Isaac's advice, Jacob went to his uncle Laban (Genesis 27:30-45). Before leaving, he received the blessing of Abraham (28:4). Laban welcomed him and offered him a job. There Jacob married Laban's daughters, Leah and Rachel. Jacob had twelve sons, each of whom became the father of a tribe. These twelve tribes developed into the nation Israel. God gave the name Israel to Jacob (Genesis 32:28). The promise to Abraham and Isaac was repeated to Jacob (35:10-12). God kept His promise and developed this family into His chosen nation, Israel.

The Family Becomes a Nation in Egypt

Of all his sons, Jacob loved Joseph most. Joseph's brothers hated him because his dreams foretold that he would reign over them. When the opportunity came, Joseph's brothers considered killing him, but at the last moment they sold him as a slave to merchants heading for Egypt (Genesis 37).

In Egypt, Joseph rose from servant to governor through God's providence. Because of God-given ability to interpret dreams (Genesis 41:16), Joseph was put in charge of Egypt's storehouses, which he had filled with food in preparation for a coming famine.

Back in Canaan, Jacob and his eleven sons soon faced starvation. Stories of plenty in Egypt brought Joseph's brothers there for food. Through these circumstances, Jacob and his family were saved from starvation in Canaan. As they left to go to Egypt, Jacob received assurance from God that his descendants would again return to the Promised Land, Canaan (Genesis 46:3, 4).

Egypt became Israel's home for four hundred and thirty years, and there Jacob's family prospered. The Egyptians held the Israelites in high honor because of Joseph's part in saving the Egyptians from the famine. The Israelites "were fruitful, and increased abundantly, and multiplied, and waxed exceeding mighty; and the land was filled with them" (Exodus 1:7).

Then the tide turned against the Israelites.

> There arose up a new king over Egypt, which knew not Joseph. And he said unto his people, Behold, the people of the children of Israel are more and mightier than we: Come on, let us deal wisely with them; lest they multiply, and it come to pass, that, when there falleth out any war, they join also unto our enemies, and fight against us, and so get them up out of the land. Therefore they did set over them taskmasters to afflict them with their burdens. . . . The more they afflicted them, the more they multiplied and grew. And they were grieved because of the children of Israel. And

the Egyptians made the children of Israel to serve with rigour: And they made their lives bitter with hard bondage. Exodus 1:8-14

As if this was not enough, the king of Egypt took a much harsher step. He ordered the midwives to kill all the sons born to the Hebrew women, but the midwives did not follow his orders (Exodus 1:15-22).

Moses and the Exodus

The Lord knew of the Hebrews' coming oppression, and He prepared a deliver, Moses. God used the order involving the midwives to bring Moses into Pharaoh's palace in preparation for leading the Hebrews to the Promised Land. Thus God's love and mercy were manifested to His people:

> The children of Israel sighed by reason of the bondage, and they cried, and their cry came up unto God by reason of the bondage. And God heard their groaning, and God remembered his covenant with Abraham, with Isaac, and with Jacob. Exodus 2:23, 24

At the right time, God called Moses to go to His people and deliver them from bondage in Egypt. He told Moses to gather the elders, go to the king of Egypt, and request that the Hebrews be allowed to go on a three-day journey to sacrifice to their God. Moses knew Pharaoh would not permit them to go for fear of losing authority over the people. God afflicted the Egyptians with ten plagues before Pharaoh would let the Hebrews leave (Exodus 3-12). The plagues came one after another, yet Pharaoh did not let the people go. Only after the tenth plague, which involved the death of all the firstborn of the Egyptians, did Pharaoh finally change his mind.

God instituted the Passover to symbolize His redemption of them from Egypt. Each Israelite family was to slay a lamb and put some of its blood on the doorposts of their house. The blood distinguished the Israelites from the Egyptians.

> The blood shall be to you for a token upon the houses where ye are: and when I [God] see the blood, I will pass over you, and the plague shall not be upon you to destroy you, when I smite the land of Egypt. And this day shall be unto you for a memorial; and ye shall keep it a feast to the Lord throughout your generations; ye shall keep it a feast by an ordinance for ever. Exodus 12:13, 14

Moses and the Israelites did as God commanded. The firstborn from the family of Pharaoh to the family of the most humble Egyptian peasant died. This tragedy changed Pharaoh's heart. He told the Israelites, "Take your flocks and your herds, as ye have said, and be gone; and bless me also" (Exodus 12:32).

"Six hundred thousand on foot that were men, beside children" left Egypt (Exodus 12:37). The time the children of Israel were in Egypt "was four hundred and thirty years" (v. 40). Through these years God multiplied seventy Israelites into a nation of six hundred thousand men, not to mention women and children.

The Giving of the Law at Sinai

"In the third month, when the children of Israel were gone forth out of the land of Egypt, the same day came they into the wilderness of Sinai" (Exodus 19:1). They camped at the base of Mount Sinai for eleven months. The record of events of the children of Israel there is given in Exodus 19 to Numbers 9.

At Sinai God again called Moses and further revealed His will for Israel, entering into a covenant relation with them that demanded their complete and total allegiance in life. In return God would have close fellowship with His people. During this time, Moses met with God on seven occasions. At the first meeting God told Moses:

> Thus shalt thou say to the house of Jacob, and tell the children of Israel; Ye have seen what I did unto the Egyptians, and how I bare you on eagles' wings, and brought you unto myself. Now therefore, if ye will obey my voice indeed, and keep my covenant, then ye shall be a peculiar treasure unto me above all people: for all the earth is mine: And ye shall be unto me a kingdom of priests, and an holy nation. Exodus 19:3-6

Moses spoke these words first to the elders and then to the people, who responded, "All that the LORD hath spoken we will do" (Exodus 19:8). The people's acceptance of God's words confirmed the covenant between them and God. Things would be different now. The Israelites were to be God's chosen people, they were to obey Him forever, and they were to be an example to others so they too could know God. The people's acceptance of God's words was important in making them a great nation whereby God could bless all the peoples of the earth.

At Mount Sinai, God revealed His will, which included the Ten Commandments. These Commandments, found in Exodus 20:3-17, were central to God's law. The first four deal with man's relationship to God, and the next six with man's relationship to man:

1. Thou shalt have no other gods before me.
2. Thou shalt not make unto thee any graven image . . . Thou shalt not bow down thyself to them, nor serve them.
3. Thou shalt not take the name of the Lord thy God in vain.
4. Remember the sabbath day, to keep it holy.
5. Honour thy father and thy mother: that thy days may be long upon the land which the Lord thy God giveth thee.
6. Thou shalt not kill.
7. Thou shalt not commit adultery.
8. Thou shalt not steal.
9. Thou shalt not bear false witness against thy neighbour.
10 Thou shalt not covet . . . any thing that is thy neighbour's

During the eleven months at Sinai, God revealed other ordinances that constituted the basic civil law in Israel (Exodus 21-23).

Moses told the people "all the words of the LORD, and all the judgments: and all the people answered with one voice, and said, All the words which the LORD hath said will we do" (Exodus 24:3). Moses wrote the words into the book of the covenant. After he reread them to the people, they again responded, "All that the LORD hath said will we do, and be obedient" (v. 7). He took the blood of sacrificed oxen, sprinkled it on the people, and then said, "Behold the blood of the covenant, which the LORD hath made with you concerning all these words" (v. 8). Through this covenant the Lord established His rule over Israel.

At this time the Lord also gave Israel instructions for the tabernacle. This tent was to serve as a sanctuary and a place of worship and offering of sacrifices. This sanctuary was the dwelling place of God among His people and was also the place where the tablets of the law were kept.

Each small detail of the tabernacle was revealed by God; no part was designed by man (Exodus 25-27). The tabernacle was situated in a courtyard that could be entered only through one door on the east side. One first entered near the altar of burnt offerings, where the sacrifices were offered. Farther ahead stood the laver, a large round bowl used by the priests for ceremonial washing and cleansing before they entered the tabernacle.

The tabernacle itself, a comparatively small, rectangular building (about 45 by 15 feet), stood at the west end of the courtyard. It was divided into two chambers. The first or outer chamber contained the golden candlestick, the table of shewbread, and the altar of incense. The second or inner chamber, the Holy of Holies, was separated from the Holy Place by a heavy curtain or veil. The central feature of the tabernacle, the ark of the covenant, was located in the Holy of Holies. On the lid of the ark, which was also known as the mercy seat, were two cherubim of gold. Their wings were outstretched toward each other, and their gaze was fixed downward on the mercy seat.

God dwelt as King among His people in the Holy of Holies. The high priest could go into His presence only once a year, on the Day of Atonement. On that day the high priest, enshrouded by a cloud of incense, entered with sacrificial blood to make atonement for his and the people's sins (Leviticus 16:11-17; Hebrews 9:7).

Aaron was the first high priest. His four sons also became priests. Two of these sons illegally burned incense and died because of their sin (Leviticus 10:1-5). The priesthood continued through the remaining two sons. They were to "teach the children of Israel all the statutes which the Lord hath spoken unto them by the hand of Moses" (Leviticus 10:11; cf. 10:6-20). The priesthood is described in Exodus 28 and 29.

Later the tribe of Levi was given the priesthood duties for remaining faithful when Israel rebelled by making the golden calf (Exodus 32:25-29). The Levites' priestly calling was to be of service to the tabernacle.

> At that time the Lord separated the tribe of Levi, to bear the ark of the covenant of the Lord, to stand before the Lord to minister unto him, and to bless in his name, unto this day. Wherefore Levi hath no part nor inheritance with his brethren; the Lord is his inheritance, according as the Lord thy God promised him. Deuteronomy 10:8, 9

They were consecrated for this service in a special ceremony (Exodus 29; Leviticus 8).

The priests officiated three kinds of offerings at the tabernacle: a drink offering, a meal offering, and an animal offering or sacrifice.

The animal offering was central. Depending on the person's resources, a bull, sheep, goat, or dove—free from blemish—was sacrificed. The blood, which made the atonement for the sins (Leviticus 1:4; 17:11), was sprinkled around the altar. The altar fire consumed the rest of the animal.

Educational Functions of the Law

Israel could not see the purpose of the law, the tabernacle, and the sacrificial offerings. The nation of Israel was the fulfillment of the promise God made to Abraham that his descendants would be a great nation and a blessing to all nations. The religious institutions in Israel served a purpose for the Jewish people at the time and were also a shadow of events to come (Colossians 2:16, 17; Hebrews 8:5; 10:1).

The law, the tabernacle, and the offerings or sacrifices were to have an educational function. Through them the Jewish people—and later all mankind—were to learn of God's will and thus become aware of sin and the need of redemption (the deliverance from the bondage and consequences of sin). Paul, an apostle of Jesus Christ, wrote that the Jews knew God's will by having "the form of knowledge and of the truth in the law" (Romans 2:20), and "by the law is the knowledge of sin" (3:20). God called for perfect obedience to the law. "Ye shall do my judgments, and keep mine ordinances, to walk therein: I am the Lord your God. Ye shall therefore keep my statutes, and my judgments: which if a man do, he shall live in them" (Leviticus 18:4, 5). This call for obedience could bring "a blessing and a curse; A blessing, if ye obey the commandments of the Lord your God, which I command you this day: And a curse, if ye will not obey the commandments of the Lord your God" (Deuteronomy 11:26-28). The curse sin brought was death: "The soul [person] that sinneth, it [he] shall die" (Ezekiel 18:4, 20).

The structure of the tabernacle revealed to man the realities of sin, its effect on man's relationship with God, and the means for man to come into the presence of God. The tabernacle, God's dwelling place, could be entered through only one door in the wall surrounding the courtyard and only by passing the altar and the laver. These items taught man the steps he needed to take before he could enter into God's presence.

Through the tabernacle the Israelites learned that their sins prevented their entrance into God's presence and that God's holiness, righteousness, and justice demanded that the sinner must die. The tabernacle taught man that only the death of a clean substitute could satisfy God's justice. The altar spoke of this substitute's death. The blood of the sacrifice, representing life, served this purpose. "The life of the flesh is in the blood: and I have given it to you upon the altar to make an atonement for your souls: for it is the blood that maketh an atonement" (Leviticus 17:11). The writer of the Book of Hebrews summarized this: "And almost all things are by the law purged with blood; and without shedding of blood is no remission" (Hebrews 9:22). The full meaning of the sacrifice and its blood was revealed progressively to the Jews.

The laver stood midway between the altar and the tabernacle. Only the priests could enter the tabernacle, and only after they had undergone a ceremonial cleansing at the laver. This ritual washing taught that more was required than the sacrifice at the altar before man could enter into God's presence. There needed to be a "washing of regeneration" that cleansed the person and made him a "new creature" (John 3:3-7; Titus 3:5; II Corinthians 5:17).

After the sacrifice at the altar and the cleansing at the laver, the priest could enter into the tabernacle's first chamber. On the right stood the table with the twelve loaves of the shewbread, "presence bread," or "the continual bread." This bread was "before the Lord continually" (Leviticus 24:8), signifying the constant communion between God and His people. On the left stood the golden candlesticks, giving the only light in the Holy Place. By this light the priests were able to serve God. The altar of incense stood before the veil that separated the Holy Place and the Holy of Holies. There incense was burned to signify prayer and worship.

The ark and mercy seat stood in the Holy of Holies, which was entered only once a year on the "day of atonement" (Leviticus 16). On that day two goats were brought before God, and lots were cast to determine which one would be sacrificed and which one would be the "scapegoat." The sacrificed goat's blood was sprinkled before and upon the mercy seat. This made an "atonement for the holy place, because of the uncleanness of the children of Israel, and because of their transgressions in all their sins" (v. 16). Aaron was to lay his hands on the head of the live goat, confessing over him all the iniquities of the children of Israel, and sending him away into the wilderness (v. 21). The first goat symbolized the covering of sins at the mercy seat, and the second goat symbolized the removal of sins by the sacrifice of the coming Christ.

The Promised Land and Its Lessons

The Jewish people spent about one year camped at Mount Sinai. After they received the law and built the tabernacle, God appeared to them in and guided them by the "pillar of cloud" (Exodus 14:24; 33:9, 10; 40:34-37; et al.) to the Promised Land. As the Israelites neared their destination, they sent twelve men to spy out the land of Canaan. These brought back a report that the land "floweth with milk and honey . . . [yet] the people be strong that dwell in the land, and the cities are walled, and very great." Only two said, "Let us go up at once, and possess it; for we are well able to overcome it" (Numbers 13:27-30). The people doubted and murmured against Moses and Aaron. They asked, Why "hath the Lord brought us unto this land, to fall by the sword? . . . were it not better for us to return into Egypt?" (14:3, 4). Because of rebellion and lack of trust, those men "from twenty years old and upward" that murmured against God would die in the wilderness.

For forty years the Israelites wandered in the wilderness because of their refusal to enter Canaan. Near the end of the period, when the people were at Kadesh, there arose a shortage of water; and the people again murmured against Moses and Aaron. The Lord appeared to Moses and Aaron and told them to assemble the people and to speak "unto the rock before their eyes; and it shall give forth his water" (Numbers 20:8). Moses, instead of speaking to the rock, struck it with his rod. Because of his disobedience, Moses was not allowed to bring the Israelites into the Promised Land.

In the fortieth year of the wilderness wanderings, Moses spoke to the people to prepare them to enter the Promised Land. He told them that their God was jealous and yet gracious. They were to follow His plan to take the Promised Land and to utterly destroy the inhabitants (Deuteronomy 2:34; 7:2). They were warned that if they made graven images, they would perish from the land, and only a few would be left to be scattered among the nations (chap. 4). The Israelites were to keep God's statutes and commandments. They were reminded that God "brought [them] forth out of the land of Egypt, from the house of bondage," and that they should "fear the Lord [their] God, and serve him" (6:12, 13). Then Moses told the people "that the Lord thy

God giveth thee not this good land to possess it for thy righteousness; for thou art a stiffnecked people" (9:6). The Canaanites possessing the land were driven out because of their exceeding wickedness. The land would be given to the Israelites to fulfill the promise made to Abraham, Isaac, and Jacob (chap. 9).

At the Lord's instructions, Moses commissioned Joshua as his successor (Numbers 27:18-23). After Moses' death Joshua took command of the people. The Lord told him to "go over this Jordan, thou, and all this people, unto the land which I do give to them." He promised that no man "would be able to stand before [them]" (Joshua 1:2, 5).

Joshua struck the land at Jericho, a strong, fortified city located in the middle of Canaan. Only by God's direct help were the Israelites able to take the city. The Lord appeared to Joshua and assured him of His presence and victory, after which He gave Joshua explicit instruction on how to take the city. Joshua was to have his armies march around the city in silence each day for six days, followed by seven trumpet-blowing priests, the ark of the covenant, and a rear guard. On the seventh day the people were to march around the city seven times with the priests blowing the trumpets. After the seventh trip, the priests were to sound a long blast, and the people were to give a great shout. God would then miraculously cause the walls of the city to fall flat. The people followed these instructions, and the walls fell, and the people took the city (Joshua 6).

After the fall of Jericho, Israel's next step met with disaster. This defeat, which happened because of disobedience to God's commands, taught the Israelites the lesson that God required absolute obedience (Joshua 7, 8). Israel's next battles were successful, for God was with them. When Israel faced five kings of Canaan in battle, God caused the sun to stand still to allow time for Joshua's complete victory (chaps. 9, 10). After this battle Joshua defeated a coalition of the northern kings, giving him control over the whole land (chaps. 11, 12). The land of Canaan was then divided among the eleven tribes of Israel. The tribe of Levi did not receive land, (14:4; cf. chaps. 13-20). Because they remained faithful when the golden calf was made at Mt. Horeb, they served in the tabernacle (Exodus 32).

When Joshua was old, he summoned Israel's elders and judges and addressed them. He told them to observe all that was written in the law of Moses, to keep separate from the nations around them, and to love the Lord their God. Joshua warned the leaders that the Lord would not continue to drive the remaining nations out of the land if the Israelites turned back and joined with any remaining remnants of the nations around them. The Israelites would perish from the good land given to them (Joshua 23, 24).

After Joshua died, the people entered into cycles of good and evil: "The children of Israel did evil in the sight of the Lord ... they forsook the Lord God of their fathers ... and followed other gods" (Judges 2:11, 12). Whenever the anger of the Lord was kindled against His people because of their sins and they fell under the power of the nations around them, the Israelites would cry out to the Lord, and He would raise up a judge to deliver them. Then after a short time the people would repeat the cycle. The Book of Judges tells of several such cycles. It was difficult for the Israelites to learn that God was holy and righteous and wanted them to obey Him.

Judges and Kings

The Book of Judges ends with a significant observation: "In those days there was no king in Israel: every man did that which was right in his own eyes" (21:25). Israel was without a king, unlike the nations around them. Israel's government was supposed to be a theocracy: God was to rule over them through His Word and His judges. Yet the people refused to listen and obey but instead did what they thought was right.

When Samuel, the last judge, became old, he appointed his sons as judges. But "his sons walked not in his ways, but turned aside after lucre, and took brides, and perverted judgment" (I Samuel 8:1-3).

The elders of Israel, disturbed by the corrupt conduct of Samuel's sons, appealed to him to give them "a king to judge us like all the nations" (I Samuel 8:5). This displeased Samuel. The Lord told him this call for a king was due to their rejection of Him. Samuel warned the people of the dangers of having a king, but they refused to listen to him. They continued to insist on having a king, and finally God allowed them to have one. Instead of the kings bringing justice and righteousness to the nation, however, they often caused the people to reject God and to fall into sin.

The first of Israel's kings was Saul (I Samuel 9:16, 17). Samuel spoke to the people about their desire for a king. He reminded them they wanted "a king [to] reign over us: when the LORD your God was your king. Now therefore behold the king whom ye have chosen, and whom ye desired! and, behold, the Lord hath set a king over you" (I Samuel 12:12, 13). He then told them, "If ye will fear the Lord, and serve him, and obey his voice, and not rebel against the commandment of the Lord, then shall both ye and also the king that reigneth over you continue following the Lord your God: But if ye will not obey . . . then shall the hand of the Lord be against you, as it was against your fathers" (vv. 14, 15).

What did their king do? Although Saul was divinely chosen, he had weaknesses. These are evident when he chose three thousand men to go against the Philistines and was met with a superior force and routed. Not waiting for Samuel, Saul offered a burnt offering on his own. Samuel told Saul, "Thou has done foolishly: thou has not kept the commandment of the Lord thy God" (I Samuel 13:13). Because of this Saul learned that his "kingdom shall not continue" (v. 14). This did not stop Saul from being foolish. He made a second mistake. He sought to kill his son Jonathan for unknowingly eating after his father had commanded his men to abstain from food while in battle (14:24, 27, 39). Saul soon showed incomplete obedience to the Lord by not destroying all of Amalek. Because of this rebellion and stubbornness, and because of rejecting the Word of the Lord, the Lord "rejected thee [Saul] from being king" (15:23). These experiences show that having a king did not solve Israel's problems.

Israel's second king, David, was devoted to God and followed His ways, although not without sin. God used David to unite the twelve tribes into one strong kingdom. He became the central figure of Old Testament history. God rewarded David's service with a promise that He would establish David's house forever (II Samuel 7). As God used Abraham to found the Messianic nation, He used David to bless the world by being the head of the Messianic family. The plan for ONE GREAT KING to come from David's family to redeem man gradually began to unfold.

The golden age of Israel occurred during the reign of Solomon, David's second son and successor. This golden age did not last long. One hundred and twenty years after its beginning, the kingdom divided into two parts. The division resulted from the apostasy of Solomon, who accommodated the pagan shrines of his many foreign wives. The Northern Kingdom, consisting of ten tribes, was called Israel; the Southern Kingdom of two tribes was called Judah.

The Northern Kingdom departed from God and fell into idolatry. None of its kings brought the people back to God. God warned the people by prophets to turn from their evil ways and to keep His commandments. "Notwithstanding they would not hear" (II Kings 17:14). Therefore, two hundred years after the division, God allowed Assyria to defeat the Northern Kingdom. These ten tribes were carried off, never to return as a nation.

The Southern Kingdom, Judah, was saved from destruction by Assyria through listening to the Prophet Isaiah's message (II Kings 19). God defended Jerusalem because of His promise to David. Yet at this time Isaiah prophesied that "the days come, that all that is in thine house . . . shall be carried into Babylon" (II Kings 20:17). The Southern Kingdom entered into a cycle of worshiping idols and then reforming. Finally the people passed the point of no return. Then Jeremiah brought them the message that Judah had become more wicked than Israel had been. The people of Judah did not realize the significance of Israel's example for them and were carried into captivity by Babylon as prophesied by Isaiah.

After seventy years in captivity, Babylon was overthrown by the Persians, and the Jews returned to Palestine. The captivity cured them of idolatry. After the return, Ezra read the law to the people and, with the aid of the Levites, "caused the people to understand the law" (Nehemiah 8:7). This brought a great revival to the remnant of believers. "Israel separated themselves from all strangers, and stood and confessed their sins, and the iniquities of their fathers" (9:2; see chaps. 8, 9).

The Prophets and the Messianic Message

Throughout Israel's history prophets arose with divine explanations of what was happening and with assurances that the people's failures did not end God's redemptive plan. The failures may appear to have slowed God's plan, but in the fullness of time it would still be carried out.

God did not give up on His people. He sent sixteen prophets who gave seventeen of the Old Testament books from Isaiah to Malachi. This prophetic period began at the time of Solomon's reign, when the apostasy of the ten tribes occurred. The greatest period of activity came just prior to Judah's overthrow, when Nebuchadnezzar, the king of Babylon, captured Jerusalem. Thirteen prophets were

Preparation for the Coming Redeemer

associated with the time of destruction (606-586 B.C.) and three with the time of restoration (536-444 B.C.).

In addition to foretelling judgment on Israel, the prophets had much to say concerning Israel's idolatry, political corruption, and immorality. The prophets also brought messages concerning the Seed promised in Genesis 3:15, although they did not understand all the details of God's redemptive plan. About this "salvation the prophets have inquired and searched diligently, who prophesied of the grace that should come unto you: Searching what, or what manner of time the Spirit of Christ which was in them did signify, when it testified beforehand the sufferings of Christ, and the glory that should follow" (I Peter 1:10, 11).

Isaiah, who prophesied at the time the Northern Kingdom was destroyed by the Assyrians, wrote the first and the largest of the prophetic books. His prophecy contains some of the clearest Messianic passages in the Old Testament. "He [Isaiah] saw his [Christ's] glory" from afar (John 12:41). Some of Isaiah's prophecies concerning Christ are:

> Behold, a virgin shall conceive, and bear a son, and shall call his name Immanuel [7:14], which being interpreted is, God with us. Matthew 1:23

> Afterward ... beyond Jordan, in Galilee of the nations. The people that walked in darkness have seen a great light. 9:1, 2, also referred to in Matthew 4:15, 16—this is a prophecy of His ministry to the Gentiles.

> Unto us a child is born, unto us a son is given: and the government shall be upon his shoulder: and his name shall be called Wonderful, Counsellor, The mighty God, The everlasting Father, The Prince of Peace. 9:6

> The voice of him that crieth in the wilderness, Prepare ye the way of the LORD, make straight in the desert a highway for our God. 40:3—this describes a forerunner; see Matthew 3:3

> He is despised and rejected of men; a man of sorrows, and acquainted with grief: and we hid as it were our faces from him; he was despised, and we esteemed him not. Surely he hath borne our griefs, and carried our sorrows: yet we did esteem him stricken, smitten of God, and afflicted. But he was wounded for our transgressions, he was bruised for our iniquities: the chastisement of our peace was upon him; and with his stripes we are healed. All we like sheep have gone astray; we have turned

every one to his own way; and the LORD hath laid on him the iniquity of us all. He was oppressed, and he was afflicted, yet he opened not his mouth: he is brought as a lamb to the slaughter, and as a sheep before her shearers is dumb, so he openeth not his mouth. He was taken from prison and from judgment: and who shall declare his generation? for he was cut off out of the land of the living: for the transgression of my people was he stricken. And he made his grave with the wicked, and with the rich in his death; because he had done no violence, neither was any deceit in his mouth. Yet it pleased the Lord to bruise him; he hath put him to grief: when thou shalt make his soul an offering for sin, he shall see his seed, he shall prolong his days, and the pleasure of the LORD shall prosper in his hand. He shall see of the travail of his soul, and shall be satisfied: by his knowledge shall my righteous servant justify many; for he shall bear their iniquities. Therefore will I divide him a portion with the great, and he shall divide the spoil with the strong; because he hath poured out his soul unto death: and he was numbered with the transgressors; and he bare the sin of many, and made intercession for the transgressors. 53:3-12

And the Gentiles shall see thy righteousness, and all kings thy glory: and thou shalt be called by a new name, which the mouth of the LORD shall name. 62:2

For the Lord GOD shall slay thee, and call his servants by another name. 65:15—God's people will be known by a new name.

Jeremiah came one hundred years after Isaiah and prophesied to Judah before the nation fell to Babylon. After the fall, he brought hope of a new covenant that would put God's law into their hearts:

Behold, the days come, saith the LORD, that I will make a new covenant with the house of Israel, and with the house of Judah: Not according to the covenant that I made with their fathers in the day that I took them by the hand to bring them out of the land of Egypt; which my covenant they brake, although I was an husband unto them, saith the LORD: But this shall be the covenant that I will make with the house of Israel; After those days, saith the LORD, I will put my law in their inward parts, and write it in their hearts; and will be their God, and they shall be my people. And they shall teach no more every man his neighbour, and every man his brother, saying, Know the LORD: for they shall all know me, from the least of them unto the greatest of them, saith the LORD: for I will forgive their iniquity, and I will remember their sin no more. Jeremiah 31:31-34; see also Hebrews 8:8-12

Preparation for the Coming Redeemer

Other Messanic prophecies are:

> And it shall come to pass afterward, that I will pour out my spirit upon all flesh. Joel 2:28—this out-pouring occurred at Pentecost; see Acts 2

> But thou, Bethlehem Ephratah, though thou be little among the thousands of Judah, yet out of thee shall he come forth unto me that is to be ruler in Israel; whose goings forth have been from of old; from everlasting. Micah 5:2—this speaks of the birthplace of the Messiah; see Matthew 2

> I will bring forth my servant the BRANCH . . . I will remove the iniquity of that land in one day. Zechariah 3:8, 9

> Thy King cometh unto thee: he is just, and having salvation; lowly, and riding upon an ass. Zechariah 9:9; see John 12:15

These prophecies, along with others (thirty pieces of silver, Zechariah 11:12—see Matthew 27:3; his hands pierced, Zechariah 12:10; 13:6; cf. John 19:37; the Smitten Shepherd, Zechariah 13:7; cf. Matthew 26:31; Mark 14:27), give details of Christ's life that were literally fulfilled at His first coming.

Malachi, the last Old Testament book, describes the final preparation for the Messiah. "Behold, I will send my messenger, and he shall prepare the way before me" (Malachi 3:1). "Behold, I will send you Elijah the prophet before the coming of the great and dreadful day of the Lord: And he shall turn the heart of the fathers to the children, and the heart of the children to their fathers, lest I come and smite the earth with a curse" (4:5, 6). This prophecy of Elijah was fulfilled in John the Baptist's ministry (see Matthew 3; 17:11-13).

After the promise and plan for Christ's coming had been given, no prophetic voice was heard for four hundred years. This was a period to study the details of the written Word concerning this plan. Great reverence for the Scriptures existed among the Jews. The synagogue, which came into prominence during the Babylonian captivity, became important as a center of Sabbath worship and a meeting place. The Gospels show that many synagogues existed throughout Palestine, and Acts show they existed in many other parts of the Roman world. Here the Scriptures were read and discussed. Its leaders, the elders, exercised discipline and oversaw the people's morals.

During this four-hundred-year period, the Jews were scattered throughout the known world. This prepared them to fulfill their mission to make known the Hope of Israel.

In the Fullness of Time

Finally, "when the fulness of the time was come, God sent forth his Son, made of a woman, made under the law, to redeem them that were under the law" (Galatians 4:4, 5). The plan of redemption was fulfilled when all the conditions were right—when the proper political, economic, moral, and religious conditions converged. The time was right for the rapid spread of the Good News of God's provision for redeeming lost man from his sinful condition. Some of the conditions contributed to "the fulness of the time" were:

1. Politically, the world was unified under the Roman government. This was a time of peace, when national frontiers were open to permit the Good News to travel freely. The people were not concerned with fears of war and had time to listen to the news of God's redemption. The Roman Empire also had good roads, which made it possible for the first missionaries to travel freely. Also, the language barrier was broken down. Throughout the empire most people were bilingual, with Greek being the common trade language. This made it possible for the New Testament books to be read in all areas of the empire. The missionaries could tell the story everywhere and know it could be understood.

2. Economically, the world was not prosperous. Poverty was commonplace. Two out of three men were slaves. These factors worked together to make life depressing. In contrast to this the Good News appeared as a bright light, and many men were ready to listen. Always man more readily turns to religion in times of economic depression than in times of prosperity.

3. Morally, the people were bankrupt. The first chapter of Romans describes the conditions of that day. Moral depravity caused downtrodden men to want to turn to something better.

4. Religiously, the old man-made gods and idols did not satisfy man's inner need to the be right with his Creator. The religions of the

day were being rejected. Caesar worship was forced upon many, but this man-made "deity" did not satisfy. Spiritually and morally there was a growing vacuum that men were eager to have filled.

In summary, the political, economic, moral, and religious climate blended together to make the times right for the revelation of God's program of redemption. The Good News about God's Son coming to redeem man from his sinful condition would spread rapidly.

Chapter 3

The Appearance of the Redeemer

The Birth of the Redeemer

"When the fulness of the time was come," God prepared to send His Son into the world to redeem fallen man (Galatians 4:4). The first step occurred "in the days of Herod, the king of Judaea" (Luke 1:5), and involved a priest named Zacharias and his wife, Elisabeth. "They were both righteous before God, walking in all the commandments and ordinances of the Lord blameless" (v. 6). They had no children and little hope of ever having any, since they were old.

It was customary to cast lots to determine which priest would "burn incense when he went into the temple of the Lord" (Luke 1:9). While Zacharias was ministrering in the temple, he was chosen by lot to carry out this duty. A priest was granted this privilege but once. During this service the angel Gabriel appeared to Zacharias and told him that even though he and his wife were old, they would have a son. Furthermore, Zacharias was to call this son John. "He shall be great in the sight of the Lord, and shall drink neither wine nor strong drink; and he shall be filled with the Holy Ghost. . . . And many of the children of Israel shall he turn to the Lord their God. And he shall go before him in the spirit and power of Elias [Elijah], to turn the hearts of the fathers to the children, and the disobedient to the wisdom of the just; to make ready a people prepared for the Lord" (vv. 15-17). John's ministry was foretold in Isaiah: "Behold, I send my messenger before thy face, which shall prepare thy way before thee. The voice of one crying in the wilderness, Prepare ye the way of the Lord, make his paths straight" (Mark 1:2, 3, from Isaiah 40:3; cf. Matthew 11:10; Luke 7:27).

The Appearance of the Redeemer

Six months after Elisabeth's conception, the same angel Gabriel appeared

> to a virgin espoused to a man whose name was Joseph, of the house of David; and the virgin's name was Mary. And the angel came in unto her, and said, Hail, thou that art highly favoured, the Lord is with thee: blessed art thou among women. And when she saw him, she was troubled at his saying, and cast in her mind what manner of salutation this should be. And the angel said unto her, Fear not, Mary: for thou hast found favour with God. And, behold, thou shalt conceive in thy womb, and bring forth a son, and shalt call his name JESUS. He shall be great, and shall be called the Son of the Highest: and the Lord God shall give unto him the throne of his father David: And he shall reign over the house of Jacob for ever; and of his kingdom there shall be no end. Then said Mary unto the angel, How shall this be, seeing I know not a man? And the angel answered and said unto her, The Holy Ghost shall come upon thee, and the power of the Highest shall overshadow thee: therefore also that holy thing which shall be born of thee shall be called the Son of God. Luke 1:27-35

The angel appeared to Joseph also and explained what was to happen: "Joseph, thou son of David, fear not to take unto thee Mary thy wife: for that which is conceived in her is of the Holy Ghost. And she shall bring forth a son, and thou shalt call his name JESUS: for he shall save his people from their sins" (Matthew 1:20, 21).

These events were foretold "by the prophet, saying, Behold, a virgin shall be with child, and shall bring forth a son, and they shall call his name Emmanuel, which being interpreted is, God with us" (Matthew 1:22, 23; from Isaiah 7:14). Jesus was the Seed of the woman (Genesis 3:15) and not the man. Jesus' supernatural birth was the way God chose to bring His Son, the Holy One who would save His people from sin, into the world. The conception of the Virgin Mary by the Holy Spirit combined in One Person the divine nature of God and sinless human nature (John 1:1, 14). God sent "his own Son in the likeness of sinful flesh" (Romans 8:3), becoming "of no reputation . . . made in the likeness of men" (Philippians 2:7). "As the children are partakers of flesh and blood, he also himself likewise took part of the same" (Hebrews 2:14). When Jesus took on Himself a human body and human nature, He did not partake of sin. He was without sin (Hebrews 4:15; I Peter 2:22; II Corinthians 5:21). Notice, too, that Mary and Joseph were of the lineage of David (Matthew 1:16; Luke 3:23, 31), from which the prophets foretold the Messiah would come.

"Jesus was born in Bethlehem of Judaea in the days of Herod the King" (Matthew 2:1). Micah foretold that Jesus' birth would be in Bethlehem (Micah 5:2). Caesar Augustus, the Roman emperor, decreed that every one should return to his own city to be enrolled (or registered) for taxation. Mary and Joseph, Jesus' parents, lived in Nazareth and went to "the city of David, which is called Bethlehem" (Luke 2:1-7), since they were of the house and lineage of David.

Although He was the Son of God and had dwelt in the courts of heaven, Jesus had a humble birth. Not one room was available at the inns of Bethlehem for His mother when the time came for His birth. Only a stable was available, and His bed was a manger (Luke 2:7). Nevertheless, His birth was notable. Angels announced His birth to "shepherds abiding in the field, keeping watch over their flock by night" (v. 8). They brought "good tidings of great joy, which shall be to all people. For unto you is born this day in the city of David a Saviour, which is Christ the Lord" (vv. 10, 11).

In the humble birth of Jesus, the Creator of the universe laid aside the use of some of His divine attributes to become a true man. This Child, born in Bethlehem, was the Word who had made all things. He came to this world, yet "the world knew him not. He came unto his own, and his own [the Jews] received him not.... The Word was made flesh, and dwelt among us ... full of grace and truth" (John 1:10, 14; see 8:58; 17:5; and Philippians 2:6-8 for evidence of His preexistence).

The term *incarnation* is used to describe the Son of God becoming flesh, that is, man. It is one of the most incomprehensible facts of history. How the divine and human attributes existed together in the incarnate Son of God is difficult to understand. The Bible teaches that the Son had a divine nature (Isaiah 9:6; Jeremiah 33:14-16; Malachi 3:1, 2; John 1:1-3, 14; 5:17, 18; Romans 8:3, 4; Colossians 1:19; Hebrews 1:2, 3). The Bible teaches too that He had a human nature (Matthew 26:26, 28, 36; Luke 23:46; 24:39; John 1:14; 8:40; 11:33; Acts 2:22; Romans 5:15; I Corinthians 15:21; I Timothy 2:5; 3:16; I John 4:2).

How and why the Son of God surrendered His divine rights can be understood only by seeing the holiness and love of God in response to the sinfulness of man. Only then can we begin to appreciate Jesus' redemptive suffering for man.

The incarnation was essential to God's plan to redeem man from sin. The law was never meant to save men. Its purpose was to show them that they were sinners. Only an incarnated God-Man by His self-sacrifice could redeem man. "What the law could not do, in that it was weak through the flesh, God sending his own Son in the likeness of sinful flesh, and for sin, condemned sin in the flesh: That the righteousness of the law might be fulfilled in us" (Romans 8:3, 4). God's Son came "to give his life a ransom for many" (Matthew 20:28).

Eight days after His birth, Jesus, the Redeemer, was circumcised in accordance with the Mosaic law and as a consequence of His humanity. The Son of God took on human flesh when He was born of woman. Since He lived under the law and came to fulfill all righteousness, His circumcision was the first step in His lifelong obedience to the law. This also served to identify Him with the promise made to Abraham that "in thy seed shall all the nations of the earth be blessed because thou hast obeyed my voice" (Genesis 22:18).

The law required every firstborn to be consecrated to the Lord. If the firstborn was a male child, he was to be presented to the Lord. "As it is written in the law of the Lord, Every male that openeth the womb shall be called holy to the Lord. And to offer a sacrifice according to that which is said in the law." Therefore, Jesus' parents took Him to the temple in Jerusalem to be presented to the Lord (Luke 2:23, 24; cf. Exodus 13:2, 13; Numbers 18:15, 16).

Simeon, a righteous and devout man, had been waiting day and night for the consolation of Israel. The Holy Spirit revealed to him that he would not die before he had seen the Christ. When the Christ Child was brought to the temple, Simeon quickly recognized Him: "Lord, now lettest thou thy servant depart in peace, according to thy word: For mine eyes have seen thy salvation, which thou hast prepared before the face of all people; a light to lighten the Gentiles, and the glory of thy people Israel" (Luke 2:29-32).

Anna, a prophetess and an elderly widow who stayed at the temple day and night fasting and praying, also recognized Jesus as being the Christ. "She coming in that instant gave thanks likewise unto the Lord, and spake of him to all them that looked for redemption in Jerusalem" (Luke 2:36-38).

Joseph, being warned by the angel of the Lord of Herod's hostility toward the Child, fled to Egypt with his family. This fulfilled what "was spoken of the Lord by the prophet, saying, Out of Egypt have I called my son" (Matthew 2:13-15; from Hosea 11:1). When Joseph, Mary, and the Child returned to Israel after the death of Herod, they found that Herod's son Archelaus reigned. Being afraid of Archelaus and being warned by God, the young family withdrew to Galilee, where they took up residence in Nazareth. As the prophets had said, "He shall be called a Nazarene" (v. 23).

Little is known of Jesus' early life. Luke tells us that Jesus "grew, and waxed strong in spirit, filled with wisdom: and the grace of God was upon him" (Luke 2:40). Being from a poor family, Jesus probably received no formal education, only training from His parents as required by the law and instruction at the synagogue. He studied the Scriptures Himself, and His training and development were extensive. By the age of twelve, when He was taken to Jerusalem and was unintentionally left there by His parents (they thought He was with relatives), Jesus already possessed great wisdom. When His parents found Him, He was "in the temple, sitting in the midst of the doctors, both hearing them, and asking them questions. And all that heard him were astonished at his understanding and answers" (Luke 2:46, 47). When asked about His remaining behind, He said, "How is it that ye sought me? wist ye not that I must be about my Father's business?" (v. 49). At this early age, He was already conscious of His divine mission.

John the Baptist Prepares the Way

As Jesus grew in mind, body, and wisdom, John the Baptist, whose birth was also foretold by the angel Gabriel, prepared for his ministry. John "grew, and waxed strong in the spirit, and was in the deserts till the day of his shewing unto Israel" (Luke 1:80). John not only grew physically, but he grew spiritually. He lived in the wilderness, apparently away from the distractions found among men, and there received the word of God. John did not receive the priest's normal education. At the end of this preparation, probably by age thirty, "the word of God came unto John . . . . And he came into all the country about Jordan, preaching the baptism of repentance for the remission of sins" (Luke 3:2-4). Jesus said that for those who would receive it, John the Baptist was Elijah whom the prophet Malachi had spoken of (Malachi 3:1; 4:5, 6; cf. Matthew 11:13-15; Luke 1:17). John spoke as the prophet Isaiah had prophesied: "The voice of one crying in the wilderness, Prepare ye the way of the Lord, make his paths straight" (Matthew 3:3). Many people responded to John's message, confessed their sins, and were baptized (v. 6).

Many leaders of the Jewish religious sects, the Pharisees and Sadducees, came for baptism too. This surprised John since he knew their high opinions of themselves and their arrogant view that everything was all right with them since they could say, "We have Abraham [as] our father" (Matthew 3:9). John confronted them, "O generation of vipers, who hath warned you to flee from the wrath to come?" (v. 7). He warned them not just to come for baptism but to repent as others had. This repentance was to be more than words: they had to bear "fruits meet for repentance.... every tree which bringeth not forth good fruit is hewn down, and cast into the fire" (Matthew 3:8, 10; cf. Isaiah 40:3; Mark 1:3; Luke 3:4-6; John 1:23).

John's ministry was not an end in itself. He knew he was preparing the way for One to follow: "I indeed baptize you with water unto repentance: but he that cometh after me is mightier than I, whose shoes I am not worthy to bear: he shall baptize you with the Holy Ghost, and with fire" (Matthew 3:11).

John Baptizes Jesus

While John was baptizing and preaching his message, Jesus left Galilee and went to him to be baptized. "John forbad him, saying, I have need to be baptized of thee, and comest thou to me?" (Matthew 3:14). John felt unworthy; he needed Jesus. Jesus answered him, "Suffer [let] it to be so now: for thus it becometh us to fulfill all righteousness" (v. 15). John wanted to fulfill all the God-given instructions for the Jewish people, thus Jesus was baptized. Immediately "the heavens were opened unto him, and he [John] saw the Spirit of God descending like a dove, and lighting upon him [Jesus]: And lo a voice from heaven, saying, This is my beloved Son, in whom I am well pleased" (v. 16; cf. John 1:29-34). Jesus' receiving the Holy Spirit and the Voice from heaven in the presence of the multitudes were a testimony that Jesus' ministry was beginning. Soon after this "John seeth Jesus coming unto him, and saith, Behold the Lamb of God, which taketh away the sin of the world" (John 1:29). John clearly saw Christ's work as the Savior, the

One who would take away the sins of the world. John recognized that his "forerunner" commission would soon be fulfilled and that he would fade away as Jesus' ministry increased. John said, "He must increase, but I must decrease" (3:30). John recognized that Jesus "cometh from above [and] is above all. . . . he whom God hath sent speaketh the words of God. . . . The Father loveth the Son, and hath given all things into his hand. He that believeth on the Son hath everlasting life" (vv. 31, 34-36).

Jesus' Temptations

After Jesus' baptism, the full extent of His ministry became evident. He was soon confronted with important decisions about His life. "Immediately the spirit driveth him into the wilderness" (Mark 1:12), where He spent forty days alone in prayer, meditation, and fasting. During this time He faced temptations from the devil (Matthew 4:1-11; Mark 1:12, 13; Luke 4:1-13).

After fasting forty days, Jesus became hungry. The tempter came to Him and started with the same approach used against Adam and Eve in the Garden of Eden (Genesis 3:1), questioning the Word of God. Satan said, "If thou be the Son of God, command that these stones be made bread" (Matthew 4:3). Jesus knew He was the Son of God and did not distrust His Father; therefore He refused to obey Satan's demand for proof of His Sonship. Jesus trusted in and appealed to His Father's Word to defend Himself from Satan's first temptation, saying, "It is written, Man shall not live by bread alone, but by every word that proceedeth out of the mouth of God" (v. 4).

The words Jesus spoke are part of Moses' address to Israel concerning the importance of keeping God commandments. Moses said, "All the commandments which I command thee this day shall ye observe to do, that ye may live" (Deuteronomy 8:1). He told them they should remember their forty years in the wilderness and how it "humbled thee, and to prove thee, to know what was in thine heart, whether thou wouldest keep his commandments, or no" (v. 2). God had taught them that man cannot live "by bread only, but by every word that proceedeth out of the mouth of the LORD doth man live" (v. 3). Thus Satan's challenge to Jesus was on the wrong issue. Jesus could have turned the stones into bread, but it was more important to follow the word of His Father. Jesus would not distrust or tempt God by ignoring any part of it. Jesus rejected Satan's appeal in this first temptation and passed His first challenge to solve man's most important spiritual need (cf. Luke 4:1-4; Deuteronomy 8:3).

The devil, knowing that Jesus accepted the Word as truth, next used the Word incorrectly to tempt Him. He took Jesus to "the holy city, and setteth him on a pinnacle of the temple, and saith unto him, If thou be the Son of God, cast thyself down: for it is written, He shall give his angels charge concerning thee: and in their hands they shall bear thee up, lest at any time thou dash thy foot against a stone" (Matthew 4:5-6; cf. Psalm 91:11-12). Once more the devil demanded proof that Jesus was the Son of God, and Jesus again did not yield to Satan's request. Satan knew Jesus was the Son of God. For Jesus to follow any of Satan's requests would have been wrong, including his request for additional proof of Jesus' deity. To defeat Satan's demand, Jesus appealed to Scripture again: "Thou shalt not tempt the Lord thy God." Satan misused the Scripture he quoted because he sought to stress one Scripture and disregard others that would clarify its meaning (Matthew 4:7; cf. Luke 4:5-12).

Next the devil showed Jesus "all the kingdoms of the world, and the glory of them; and saith unto him, All these things will I give thee, if thou wilt fall down and worship me" (Matthew 4:8). The devil challenged Jesus to seek an earthly kingdom by worshiping him rather than God. But Jesus replied from Scripture, "Thou shalt worship the Lord thy God, and him only shalt thou serve" (v. 10; cf. Deuteronomy 6:13; I Chronicles 21:1). After Jesus withstood these temptations, the devil left Him, but only until a better opportunity came to further tempt Him (Luke 4:13; cf. Matthew 4:11).

The temptations of Jesus serve to let man know that temptation in itself is not sin, and that man has a Savior who was "in all points tempted like as we are, yet without sin" (Hebrews 4:15). He was like "his brethren [man], that he might be a merciful and faithful high priest in things pertaining to God, to make reconciliation for the sins of the people. For in that he himself hath suffered being tempted, he is able to succour [help] them that are tempted" (Hebrews 2:17, 18). By withstanding temptations, Jesus ultimately would began a series of events that defeat the power of sin and bring redemption to man.

Jesus is described as "the Lamb of God" (John 1:29), "a lamb without blemish and without spot" (I Peter 1:19; cf. Hebrews 9:14), and one who "did no sin, neither was guile found in his mouth" (I Peter 2:22). The word *lamb* connotes sacrifice to the Hebrew mind.

This "lamb without blemish" was the Sacrifice to be offered for man's sin.

Throughout His life Jesus faced temptations from the devil, who wanted to prevent the Lamb from becoming the sacrifice for the world's sins. Jesus, however, did not yield to Satan but remained absolutely sinless by completely obeying God's will. Later He challenged His enemies, "Which of you convinceth me of sin?" (John 8:46). They could not point to any sin in His life. God had Jesus come into the world as a perfect man, "who knew no sin; that we might be made the righteousness of God in him" (II Corinthians 5:21). Since He was sinless, Jesus was qualified to be the Mediator between God and man (I Timothy 2:5).

Jesus' Ministry

After the temptations Jesus continued to live in full obedience to God's will, testifying that "I do always those things that please him" (John 8:29). He was the perfect man, the last Adam, the life-giving spirit (I Corinthians 15:45; cf. John 5:21; Romans 8:2; Hebrews 9:14). His perfection totally controlled His character and conduct.

Sometime later, Jesus approached John and two of his disciples, and John again bore witness to Him: "Behold the Lamb of God! And the two disciples heard him speak, and they followed Jesus" (John 1:36, 37). One of these disciples, Andrew, went and found "his own brother Simon, and saith unto him, We have found the Messias [the Christ]" (v. 41). Jesus was the Anointed One the Jews were looking for (Isaiah 61:1; Luke 4:18). Andrew brought Simon to Jesus, who told Simon that he would soon be called Cephas. "Cephas" is Aramaic, which by interpretation is "Peter," and this latter name means stone (John 1:40-42). Later we will see the significance of this change of name.

Then Jesus met Philip on His way to Galilee and "saith unto him, Follow me" (John 1:43). Philip followed. Philip soon found Nathanael and told him, "We have found him, of whom Moses in the law, and the prophets, did write" (v. 45). Nathanael must have been a student of the Word, since he understood Philip's remarks. After his meeting with Jesus, Nathanael recognized that Jesus was "the Son of God . . . the King of Israel" (v. 49).

Jesus, with His mother and disciples, went to a marriage at Cana in Galilee. During the marriage feast the supply of wine failed. Because she knew that her Son was able to perform miracles, Jesus' mother spoke to Him about the situation. He responded to her request by saying, "Woman, what have I to do with thee? mine hour is not yet come" (John 2:4). To us Jesus' response might seem somewhat disrespectful. In the Jewish culture the response was entirely appropriate. In a sense Jesus was saying, "What have I to do with the shortage of wine?" Jesus may have been mildly displeased with the situation, but He still responded, asking that six stone jars of about twenty or thirty gallons each be filled with water. Then He told the servants to draw some of the liquid and take it to the overseer of the feast. The governor found the sample was good wine. This miracle "manifested forth his glory" (v. 11), and caused His disciples to believe on Him. This was the first of Jesus' miracles, the first of His signs that attested to His deity (cf. 20:30, 31).

Soon after this Jesus went to Jerusalem for the Passover. There He was shocked to see that the temple, dedicated to God, had become a place where money changers were selling oxen, sheep, and pigeons. Jesus' holy wrath and indignation moved Him to drive the animals out of the temple courts. "Take these things hence," Jesus commanded, and "make not my Father's house an house of merchandise" (John 2:16).

The Jews inquired by what authority Jesus cleansed the temple and asked for a sign from Him. He answered by referring to a coming event: "Destroy this temple, and in three days I will raise it up" (John 2:19). Although this would be a most convincing sign, the Jews did not understand the meaning of His words. They thought only of the forty-six years needed to build the temple. They did not realize that Jesus was referring to His body, which He would raise in three days after He gave His life to reconcile man to God.

Nicodemus, a ruler of the Jews, was probably one of those who believed in Jesus because of the signs He did (John 2:23). Nicodemus' faith was weak, so he "came to Jesus by night, and said unto him, Rabbi, we know that thou art a teacher come from God: for no man can do these miracles that thou doest, except God be with him" (John 3:2). Bypassing the normal greeting, Jesus spoke to Nicodemus about salvation. "Verily, verily, I say unto thee, Except a man be born of water and of the Spirit, he cannot enter into the kingdom of God" (v. 5). No one can see (or comprehend) the kingdom of God unless he has a change of heart. This was hard for Nicodemus to understand. "That which is born of the flesh is flesh;

and that which is born of the Spirit is spirit" (v. 6). This rebirth, the regeneration of sinful man, was not a natural but a spiritual matter. Jesus reminded Nicodemus that he does not marvel about natural things he does not understand (for instance, where the wind comes from or goes to). So it is with everyone who is born of the Spirit. The rebirth would be as real as the wind's effects on a person's life, even though he might not understand how it occurs.

Nicodemus inquired further with this question: "How can these things be?" (John 3:9). Jesus replied,

> Art thou a master of Israel, and knowest not these things? Verily, verily, I say unto thee, We speak that we do know, and testify that we have seen; and ye receive not our witness. If I have told you earthly things, and ye believe not, how shall ye believe, if I tell you of heavenly things? And no man hath ascended up to heaven, but he that came down from heaven, even the Son of man which is in heaven. And as Moses lifted up the serpent in the wilderness, even so must the Son of man be lifted up: That whosoever believeth in him should not perish, but have eternal life. John 3:10-15

Next follows a summary of the central truth of the Gospel:

> For God so loved the world, that he gave his only begotten Son, that whosoever believeth in him should not perish, but have everlasting life. For God sent not his Son into the world to condemn the world; but that the world through him might be saved. He that believeth on him is not condemned: but he that believeth not is condemned already, because he hath not believed in the name of the only begotten Son of God. And this is the condemnation, that light is come into the world, and men loved darkness rather than light, because their deeds were evil. For every one that doeth evil hateth the light, neither cometh to the light, lest his deeds should be reproved. But he that doeth truth cometh to the light, that his deeds may be made manifest, that they are wrought in God. John 3:16-21

After His meeting with Nicodemus, Jesus went into Judea where He continued teaching about the kingdom of God. Then Jesus went to Galilee by way of Samaria. During this journey He rested at a well dug years before by Jacob. While Jesus was there, a Samaritan woman came to draw water. Jesus asked her for a drink. This surprised some of His followers since Jews held Samaritans in contempt. They were of mixed blood because of a forced mingling

The Appearance of the Redeemer

during the eighth century B.C. Assyrian occupation of Israel, and they had developed a monotheistic religion similar to the Jews.

During her conversation with Jesus, the Samaritan woman raised a point that caused heated arguments between the Jews and the Samaritans. Was Mount Gerizim or Jerusalem the place where men were to worship? The Samaritans had built a temple at Mount Gerizim when the Jews had refused their help to rebuild the temple after the Jews return from the Babylonian captivity. Jesus replied, "The hour cometh, when ye shall neither in this mountain, nor yet at Jerusalem, worship the Father. . . . the true worshippers shall worship the Father in spirit and in truth: for the Father seeketh such to worship him. God is a Spirit: and they that worship him must worship him in spirit and in truth" (John 4:21-24). Jesus stressed that attitude and spirit were more important than the place of worship.

Passing through Samaria, "Jesus came into Galilee, preaching the gospel of the kingdom of God, and saying, The time is fulfilled, and the kingdom of God is at hand: repent ye, and believe the gospel" (Mark 1:14, 15; see also Matthew 4:23-25). Jesus immediately drew popular support. The people "were astonished at his doctrine: for he taught them as one that had authority, and not as the scribes" (v. 22). He did not follow the Jewish scribes' customary practice of citing various authorities for His statements. Instead, He spoke truth that stood on its own strength; it needed no authorities to support it.

Early in His ministry in Galilee, Jesus returned to the town of "Nazareth, where he had been brought up" (Luke 4:16). During His stay there He attended the Sabbath worship service at the synagogue and addressed the congregation. He

> stood up for to read. And there was delivered unto him the book of the prophet Esaias [Isaiah]. And when he had opened the book, he found the place where it was written, The Spirit of the Lord is upon me, because he hath anointed me to preach the gospel to the poor; he hath sent me to heal the brokenhearted, to preach deliverance to the captives, and recovering of sight to the blind, to set at liberty them that are bruised, to preach the acceptable year of the Lord. And he closed the book, and he gave it again to the minister, and sat down. And the eyes of all them that were in the synagogue were fastened on him. vv. 16-20; cf. Isaiah 61:1

He then declared, "This day is this scripture fulfilled in your ears" (Luke 4:21). The Jews first spoke well of him "and wondered at the gracious words," but remembering that He was Joseph's son, they rejected Him. He told them, "Verily I say unto you, No prophet is accepted in his own country" (v. 24). They were "filled with wrath" toward him and "thrust him out of the city" (vv. 28, 29). They took Him to the brow of a hill and would have killed Him, but He miraculously left, and "passing through the midst of them went his way" (Luke 4:30). After the Nazareth Jews rejected Him, Jesus left their town and went to Capernaum, which He made His headquarters for approximately the next eighteen months.

The Kingdom of God

The Gospels emphasize Jesus' role as a master or teacher (Matthew 4:23; 7:29; 9:35; 11:1; 12:38; Mark 5:35; Luke 18:18; John 1:38; 3:2; 13:13), and as a preacher (Matthew 4:17, 23; 9:35; 11:1; Mark 1:14, 38, 39; Luke 4:44; 8:1), and record many of His teachings. Several of these shed light on the plan of redemption. A central statement in Jesus' ministry was that "the kingdom of God is at hand: repent ye, and believe the gospel" (Mark 1:15). (Mark and Luke use the term "kingdom of God" while Matthew uses the term "kingdom of heaven," possibly because he wrote to Jewish readers who were reluctant to speak the name of God.)

The concept of the kingdom was not new to Jesus' hearers. The Jews had long referred to God as One having sovereign rule over man and His creatures. During the past this included God's rule over Israel, but the political sovereignty ceased with the destruction of Jerusalem by the Babylonians. Nevertheless the idea of the kingdom remained with the Jews. For centuries they looked forward to once again being a kingdom through which God would reign over His people. This anticipation caused many Jews to think only in political terms. Too many Jews could not forget that Israel was once a theocracy that God ruled through their kings. Centuries had passed since the Jews had been carried into captivity by the Babylonians; yet some Jews believed the Roman rule would be broken and Israel would again be restored as a sovereign, political kingdom.

There are two aspects to the kingdom: a present spiritual kingdom and a future literal kingdom. The future literal kingdom, composed of both Jews and Gentiles, will be ruled by Christ the King. The political kingdom the Jews were looking for would "be trodden down [by] the Gentiles, until the times of the Gentiles be fulfilled" (Luke

21:24; cf. Romans 11:25). This is the subject of the last chapter of this book.

Until then there will be a spiritual kingdom where God rules in the hearts of those who follow the redemptive plan brought by Jesus Christ. Jesus used the term *kingdom* as an analogy of the spiritual rule of God over men in this age. He never gave a definition of the kingdom but taught what it was like through parables. He taught that the kingdom of God is like sown seed that can be snatched away, choked out by weeds, or grow to maturity and produce a crop (Matthew 13:3-9, 18-30, 36-43; cf. Mark 4:1-20; Luke 8:4-15). The kingdom of God would coexist with evil and face opposition from the evil one, the devil. The kingdom of God is like a grain of mustard seed (Matthew 13:31, 32; cf. Mark 4:30-32) and like leaven that grows to something great from something small and works throughout the world (Matthew 13:33; cf. Luke 13:20, 21). These parables show the kingdom will grow and spread through the world.

The kingdom is like a treasure hidden in a field (Matthew 13:44) and like a fine pearl (v. 45), which when found is worth an all-out effort to obtain. The kingdom of God is worth an all-out effort to enter it. This does not mean that entrance can be earned by works of the law, but that the seeker should repent, believe, and follow Jesus unreservedly. The kingdom is like a fishing net in which both bad fish and good fish are caught, but in the end they are separated, and the bad are thrown out (vv. 47-50). Only at the end will the godly followers of Christ and the ungodly be separated. In summary, these parables show the kingdom of God and the evil kingdom will exist side-by-side. At the end of this age, there will be a separation of good and evil, and the children of the King will live in a glorious kingdom.

The spiritual kingdom would be established by God's grace and the work of the Holy Spirit, making it possible for men individually to submit themselves to God. Men would have to forget about being great and become as little children to enter this kingdom. Jesus stated, "Except ye be converted, and become as little children, ye shall not enter into the kingdom of heaven" (Matthew 18:3). This implies men must be reborn (see John 3:3-7), giving them a new relationship with God. The kingdom of God referred simply to this reestablished rule of God in the hearts of men. Men would return to a relationship to God approximating the one they had before the Fall. They would have to repent, or turn from their rebellion against God and trust and obey Him. Each one must "humble himself as ... [a] little child" (v. 4). Little children show humility by trusting and depending on others. In this case the wayward in humility must rely solely on Jesus to bring forth the necessary conversion. This is "good news" for those who repent and believe. The term *good news* translates the Greek term *euaggelion*, which is usually translated *gospel*.

The kingdom of God is separate from and opposed to the kingdom of this world, which is composed of children of Satan (Matthew 13:38; John 8:44) and is ruled by Satan (Ephesians 2:2). The object of the kingdom of God is to overthrow the kingdom of darkness by defeating Satan's power over man (Matthew 12:22-30; Romans 13:12) and by giving him a new nature through the rebirth (John 3:3; Ephesians 4:22, 23; Colossians 3:9, 10; I Peter:1:23; 2:2). This new man is "not of the world but ... chosen ... out of the world" (John 15:19; 17:14). The Father gives them to Jesus "out of the world" (17:6). Jesus further explained that "they are not of the world, even as I am not of the world" (v. 16).

The phrase "kingdom of God" bears witness also to the spiritual nature of the kingdom, which has its origin and source in God. To the Pharisees who asked Christ about His coming kingdom, Jesus replied, "The kingdom of God cometh not with observation. Neither shall they say, Lo here! or, lo there! for, behold, the kingdom of God is within you" (Luke 17:20, 21). It was not a kingdom patterned after Israel with "signs to be observed" (v. 20 RSV), that is, with rituals, regulations to be observed, a political state, etc. The Greek term *entos* translated "within you" means "within you, in your heart," and is sometimes translated "among you, in your midst." Thus the RSV translates this verse: "The kingdom of God is in the midst of you," or as the footnote states, "within you" (17:21 RSV).[1] Entrance into this spiritual kingdom requires conversion or the new birth. Without it the unregenerate and spiritually unenlightened man can neither see nor enter the kingdom of God (John 3:3, 5).

The concept of the kingdom of God, where man again comes under God's rule, implies that those who belong to it possess a new set of values. The Sermon on the Mount (Matthew 5-7) is a clear example of these new standards. They deal with man's relation with his

---

[1] William Arndt and F. Wilber Gingrich, *A Greek-English Lexicon of the New Testament*, Chicago: University of Chicago Press, 1979, 2nd edition, p. 269.

brothers (5:21-26), with adultery (v. 28), with divorce (vv. 31, 32), with swearing oaths (vv. 33-37), with resisting evil (vv. 38-42), with one's enemies (vv. 43-48), with giving alms (6:1-4), with prayer (vv. 5-13), with forgiveness (vv. 14, 15), with fasting (vv. 16-18), with accumulating earthly wealth (vv. 19-21), with loyalty (v. 24), with anxiety (vv. 25-34), with judging (7:1-5), and with asking your heavenly Father to fulfill your needs (vv. 7-12).

The sermon concludes with an admonition to "enter in at the strait gate: for wide is the gate, and broad is the way, that leadeth to destruction, and many there be which go in thereat: Because strait is the gate, and narrow is the way, which leadeth unto life, and few there be that find it" (Matthew 7:13, 14). Jesus' followers are to beware of false prophets who are "ravening wolves" (vv. 7:15ff.) and to be aware that

> not every one that saith unto me, Lord, Lord, shall enter into the kingdom of heaven; but he that doeth the will of my Father which is in heaven. Many will say to me in that day, Lord, Lord, have we not prophesied in thy name? and in thy name have cast out devils? and in thy name done many wonderful works? And then will I profess unto them, I never knew you: depart from me, ye that work iniquity. Therefore whosoever heareth these sayings of mine, and doeth them, I will liken him unto a wise man, which built his house upon a rock: And the rain descended, and the floods came, and the winds blew, and beat upon that house; and it fell not: for it was founded upon a rock. And every one that heareth these sayings of mine, and doeth them not, shall be likened unto a foolish man, which built his house upon the sand: And the rain descended, and the floods came, and the winds blew, and beat upon that house, and it fell: and great was the fall of it. 7:21-27

From the above it is clear that the Sermon on the Mount presents a new set of standards that differ sharply from the law and the scribes' teachings. This sermon shows Jesus is deeply concerned about moral issues. His teachings are much deeper than Jewish legalism. "Except your righteousness shall exceed the righteousness of the scribes and Pharisees, ye shall in no case enter into the kingdom" (Matthew 5:20). The wise man will "heareth these sayings . . . and doeth them," but he does them not only in an outwardly way, as the Pharisee might, but sees and follows their inner meaning too. He will take heed to Jesus' warnings about the consequences of not following them. The result of not following these teachings is serious. It would be like building a house on sand that would not withstand a storm.

Discipleship

Throughout His ministry Jesus called men to follow Him and become His disciples. Those who accepted this call were to count the cost involved. When "a certain man said unto him, Lord, I will follow thee whithersoever thou goest" (Luke 9:57), Jesus reminded him that "foxes have holes, and birds of the air have nests; but the Son of man hath not where to lay his head" (v. 58). To follow Jesus is costly, and men had better consider it before starting out.

At this time another man accepted Jesus' call to follow Him, but he had a supposedly reasonable thing to do first: "Lord, suffer me first to go and bury my father" (Luke 9:59). When a would-be disciple hears the "Follow me," nothing should prevent his following—even if it means letting the dead bury their own dead. "Another also said, Lord, I will follow thee; but let me first go bid them farewell, which are at home at my house" (v. 61). But Jesus had to remind this person that no man who puts "his hand to the plough, and looking back, is fit for the kingdom of God" (v. 62). Again the would-be disciple is told that nothing may come between him and his following the Lord.

Matthew exemplifies the type of response for which Jesus was looking. This tax collector was sitting at his tax table when Jesus said to him, "Follow me. And he arose, and followed him" (Matthew 9:9). The Pharisees criticized Jesus for calling a tax collector to be His disciple. "Why eateth your Master with publicans and sinners?" (v. 11). To the Pharisees, Matthew was a traitor because he had sold out to the Roman government and was working for them. Jesus had to remind these religious leaders that "they that be whole need not a physician, but they that are sick. But go ye and learn what that meaneth, I will have mercy, and not sacrifice: for I am not come to call the righteous, but sinners to repentance" (vv. 12, 13). Matthew repented, changed his life, and became a worthy disciple.

At the birth of Jesus, the angels praised, "Glory to God in the highest, and on earth peace, good will toward men" (Luke 2:14). The presence of peace depends on man's response to the good news. The call to discipleship may cause friction between those who follow

The Appearance of the Redeemer

Jesus and their family members and friends who do not. Jesus reminded His disciples that He did not necessarily

> come to send peace on earth: I came not to send peace, but a sword. For I am come to set a man at variance against his father, and the daughter against her mother, and the daughter in law against her mother in law. And a man's foes shall be they of his own household. He that loveth father or mother more than me is not worthy of me: and he that loveth son or daughter more than me is not worthy of me. And he that taketh not his cross, and followeth after me, is not worthy of me. He that findeth his life shall lose it: and he that loseth his life for my sake shall find it. Matthew 10:34-39

After telling His disciples that He must suffer and be killed in Jerusalem, Jesus told them, "If any man will come after me, let him deny himself, and take up his cross, and follow me. For whosoever will save his life shall lose it: and whosoever will lose his life for my sake shall find it" (Matthew 16:24, 25; cf. Mark 8:34–9:1; Luke 9:23-27; 14:27; 17:33). *Deny himself* means to disown one's personality and desires and to yield oneself completely to the Lord. Paul wrote to the Philippians that they should have the mind that was in Christ when He emptied and humbled Himself, becoming "obedient unto death, even the death of the cross" (Philippians 2:5-8). The *cross* symbolizes the suffering—and if necessary even death—that the disciple accepts when he follows his Lord. The Lord would not be the only one to suffer; His disciples would suffer too. The cross also symbolizes crucifixion, a term Paul used to describe the Christian: "they that are Christ's have crucified the flesh with the affections and lusts" (Galatians 5:24). Those who lose their carnal life will be rewarded with everlasting life.

Luke wrote of an instance where Jesus spoke to a multitude who were interested in becoming disciples. In commenting on discipleship, Jesus first spoke about the need to "hate" family members and one's own life: "If any man come to me, and hate not his father, and mother, and wife, and children, and brethren, and sisters, yea, and his own life also, he cannot be my disciple" (Luke 14:26; cf. 12:51-53). These are hard words. The point is disciples must lay aside all interests that prevent full surrender and total loyalty to Christ. This hate can be understood by comparing it to the love Jesus demanded. He told His disciples, "A man's foes shall be they of his own household. He that loveth father or mother more than me is not worthy of me: and he that loveth son or daughter more than me is not worthy of me" (Matthew 10:36, 37). Disciples must love Jesus above all others. This will result in faithfulness and loyalty to Jesus Christ that transcends all family relationships and one's own desires. Nothing is to stand in the way of following Christ. Jesus said, "And whosoever doth not bear his cross, and come after me, cannot be my disciple" (Luke 14:27). He then mentioned that a person intending to build a tower will first estimate its cost to be sure he can finish it, and that no king would go to war without first considering if he could win. "So likewise, whosoever he be of you that forsaketh not all that he hath, he cannot be my disciple" (v. 33). Discipleship and salvation are serious matters and require a full commitment at the start and putting everything else in second place throughout life. Jesus Christ must be first place in the disciple's life.

Lest some think discipleship is a burden, Jesus said, "Come unto me, all ye that labour and are heavy laden, and I will give you rest. Take my yoke upon you, and learn of me; for I am meek and lowly in heart: and ye shall find rest unto your souls. For my yoke is easy, and my burden is light" (Matthew 11:28-30). How can discipleship be easy? The answer lies in the rebirth experience. The disciple's inner nature is changed so that he desires to do God's will and thereby finds righteousness, peace, and joy (John 14:27; 16:33; Romans 14:17; 15:13; Galatians 5:22, et al.). The inner change removes the burden, even though the disciple may suffer for the cause of Christ (Matthew 10:16-25; Luke 10:3; 21:5-19; Romans 8:17; Philippians 1:29, 30; 3:10; II Timothy 2:12; I Peter 4:12-14; 5:10).

The Only Way

Jesus' call to discipleship was a call to follow the only way of redemption. Jesus said,

> I am the bread of life. . . . this is the will of him that sent me, that every one which seeth the Son, and believeth on him, may have everlasting life: and I will raise him up at the last day. . . . Every man therefore that hath heard, and hath learned of the Father, cometh unto me. . . . He that believeth on me hath everlasting life. I am that bread of life. Your fathers did eat manna in the wilderness, and are dead. This is the bread which cometh down from heaven, that a man may eat thereof, and not die. I am the living bread which came down from heaven: if any man eat of this

The Appearance of the Redeemer 57

bread, he shall live for ever: and the bread that I will give is my flesh, which I will give for the life of the world. John 6:35, 40, 45-51

Jesus said, "I am the light of the world: he that followeth me shall not walk in darkness, but shall have the light of life" (John 8:12; cf. 9:5; 12:35, 36). Jesus is the One who frees man from his sin so he no longer walks in the darkness but in the light.

Jesus spoke to the Jews who had believed in Him: "If ye continue in my word, then are ye my disciples indeed; and ye shall know the truth, and the truth shall make you free" (John 8:31, 32). He explained that "whosoever committeth sin is the servant of sin" (v. 34). The person who is a "servant abideth not in the house for ever: but the Son abideth ever. If the Son therefore shall make you free, ye shall be free indeed" (vv. 35, 36). To be free means freedom from the power and the eternal consequences of sin. "If a man keep my saying, he shall never see death" (v. 51).

Those who seek eternal life must enter by the Door. Jesus used this metaphor to describe the purpose of His being. "Verily, verily, I say unto you, He that enterth not by the door into the sheepfold, but climbeth up some other way, the same is a thief and a robber. But he that entereth in by the door is the shepherd of the sheep" (John 10:1, 2). The sheepfold was a fenced enclosure with a door to enter; Jesus entered so others might have life. He then became the Door for others to enter. He said, "I am the door: by me if any man enter in, he shall be saved.... I am come that they might have life, and that they might have it more abundantly. I am the good shepherd: the good shepherd giveth his life for the sheep.... Therefore doth my Father love me, because I lay down my life, that I might take it again" (vv. 9-11, 17; cf. 15). In the kingdom Jesus is the only door since He is the One who gave His life so repentant men can be saved.

When one of His close friends died, Jesus restored him to life. During this event Jesus explained, "I am the resurrection, and the life: he that believeth in me, though he were dead, yet shall he live: And whosoever liveth and believeth in me shall never die" (John 11:25, 26). Jesus is the source of life and of resurrection from the dead. Neither life nor resurrection exist apart from Him. Victory over death is possible only for those who believe in Him.

Jesus said clearly that the results of hearing Him have eternal consequences:

> If any man hear my words, and believe not, I judge him not: for I came not to judge the world, but to save the world. He that rejecteth me, and receiveth not my words, hath one that judgeth him: the word that I have spoken, the same shall judge him in the last day. For I have not spoken of myself; but the Father which sent me, he gave me a commandment, what I should say, and what I should speak. And I know that his commandment is life everlasting: whatsoever I speak therefore, even as the Father said unto me, so I speak. John 12:47-50

Jesus' purpose was to save the sinner, but if the sinner rejected Him, there was no other way. The sinner will be judged by what he rejected—the word Jesus bore. Judgment will occur on the basis of God's authority. He empowered Jesus to forgive sins, as He bore witness early in His ministry (Mark 2:10; Luke 7:48).

Those who believe in Jesus and understand the love He has for them will love Him. Jesus said, "If ye love me, keep my commandments" (John 14:15). He promised He would send them a Counselor, the Holy Spirit, to guide and teach them. Jesus explained,

> He that hath my commandments, and keepeth them, he it is that loveth me: and he that loveth me shall be loved of my Father, and I will love him, and will manifest myself to him. . . . If a man love me, he will keep my words: and my Father will love him, and we will come unto him, and make our abode with him. He that loveth me not keepeth not my sayings: and the word which ye hear is not mine, but the Father's which sent me. vv. 21-24

Jesus expects those who love Him to keep His Word. Those who believe in Him and keep His word will bear fruit. "I am the true vine and my Father is the husbandman. . . . These things have I spoken unto you, that my joy might remain in you, and that your joy might be full" (John 15:1, 11). The fruit of obedience springs from the believer's life in Christ and brings glory to God and joy to Christ and to the believer.

His Mighty Works

The Gospels record many instances of Jesus performing mighty works. For example, Matthew mentioned ten specfic healings and one instance of power over natural forces in chapters 8 and 9 of his

The Appearance of the Redeemer

gospel. Jesus healed the leper (Matthew 8:2-4), healed the centurion's paralyzed servant (vv. 5-13), healed Peter's mother-in-law of a fever (vv. 14, 15), healed many with demons (v. 16), calmed the storm (vv. 23-27), healed two demoniacs (vv. 28-34), healed a paralytic (9:1-8), healed the woman with a hemorrhage (v. 20), raised the ruler's daughter from the dead (vv. 18-26), healed the two blind men (vv. 27-30), and healed the dumb demoniac (vv. 32-34).

These are a few of the miracles recorded in the Gospels. Matthew wrote that in different places, as Jesus went teaching and preaching the gospel, He healed "every sickness and every disease" (Matthew 9:35). John wrote that Jesus also did many other signs not recorded because it would take too much space to write them down (John 20:30; 21:25). These works bore witness to Him, gave Him great fame (Matthew 9:8, 26, 31, 33), and resulted in many believing in Him (John 2:11, 23; 3:2; 6:2, 14; 7:31; 9:16, 31-33; 12:18; et al.).

Although Jesus performed many miraculous works, these were not the heart of His ministry. In fact, He often tried to keep men from giving too much attention to them by asking those healed to refrain from telling others (Matthew 8:1-4; Mark 3:12; 5:43; 7:36; 8:22-26, 30; 9:9). Often He included a spiritual lesson with the works so men would see beyond the miraculous. Jesus' main ministry was spiritual. He performed miracles to support this ministry, not to hinder it. Finding solutions to physical problems must not interfere with solving man's root problems, the spiritual ones.

The Twelve Disciples

Jesus' ministry was not confined to His own labors. He appointed twelve disciples or apostles to represent Him in His ministry. They had "power against unclean spirits, to cast them out, to heal all manner of sickness and all manner of disease" (Matthew 10:1). They were sent to preach that "the kingdom of heaven is at hand" (v. 7)

Jesus warned His disciples, "I send you forth as sheep in the midst of wolves: be ye therefore wise as serpents, and harmless as doves. But beware of men: for they will deliver you up to the councils, and they will scourge you in their synagogues; and ye shall be brought before governors and kings for my sake, for a testimony against them and the Gentiles" (Matthew 10:16-18; cf. Mark 13:9; Luke 21:12). When they were brought before the authorities, Jesus promised them guidance through the Holy Spirit. They were to "take no thought how or what ye shall speak: for it shall be given you in that same hour what ye shall speak. For it is not ye that speak, but the Spirit of your Father which speaketh in you" (vv. 19, 20; cf. Mark 13:11; Luke 21:14, 15). Throughout their ministry the disciples could expect to be hated and persecuted (cf. Luke 10:3; 21:12-19).

This promised Holy Spirit "shall teach you [the apostles] all things, and bring all things to your remembrance, whatsoever I have said unto you" (John 14:26). He "will guide [the apostles] into all truth: for he shall not speak of himself; but whatsoever he shall hear, that shall he speak: and he will shew you things to come" (John 16:13; cf. vv. 14, 15; 14:16, 17; 15:26, 27; 17:7, 8, 17, 20; Acts 1:8). The reality of this promise enabled the disciples to recall and teach all the things Jesus had taught them, making it possible for them to record His word and for us to know His teachings and plan of salvation.

The persecution the disciples received was a reflection of the growing rejection Jesus was facing. "The disciple is not above his master, nor the servant above his lord. It is enough for the disciple that he be as his master, and the servant as his lord. If they have called the master of the house Beelzebub, how much more shall they call them of his household?" (Matthew 10:24, 25). The disciples could expect the same treatment as their Master received and be called the same. But this was not to deter them. They were to teach what they learned from their Master and "preach [it] upon the housetops" (v. 27) and not fear those who could kill "but rather fear him which is able to destroy both soul and body in hell" (v. 28).

John the Baptist

After fulfilling its purpose, John the Baptist's ministry ended in a tragic way. Herod the tetrarch seized John and put him in prison because he had denounced Herod's living with his brother's wife, Herodias. Herod wanted to put John to death but "feared the multitude, because they counted him as a prophet" (Matthew 14:5). At a birthday party Herodias's daughter danced and pleased Herod, "whereupon he promised with an oath to give her whatsoever she would ask" (v. 7). Prompted by her mother, the girl asked for John the Baptist's head. "The king was sorry: nevertheless for the oath's sake" (v. 9), Herod fulfilled the daughter's request (Matthew 14:1-12; cf. Mark 6:14-29; Luke 9:7-9).

The Appearance of the Redeemer

Upon hearing of John's death, Jesus withdrew to a lonely place to rest. John's death impressed on Jesus the opposition He would face, which in just a year would cause Him to give His life to redeem man. Jesus and His disciples needed rest before they resumed their strenuous ministry (Mark 6:31). The disciples had just returned from an exhausting teaching and preaching journey that drew large crowds, and they needed time to eat and rest.

Despite Jesus' desire for rest, the people continued to follow Him (Matthew 14:13; Mark 6:32, 33). His compassion moved Him to heal the sick and feed the hungry (Matthew 14:13-21; Mark 6:35-44). After Jesus sent His disciples to the other side of the Sea of Galilee by boat, He sent the people away. Jesus then went on a mountain to pray, knowing that after John's death He would soon express His love for all in the ultimate act—crucifixion. When evening had come, He went to join His disciples in the boat, walking on the sea (Matthew 14:22-36), again miraculously showing His divinity.

Increasing Opposition

The Pharisees and scribes increasingly opposed Jesus. They looked for every opportunity to find fault with Him. Once they accused His disciples of violating the traditions of the elders because the disciples did not wash their hands before they ate. Jesus rebuked the Pharisees for making the Word void by their own law, saying, "Why do ye also transgress the commandment of God by your tradition?" (Matthew 15:3). They had devised a method for avoiding the commandment to honor father and mother. Jesus told them, "Ye hypocrites, well did Esaias prophesy of you, saying, This people draweth nigh unto me with their mouth, and honoureth me with their lips; but their heart is far from me. But in vain they do worship me, teaching for doctrines the commandments of men" (vv. 7-9; cf. Mark 7:1-13).

Jesus explained to the people that it is not what one eats with unwashed hands that defiles a person "but that which cometh out of the mouth" (Matthew 15:11; Mark 7:15). What proceeds out of the mouth comes from the heart, Jesus said, and this defiles the man. "For out of the heart proceed evil thoughts, murders, adulteries, fornications, thefts, false witness, blasphemies" (Matthew 15:19; cf. Mark 7:14-23). The disciples noted that this statement offended the Pharisees. Jesus told them, "Every plant, which my heavenly Father hath not planted, shall be rooted up. Let them alone: they be blind leaders of the blind. And if the blind lead the blind, both shall fall into the ditch" (Matthew 15:13, 14).

The Pharisees did not forget Jesus, for they soon returned to ask for a sign. He again rebuked them by telling them they knew how to tell whether the weather would be fair or stormy by looking at the sky. He told them, "O ye hypocrites, ye can discern the face of the sky; but can ye not discern the signs of the times?" (Matthew 16:3). He said, "A wicked and adulterous generation seeketh after a sign; and there shall no sign be given unto it, but the sign of the prophet Jonas" (v. 4; cf. Mark 8:10-12).

These are just two instances of the conflict between Jesus and the Pharisees. Earlier they created conflicts over fasting (Matthew 9:14-17; Mark 2:18-28; Luke 5:33-38), plucking heads of grain and healing on the Sabbath (Matthew 12:1-14; Mark 2:23-3:5; Luke 6:1-11), an immoral woman's anointing Jesus' feet with ointment while at a Pharisee's house (Luke 7:36-50), healing a lame man at the pool of Bethesda (John 5:1-18), and what to do with a woman caught in adultery (John 8:1-11).

Jesus' View of Scripture

Since a conflict arose between Jesus and the Jewish leaders over the Scriptures, it is well for us to understand Jesus' attitude toward Scripture. He treated Scripture as the Word of God, the revelation of God to Israel. Jesus once stated that "the scripture cannot be broken" (John 10:35), and that He did not come to destroy the law or the prophets but to fulfill them (Matthew 5:17). He warned that

> whosoever therefore shall break one of these least commandments, and shall teach men so, he shall be called the least in the kingdom of heaven: but whosoever shall do and teach them, the same shall be called great in the kingdom of heaven. For I say unto you, That except your righteousness shall exceed the righteousness of the scribes and Pharisees, ye shall in no case enter into the kingdom of heaven. Matthew 5:19-20

When Jesus reproved the scribes and Pharisees, He did so because their legalistic approach to the Scriptures often voided the Word of God. They had built up a system of traditions not based on the Scriptures. Jesus did not oppose these people because they wanted to follow God's will but because they misunderstood His will and refused to be corrected. Desiring that all men do God's will, Jesus took every opportunity to explain more clearly the Sabbath commandment, fasting, alms giving, praying, and other laws of God.

In many cases Jesus reestablished the original purpose of the law. He reestablished, for example, the permanence of the marriage bond. The Mosaic law permitted divorce because of the hardness of man's heart. Jesus did not allow any reasons for divorce. The exception found in Matthew appears to be for the breaking of an engagement because of fornication. Matthew's Gospel was written to Jewish readers who held a high view of the betrothal period, requiring a formal divorce to break it (Matthew 1:18-22; 19:1-12).

During one of His confrontations with the Jews, Jesus told them their "father Abraham rejoiced to see my day: and he saw it, and was glad" (John 8:56). The Old Testament saints looked forward in faith to Him, but they "all died in faith, not having received the promises, but having seen them afar off" (Hebrews 11:13; see also 11:39, 40). Jesus told His disciples, "Blessed are your eyes, for they see: and your ears, for they hear. For verily I say unto you, that many prophets and righteous men have desired to see those things which ye see, and have not seen them: and to hear those things which ye hear, and have not heard them" (Matthew 13:16, 17; cf. Luke 10:23, 24). Peter later wrote, "Of which salvation the prophets have inquired and searched diligently, who prophesied of the grace that should come unto you: Searching what, or what manner of time the Spirit of Christ which was in them did signify, when it testified beforehand the sufferings of Christ, and the glory that should follow" (I Peter 1:10, 11). Jesus clearly spoke to His disciples about His being the One to whom the Scriptures pointed (see Luke 24:27, 44ff.).

Peter's Confession

At first the apostles did not fully understand Jesus' mission. Its significance developed slowly throughout His ministry. An example of this can be seen in Peter. He was introduced to Jesus by Andrew, his brother, and was told at the time that they had "found the Messias, which is, being interpreted, the Christ" (John 1:41). The full impact of these words did not come to Peter until three years later.

As Jesus and His disciples came to Caesarea Philippi, He asked them, "Whom do men say that I the Son of man am?" (Matthew 16:13). After the disciples mentioned some of the common opinions as to Jesus' identity, He asked, "But whom say ye that I am?" (v. 15). Peter spoke first, as he often did, making a confession, "Thou art the Christ, the Son of the living God" (v. 16). Peter received Jesus' commendation for his answer. The meaning of Jesus' ministry was just beginning to become plain to His disciples. Jesus told Peter that his understanding was not the result of human intelligence; rather, the Father had revealed it to him. Jesus told Peter, "Thou art Peter, and upon this rock I will build my church; and the gates of hell shall not prevail against it. And I will give unto thee the keys of the kingdom of heaven: and whatsoever thou shalt bind on earth shall be bound in heaven: and whatsoever thou shalt loose on earth shall be loosed in heaven" (vv. 18-20; cf. Mark 8:27-30; Luke 9:18-21).

There is much confusion about "binding and loosing." Jesus twice referred to this concept, once in a teaching sense and once in a disciplinary sense.

The "binding and loosing" Jesus spoke to Peter of is used in a teaching sense. Binding and loosing thus becomes a method of teaching about the kingdom whereby the meaning of God's Word would be unlocked so that men can understand and be saved. These disciples quickly grasped this as a teaching concept since "keys" were the symbol of the scribes, the teachers of the law.[2] Thus the "keys" were keys to understanding. The basis for saving and condemning was already decided in the "courts" of heaven. Those who believed that Jesus was the Christ and followed Him would find heaven's door opened to them. Those who rejected and refused Christ would find heaven's door shut tightly against them. Thus as a teaching method, making the gospel message clear would have either a binding or loosing affect on those who heard.

These keys were initially given to Peter (Acts 2), but Acts 15 shows the keys were given also to the apostles in general. They were called together to a conference in Jerusalem to consider the question how the Mosaic law related to the Gentiles. Peter did not decide this question on his own, as if he alone had the keys to the kingdom.

Jesus promised a "Comforter, which is the Holy Ghost, whom the Father will send in my name, he shall teach you all things, and bring all things to your remembrance, whatsoever I have said unto you"

---

[2]G. Campbell Morgan, *The Gospel According to Matthew*, Old Tappan, N.J.: Fleming Revell Co., p. 215.

(John 14:26). This promise is most significant; it ties the apostles' remembrance of Jesus' words to Jesus Christ Himself. He promised that the Holy Spirit would guide the apostles in their teaching and writing, enabling them to recall and teach all things He had taught them. This promise was made again before His ascension (Acts 1:8).

In his letter to the Ephesian church, Paul alluded to Jesus' teaching when he wrote about "the household of God ... built upon the foundation of the apostles and prophets, Jesus Christ himself being the chief corner stone" (Ephesians 2:19, 20). The church was built by the apostles, as a group, who possessed the keys. These keys enabled them to build Jesus' church and to put the word of God into a written form after Jesus' resurrection. This enabled the Christians to know about the redemptive events and God's will for their lives.

The Transfiguration

Soon after Peter's confession, the Transfiguration confirmed that Jesus was the Son of God. Jesus took Peter, James, and John to the top of a high mountain, and there He "was transfigured before them; and his face did shine as the sun, and his garments was white as light. And, behold, there appeared unto them Moses and Elias talking with him" (Matthew 17:2, 3). This was a new experience for these disciples. They reacted by wanting to build booths for the three men. At this point "a bright cloud overshadowed them, and behold a voice out of the cloud, which said, This is my beloved Son, in whom I am well pleased; hear ye him" (v. 5). The disciples were filled with awe.

The Transfiguration then came to a sudden end. Returning from the mountain, Jesus told His disciples, "Tell the vision to no man, until the Son of man be risen again from the dead" (Matthew 17:9). The disciples then asked Him about Elijah returning before the Messiah was to come. Jesus explained that Elijah had come, but "they knew him not, but have done unto him whatsoever they listed [pleased]. Likewise shall also the Son of man suffer of them" (v. 12). The disciples understood that He was speaking of John the Baptist (v. 13; cf. Mark 9:2-13; Luke 9:28-36).

Peter recalled the Transfiguration in his second epistle: "For we have not followed cunningly [cleverly] devised fables [myths] ... [we] were eyewitnesses of his majesty. For he received from God the Father honour and glory, when there came such a voice to him from the excellent glory, This is my beloved Son, in whom I am well pleased, And this voice which came from heaven we heard, when we were with him in the holy mount" (II Peter 1:16-18). The Transfiguration was one of three events that included a verbal witness from God (cf. Matthew 3:17; John 12:28).

Jesus Foretells His Death and Resurrection

After Jesus announced to Peter that He would build His church, and before the Transfiguration, Jesus began "to shew unto his disciples, how that he must go unto Jerusalem, and suffer many things of the elders and chief priests and scribes, and be killed, and be raised again the third day" (Matthew 16:21). Peter did not believe this should happen and rebuked Jesus for making such a statement. Jesus told Peter, "Get thee behind me, Satan: thou art an offence unto me: for thou savourest not the things that be of God, but those that be of men" (v. 23; see also 17:22, 23; cf. Mark 9:31, 32; Luke 9:44, 45).

Jesus planned to go to Jerusalem for the Passover, but some Pharisees warned Him that Herod planned to kill Him. He told them,

> Nevertheless I must walk today, and tomorrow, and the day following: for it cannot be that a prophet perish out of Jerusalem. O Jerusalem, Jerusalem, which killest the prophets, and stonest them that are sent unto thee; how often would I have gathered thy children together, as a hen doth gather her brood under her wings, and ye would not! Behold, your house is left unto you desolate: and verily I say unto you, Ye shall not see me, until the time come when ye shall say, Blessed is he that cometh in the name of the Lord. Luke 13:33-35; cf. Matthew 23:37-39

On His way to the city, Jesus explained more of His plans: "Behold, we go up to Jerusalem; and the Son of man shall be betrayed unto the chief priests and unto the scribes, and they shall condemn him to death, And shall deliver him to the Gentiles to mock, and to scourge, and to crucify him: and the third day he shall rise again" (Matthew 20:18, 19; cf. Mark 10:32-34; Luke 18:31-33). He explained this further when He answered the question of the wife of Zebedee about allowing her two sons to sit on His right and left in His kingdom:

> Ye know that the princes of the Gentiles exercise dominion over them, and they that are great exercise authority upon them. But it shall not be so among you: but whosoever will be great among you, let him be your

The Appearance of the Redeemer

minister; And whosoever will be chief among you, let him be your servant: Even as the Son of man came not to be ministered unto, but to minister, and to give his life a ransom for many. Matthew 20:25-28; cf. Mark 10:42-45

The purpose of Jesus' coming to the earth was to save the world (John 12:47; cf. 3:17). He was the Good Shepherd, who came "that [men] might have life, and that they might have it more abundantly.... The good shepherd giveth his life for the sheep.... I lay down my life, that I might take it again. No man taketh it from me, but I lay it down of myself. I have power to lay it down, and I have power to take it again.... This commandment have I received from my Father" (John 10:10-18). Jesus would give His life voluntarily to ransom man from the eternal consequences and power of sin.

The Last Passover

When Jesus approached Jerusalem, He sent two of His disciples to obtain a donkey and her colt. This fulfilled the prophecy concerning His entry: "Tell ye the daughter of Sion, Behold, thy King cometh unto thee, meek, and sitting upon an ass, and a colt the foal of an ass" (Matthew 21:5; cf. Zechariah 9:9). They

brought the ass, and the colt, ... and they set him thereon. And a very great multitude spread their garments in the way; others cut down branches from the trees, and strawed them in the way. And the multitudes that went before, and that followed, cried, saying, Hosanna to the son of David: Blessed is he that cometh in the name of the Lord; Hosanna in the highest. And when he was come into Jerusalem, all the city was moved, saying, Who is this? And the multitude said, This is Jesus the prophet of Nazareth of Galilee. Matthew 21:7-11; cf. Mark 11:1-10; Luke 19:28-40; John 12:12-19

The King, in weakness and poverty, entered Jerusalem. A triumphant entry it was, with a king riding on a beast of burden that no "political" king would ever ride, dressed in a homemade, seamless, woven garment, riding on streets covered with palm limbs—a person from Nazareth who Pilate and the Romans ignored. Only the common people were stirred up, and of course some Jewish leaders were miffed because they were not the center of attention. What a triumphant entry for the KING of KINGS!

Even as the triumphant entry was in progress, some people opposed what was happening. "Some of the Pharisees from among the multitude said unto him, Master, rebuke thy disciples. And he answered and said unto them, I tell you that, if these should hold their peace, the stones would immediately cry out" (Luke 19:39, 40; cf. Matthew 21:15, 16). Some Pharisees opposed Jesus' triumphant entry—they wanted Jesus the Messiah ignored. Jesus did not rebuke His disciples, for something of great importance was happening, and if they did not cry out the stones would.

As Jesus approached the city, He could see its magnificent temple. The great temple, covered with brilliant plates of gold, stood in an immense square, along with many structures of white marble. The city, an emblem of stability and prosperity, was surrounded with great walls. Yet Jesus saw more, and He wept over the city, saying,

> If thou hadst known, even thou, at least in this thy day, the things which belong unto thy peace! but now they are hid from thine eyes. For the days shall come upon thee, that thine enemies shall cast a trench about thee, and compass thee round, and keep thee in on every side, And shall lay thee even with the ground, and thy children within thee; and they shall not leave in thee one stone upon another; because thou knewest not the time of thy visitation. Luke 19:41-44; cf. Matthew 24:2; Mark 13:2

Even as He listened to the hosannas, Jesus realized what the results of the Jews' rejection of Him would mean for the city's future.

Jerusalem normally had many visitors during the Passover, but this season held exceptional excitement. Because Jesus' ministry had caught the attention of so many, the whole city was aroused by His entry. But the crowds who spread the palm branches and shouted the hosannas no doubt failed to realize that they too were fulfilling Zechariah's prophecy and thus identifying Jesus as the Messiah.

Just before going to Jerusalem, Jesus had raised Lazarus from the dead. "For this cause the people also met him, for that they heard that he had done this miracle" (John 12:18). The Jewish leaders resented Jesus' popularity and the converts that resulted from the raising of Lazarus; therefore the Sanhedrin council had raised the question,

> What do we? for this man doeth many miracles. If we let him thus alone, all men will believe on him: and the Romans shall come and take away both our place and nation. And one of them, named Caiaphas, being the

The Appearance of the Redeemer

high priest that same year, said unto them, Ye know nothing at all, nor consider that it is expedient for us, that one man should die for the people, and that the whole nation perish not. And this spake he not of himself: but being high priest that year, he prophesied that Jesus should die for that nation; and not for that nation only, but that also he should gather together in one the children of God that were scattered abroad. John 11:47-52

From that day forward the problem of Jesus was decided for the Jewish leaders; they would seek a way to put him to death (John 11:53). They seemed more concerned about preserving their institutions than understanding what Jesus' signs meant. Thus as Jesus' entry to Jerusalem drew such excitement, the leaders became fearful that everyone would believe in Him. They felt helpless and said one to another, "Perceive ye how ye prevail nothing? behold, the world is gone after him" (12:19).

Events in Jerusalem

The next day Jesus went to the temple, and for the second time He drove out all who sold and bought in the temple. He "overthrew the tables of the moneychangers . . . and said unto them, It is written, My house shall be called the house of prayer; but ye have made it a den of thieves" (Matthew 21:12, 13; cf. Mark11:15-17; Luke 19:45, 46). Three years earlier, at the beginning of His ministry, He had cleansed the temple. The changing of money and the selling of sacrifices were so profitable that the evildoers had returned. This second cleansing further identified Jesus as the Messiah, for it showed that He had authority from God to take charge of the temple. The second cleansing also brought strong response from the chief priests and scribes when they heard what happened. They "sought how they might destroy him: for they feared him, because all the people was astonished at his doctrine" (Mark 11:18).

The next day the chief priests and elders came to challenge Jesus' authority in the hope of blocking His progress. Jesus had clearly told of His mission before He came to Jerusalem. Now, with His triumphal entry and with the cleansing of the temple, it was clear to all what was happening; but the leaders and many of the people were stubborn and refused to believe. When Jesus returned to the temple the next day, they "came unto him as he was teaching, and said, By what authority doest thou these things? and who gave thee this authority?" (Matthew 21:23). This was a good question; yet it was not asked in hope of finding an answer. The Jewish leaders knew what He was teaching and who He claimed to be, but they were not interested in an answer. They wanted only to challenge Him. Jesus replied, "I also will ask you one thing, which if ye tell me, I in like wise will tell you by what authority I do these things. The baptism of John, whence was it? from heaven, or of men?" (vv. 24, 25). They did not answer because they realized if they said John's baptism was from heaven, He would then ask, "Why did ye not then believe him?" (v. 25). If they said, "Of men," they knew the people would react, for all men held John as a prophet. So they did not answer, and neither did Jesus (cf. Mark 11:27-33; Luke 20:1-8).

In response to the Jews' challenge, Jesus spoke three parables to warn the people of the stubbornness and blindness of the Jewish leaders. The first, a parable about two sons, showed that the Jewish leaders were unprepared to receive Him. A "lower people," not the chosen ones, were ready. The second, a parable about the vineyard, showed that the Jews had repeatedly killed God's prophets and were about to kill His Son. Had they not read in the Scriptures, "The stone which the builders rejected, the same is become the head of the corner: this is the Lord's doing, and it is marvellous in our eyes?" (Matthew 21:42). This time their rejection would mean that "the kingdom of God shall be taken from [them], and given to a nation bringing forth the fruits thereof" (v. 43). The third parable, about a marriage feast, showed how an invitation that was refused was given to others. Similarly, Jesus had invited the Jews to follow, but since they refused, He would now invite others (Matthew 21:28-22:14; cf. Mark 12:1-11; Luke 20:9-18).

The point of these parables is, "For many are called, but few are chosen" (Matthew 22:14). Hearing this, the Jewish leaders surely recalled Jesus' earlier comments that "the kingdom of God shall be taken from you [Jews], and given to a nation bringing forth fruit" (Matthew 21:43). The chief priests and the Pharisees understood that Jesus was speaking of them. From then on they attempted to arrest Him but feared the multitudes who saw Him as a prophet. The leaders would have to turn the masses against Him before He could be arrested (Matthew 21:45, 46; Mark 12:12; Luke 20:19, 20).

"Then went the Pharisees, and took counsel how they might entangle him in his talk" (Matthew 22:15). They decided upon three questions. The first concerned taxes. "Is it lawful to give tribute unto Caesar, or not?" (v. 17). Jesus, aware of their evil intention, told them bluntly, "Why tempt ye me, ye hypocrites?" (v. 18). Taking a coin with Caesar's image on it, He gave them a simple answer: "Render ... unto Caesar the things which are Caesar's; and unto God the things that are God's" (v. 21; cf. Mark 12:13-17; Luke 20:21-26).

The Sadducees' second question concerned resurrection and marriage in heaven. The affect of this question (and Jesus' answer) on the people was just the opposite from what the Sadducees had wanted. "When the multitude heard this, they were astonished at his doctrine" (Matthew 22:33; Mark 12:18-27; Luke 20:27-40).

The third question came from the Pharisees: "Master, which is the great commandment in the law?" (Matthew 22:36). This query had become a favorite of this group who frequently discussed the law. He quickly answered, "Thou shalt love the Lord thy God with all thy heart, and with all thy soul, and with all thy mind. This is the first and great commandment. And the second is like unto it, Thou shalt love thy neighbor as thyself. On these two commandments hang all the law and the prophets" (vv. 37-40; cf. Mark 12:28-34).

After answering these three questions, while the Pharisees were still gathered together, Jesus asked them, "What think ye of Christ? whose son is he?" (Matthew 22:42). They quickly replied that He was the son of David. Then Jesus asked them, "How then doth David in spirit call him Lord, saying, The LORD said unto my Lord, Sit thou on my right hand, till I make thine enemies thy footstool? If David then call him Lord, how is he his son?" None of them could answer; thus they dared not ask Him additional questions (vv. 43-45; cf. Mark 12:35-37; Luke 20:41-44).

Jesus then spoke to the crowds about the false leadership and hypocrisy of the scribes and Pharisees. They were the ones who "say, and do not" (Matthew 23:3), who put "heavy burdens" (v. 4) on men's shoulders, but would not assist others in moving them. They "shut up the kingdom of heaven against men" (v. 13) because they would neither enter nor allow others to enter. Jesus spoke woe unto them, pointing out they were "blind guides, which strain at a gnat, and swallow a camel ... full of extortion and excess ... full of dead men's bones" (vv. 24, 25, 27). They were the same as their fathers who shed the blood of the prophets. "O Jerusalem, Jerusalem, thou that killest the prophets, and stonest them which are sent unto thee, how often would I have gathered thy children together, even as a hen gathereth her chickens under her wings, and ye would not! Behold, your house is left unto you desolate. For I say unto you, Ye shall not see me henceforth, till ye shall say, Blessed is he that cometh in the name of the Lord" (vv. 37-39; Mark 12:38-40; Luke 20:45-47).

Jesus' words were strong and frank. There was no further need to avoid offending the Jewish religious leaders. They had shown their true colors by their constant attempts to entangle Him by His words.

The Jews had rejected Jesus although "he had done so many miracles before them, yet they believed not on him" (John 12:37). Their rejection fulfilled Isaiah's prophecy (Isaiah 53:3). The Jews' rejection was not complete, however, for some believed; "but because of the Pharisees they did not confess him, lest they should be put out of the synagogue: For they loved the praise of men more than the praise of God" (John 12:42, 43).

Jesus came to the world as a light. Those who hear and obey His sayings, He will not judge. "I came not to judge the world, but to save the world" (John 12:47). But those who have rejected Him have a judge. "The word that I have spoken, the same shall judge him in the last day" (v. 48). The mission of Jesus, who was sent from God to bring eternal life to those who receive Him as Lord and Savior, was now close to being fulfilled.

After Jesus taught His disciples about the destruction of Jerusalem and the end of the world (Matthew 24 and 25), He turned to His disciples and said, "Ye know that after two days is the feast of the passover, and the Son of man is betrayed to be crucified." The opposition to Jesus had reached the point where "assembled together the chief priests, and the scribes, and the elders of the people, unto the palace of the high priest, who was called Caiaphas, And consulted that they might take Jesus by subtilty, and kill him" (Matthew 26:1-5; cf. Mark 14:1, 2; Luke 22:1, 2). They covenanted with one of the disciples to deliver Jesus for thirty pieces of silver (Matthew 26:15).

The Lord's Supper

Jesus told His disciples to prepare for the Passover, since His time was at hand. During this supper He instituted two ordinances to be observed by His followers: communion and foot washing. "Jesus took bread, and blessed it, and brake it, and gave it to the disciples, and said, Take, eat; this is my body. And he took the cup, and gave

The Appearance of the Redeemer

thanks, and gave it to them, saying, Drink ye all of it; for this is my blood of the new testament, which is shed for many for the remission of sins" (Matthew 26:26-28; cf. Mark 14:22-25; Luke 22:17-20; I Corinthians 11:23-26). The bread is taken in memory of Christ's broken body. The cup recalls Christ's shed blood. Communion symbolizes the new covenant brought into effect by His blood.

After supper Jesus "poureth water into a basin, and began to wash the disciples' feet, and to wipe them with the towel" (John 13:5). After having washed their feet, he explained what he had done. He told them, "Ye call me Master and Lord: and ye say well; for so I am. If I then, your Lord and Master, have washed your feet, ye also ought to wash one another's feet. For I have given you an example, that ye should do as I have done to you. . . . If ye know these things, happy are ye if ye do them" (John 13:13-15, 17). Jesus used the occasion of the Lord's Supper to introduce a new ordinance that reminded disciples of brotherly service. This is an example all Christians should practice, and they will receive a blessing from obedience.

After the Lord's Supper, Jesus and His disciples went to the Mount of Olives. There Jesus warned the disciples that "it is written, I will smite the shepherd, and the sheep of the flock shall be scattered" (Matthew 26:31). They would all desert Him, and He would have to face His crucifixion alone (cf. Mark 14:26-31; Luke 22:31-38).

Jesus then went to a place called Gethsemane. He told the three disciples with Him that His soul was very sorrowful, even to death, and that they should stay near as He went to pray.

> And he went a little further, and fell on his face, and prayed, saying, O my Father, if it be possible, let this cup pass from me: nevertheless not as I will, but as thou wilt. And he cometh unto the disciples, and findeth them asleep, and saith unto Peter, What, could ye not watch with me one hour? Watch and pray, that ye enter not into temptation: the spirit indeed is willing, but the flesh is weak. He went away again the second time, and prayed, saying, O my Father, if this cup may not pass away from me, except I drink it, thy will be done. And he came and found them asleep again: for their eyes were heavy. And he left them, and went away again, and prayed the third time, saying the same words. Then cometh he to his disciples, and saith unto them, Sleep on now, and take your rest: behold, the hour is at hand, and the Son of man is betrayed into the hands of sinners. Rise, let us be going: behold, he is at hand that doth betray me. Matthew 26:39-46; cf. Mark 14:32-42; Luke 22:39-46

At that moment, Judas, one of the twelve, brought soldiers and a crowd to seize Jesus. To identify Jesus, Judas greeted Him with a kiss. The soldiers who were sent from the chief priests and elders took Jesus. He could have called many legions of angels to protect Himself; however, He knew the time of His suffering had come. Instead of avoiding His enemies as He had done earlier, He submitted to them, thus fulfilling Scriptures (see Matthew 26:47-56; Mark 14:43-50; Luke 22:47-53; John 18:3-11).

The Trial

The events that followed brought Jesus before the high priest (Caiaphas), the scribes, and the elders for trial. These leaders "sought false witness against Jesus, to put him to death; But found none: yea, though many false witnesses came, yet found they none" (Matthew 26:59, 60). In the Jewish law a minimum of two witnesses was required to support a charge. Apparently these witnesses reported isolated instances with no two agreeing (Deuteronomy 19:15). More and more witnesses were called until finally two came forth with the same charge: that Jesus had said, "I am able to destroy the temple of God, and to build it in three days" (Matthew 26:61). Since any threat against the temple could result in the death sentence, this charge was quickly pursued.

The high priest asked Jesus for an answer to the charge, but He remained silent since no evidence had been produced. Then the high priest put forth another question: "I adjure thee by the living God, that thou tell us whether thou be the Christ, the Son of God" (Matthew 26:63). Since this question was prefaced with the oath of the covenant, Jesus had to answer. To remain silent would have been criminal. To answer falsely was impossible for Him. This was the time for Jesus to speak the truth; therefore, He affirmed that He was the Christ. "Jesus saith unto him, Thou hast said: nevertheless I say unto you, Hereafter shall ye see the Son of man sitting on the right hand of power, and coming in the clouds of heaven" (v. 64).

The time had come for Jesus' mission to be fulfilled; His crucifixion would result from His own testimony. The high priest quickly cried, "He hath spoken blasphemy; what further need have we of witnesses? behold, now ye have heard his blasphemy" (Matthew 26:65). Instead of acknowledging Jesus' claim, the Jews used it to condemn Him to death. There was no longer a need for witnesses since all had heard Him. "What think ye? They answered and said, He is guilty of death" (v. 66). The religious leaders quickly treated Him as a condemned criminal by spitting at Him and striking Him (vv. 67, 68; cf. Mark 14:53-65; Luke 22:66-71; John 18:12-24).

"When the morning was come, all the chief priests and elders of the people took counsel against Jesus to put him to death: And when they had bound him, they led him away, and delivered him to Pontius Pilate the governor" (Matthew 27:1, 2; Mark 15:1; Luke 23:1; John 18:28). Jesus was taken to Pilate because the Romans had taken the power of imposing the death penalty away from the Jews (John 18:31). These events fulfilled the prophecies Jesus had spoken of earlier (Matthew 20:18ff.).

After interviewing the Jews concerning the charges against Jesus and talking to Him personally, Pilate said, "I find no fault in this man.... And [the chief priests and multitudes] were the more fierce, saying, He stirreth up the people, teaching throughout all Jewry, beginning from Galilee to this place" (Luke 23:4, 5).

Hearing that Jesus was a Galilean and thus belonged under Herod's jurisdiction, Pilate sent Him to Herod. Herod, glad to have this noted Jesus sent to Him, questioned Jesus, but "he answered him nothing" (Luke 23:9). Herod and his soldiers then "mocked him, and arrayed him in a gorgeous robe, and sent him again to Pilate" (v. 11).

Pilate told the chief priests, rulers, and people: "I, having examined him before you, have found no fault in this man touching those things whereof ye accuse him: No, nor yet Herod: for I sent you to him; and, lo, nothing worthy of death is done unto him. I will therefore chastise him, and release him" (Luke 23:14-16).

Pilate may have wanted to release Jesus because Pilate realized it was out of "envy they had delivered him" (Matthew 27:18). Pilate sought to free Jesus according to the custom of releasing a notorious prisoner at the time of the Passover feast. He offered to release to the Jews either a murderer and robber named Barabbas or Jesus. Pilate did not offer to release Jesus directly because, if he did, the Jews would cried out that he was not Caesar's friend (John 19:12).

In an attempt to get the people to ask for Barabbas's death, Pilate pointed out that neither he nor Herod had found any crime against Jesus, but that he would submit Jesus to scourging as punishment. By choosing Jesus the Jews could prevent the notorious Barabbas from being released. At the same time their thirst for vengeance against Jesus could be satisfied. The Jewish leaders persuaded the people to forget any good feelings they had for Jesus and to ask freedom for the murderer Barabbas. Apparently none of Jesus' followers were present, or if they were, they did not attempt to change the crowd's views. Pilate released Barabbas and Jesus faced death.

Then Pilate asked, "What shall I do then with Jesus which is called Christ?" (Matthew 27:22). Quickly the people put forth their leaders' views and shouted, "Let him be crucified" (v. 22). Pilate responded, "Why, what evil hath he done?" (v. 23). No longer rational, the people could only shout all the more, "Let him be crucified. When Pilate saw that he could prevail nothing, but that rather a tumult [riot] was made" (vv. 23, 24), he used the Jewish symbol of washing his hands to show he was free of any guilt in the decision. He then told the crowd, "I am innocent of the blood of this just person: see ye to it. Then answered all the people, and said, His blood be on us, and on our children" (vv. 24, 25). Jesus was then delivered to be crucified (cf. Mark 15:7-15; Luke 23:13-25; John 18:38–19:16).

The Crucifixion

Jesus was quickly prepared for crucifixion. The soldiers showed their contempt and mockery by putting a scarlet robe and a crown of thorns on Him and by shouting, "Hail, King of the Jews!" (Matthew 27:29). These acts ridiculed both Jesus and the Jews by making light of their national expectation of a Messiah. The soldiers responded by spitting on Jesus, striking Him, and finally stripping Him of the robe and redressing Him in His own clothes. Led to a place called *Golgotha*, which means "the place of a skull," He was crucified (v. 33). They placed above His head the charges against Him written in Greek, Latin, and Hebrew: "Jesus of Nazareth the King of the Jews" (John 19:19). Many of the Jews protested this wording. They wanted it to read, "He said, I am King of the Jews" (v. 21). Pilate would not allow the sign to be changed: "What I have written I have written." Unknowingly he left a sign that accurately described Jesus (v. 22; cf. Matthew 27:27-37; Mark:15:16-26; Luke 23:27-38).

As Jesus hung on the cross, He faced more jeers from the very people whose hope lay in Him. The passersby shouted, "Thou that destroyest the temple, and buildest it in three days, save thyself. If thou be the Son of God, come down from the cross" (Matthew

27:40). The Jewish leaders also mocked Him: "He saved others; himself he cannot save. If he be the King of Israel, let him now come down from the cross, and we will believe him. He trusted in God; let him deliver him now" (vv. 42, 43; cf. Mark 15:29-32; Luke 23:35-37).

Crucifixion was one of the cruelest forms of death ever devised. Designed to make death as lingering and painful as the body could endure, crucifixion was also considered the most shameful punishment possible. Jesus—the Innocent One, the Son of God, the Creator—by enduring crucifixion died a death of untold physical and mental suffering. The physical pain seems enough, but the mental suffering must have been beyond words when one realizes who Jesus is and what He endured as men rejected Him, while He suffered for their sins. He refused the mixture of strong wine and myrrh, which would have deadened the pain. He came into the world to die for men's sins, and He bore the full extent of suffering. Since His death was a voluntary sacrifice, He prayed, "Father, forgive them; for they know not what they do" (Luke 23:34). He desired forgiveness for those who brought about His death.

Darkness gathered over the land for the last three hours Jesus hung on the cross (Matthew 27:45; Luke 23:44). We are not told the cause or the meaning of this darkness. We do know this event was a testimony that He was the Light of the world. As we will see later, it was one of the events that caused the centurion and other soldiers who crucified Christ to say, "Truly this was the Son of God" (v. 54).

The darkness brought a deep sense of loneliness to Christ. About the ninth hour (three o'clock in the afternoon), Jesus cried out with a loud voice, "Eli, Eli, lama sabachthani," which means, "My God, My God, why hast thou forsaken me?" (v. 46; cf. Mark 15:33-35). This has also been translated, "My God, My God, to what sort of persons hast thou left me?"[3] This gives the thought that God, by withdrawing His protective hand that was over His Son, left Him to suffer at the hands of His enemies without any hope of physical deliverance.

Jesus knew when He was near the point of death. John wrote, "Jesus knowing that all things were now accomplished, that the scripture might be fulfilled, saith I thirst" (John 19:28). Suffering thirst, He needed a drink to moisten His throat for His last cry. At the

---

[3] R. C. H. Lenski, *Interpretation of St. Mark's Gospel*, Columbus, Ohio: Wartburg Press, 1946, p. 717.

time when the Passover lamb was slaughtered, Jesus cried with a loud voice, "It is finished," and yielded His spirit (John 19:30; Luke 23:46). Jesus' death finished His redemptive work. By giving His blood, the life of the body, He died once for all men's sins (Hebrews 9:12, 14, 26; cf. Romans 6:10).

At the moment of Jesus' death, the temple veil, which separated the Holy Place and the Holy of Holies, ripped from top to bottom into two pieces. The torn veil symbolized the end to the old covenant's system of sacrifice and worship. The temple was no longer needed after He accomplished His work on the cross.[4] The torn veil had served its purpose in preparing man for the Christ. The torn veil further—and more significantly—signifies that access to God is now available to all who enter through the Door and the Bread of Life. There is no further need for additional sacrifices or for a high priest since Christ "offered one sacrifice for sins for ever" (Hebrews 10:12; cf. 7:26-28). Later this will be discussed in detail.

Other events, such as earthquakes and the opening of graves, also occurred at Jesus' death. Some dead persons rose after Jesus' resurrection and appeared in Jerusalem (Matthew 27:51-54; Mark 15:38). A centurion, seeing these things, "feared greatly, saying, Truly this was the Son of God" (Matthew 27:54; cf. Mark 15:39; Luke 23:47). The multitudes assembled "to that sight, beholding the things which were done, smote their breasts, and returned" (Luke 23:48).

Since He had hung on the cross for a relatively short time, Jesus did not die because of the physical punishment His body received. He voluntarily gave up His spirit before His body would have normally died (cf. John 10:17, 18). Thus He gave His life as a ransom for man, as a sacrifice that would finally restore man to His original position before God. His death at the ninth hour occurred at the time of the evening sacrifice; thus He became "the Lamb of God, which taketh away the sin of the world" (1:29).

As the Sabbath approached, the Jews went to Pilate to ask that the legs of Jesus and the other two men crucified with Him be broken, so the victims would die. Then their bodies could be removed before the

---

[4] Yet the temple and its sacrificial system did continue in operation until A.D. 70. For a time even the disciples frequented it (Acts 2:46; 3:1; 5:20, 25, 42; 21:26).

Sabbath. The law required that a body should not be left hanging overnight (Deuteronomy 21:23). Since the forthcoming Sabbath was a "high day" (it was both a Sabbath and the second Paschal day), the Jews felt even stronger about this matter; so Pilate granted their wish. When the soldiers came to Jesus, they found Him already dead; therefore, they did not break His legs. When one of the soldiers pierced Jesus' side with a spear, blood and water came forth, evidence that He was dead. "These things were done, that the scripture should be fulfilled, A bone of him shall not be broken. And again another scripture saith, They shall look on him whom they pierced" (John 19:36, 37). Thus the Scriptures concerning the Paschal Lamb (Exodus 12:46; Numbers 9:12) and the righteous, suffering Servant (Psalm 34:19-22) were fulfilled.

The Burial of Jesus

With the Sabbath rapidly approaching, one of Jesus' disciples, a rich man named Joseph, asked Pilate for Jesus' body. After Joseph received permission to bury it, he and Nicodemus wrapped the body with linen cloth and spices according to Jewish burial custom and placed it in a new tomb near the place of crucifixion. The tomb was closed by rolling a huge stone across the opening (Matthew 27:57-61; Mark 15:42-47; Luke 23:50-56; John 19:31-42).

The next day the Jews, remembering that Jesus had said He would rise again after three days, asked Pilate to have the tomb sealed and guarded by soldiers. The Jews feared that Jesus' disciples would "steal him away, and say unto the people, He is risen from the dead: so the last error shall be worse than the first" (Matthew 27:64). Pilate instructed the soldiers to "make it as sure as ye can" (v. 65). There would be no way for the disciples to take the body from the tomb.

The Resurrection

In the disciples' minds the last week of Jesus' life began on a triumphant note with His entry into Jerusalem but ended in despair with His death on the cross. Everything that had recently looked so promising now seemed hopeless. The crucifixion was so real the disciples forgot about their Master's statement that He would rise after three days. Obviously they did not catch the full meaning of His teaching, for "as yet they knew not the scripture, that he must rise again from the dead" (John 20:9).

Since Jesus died just before the Sabbath, there had not been sufficient time for His burial. Therefore, the disciples decided to return after the Sabbath to complete the burial. At the dawn of

> the first day of the week, came Mary Magdalene and the other Mary to see the sepulchre. And, behold, there was a great earthquake: for the angel of the Lord descended from heaven, and came and rolled back the stone from the door, and sat upon it. His countenance was like lightning, and his raiment white as snow: And for fear of him the keepers did shake, and became as dead men. And the angel answered and said unto the women, Fear not ye: for I know that ye seek Jesus, which was crucified. He is not here: for he is risen, as he said. Come, see the place where the Lord lay. Matthew 28:1-6; cf. Mark 16:1-6; Luke 24:1-7

Because death had been unable to keep its power over Him, the prophecy was fulfilled concerning Christ that God would "not leave my soul in hell [Sheol]" (Psalm 16:10; cf. Acts 2:27, 31). The Old Testament term *Sheol* refers to the place of the dead, not the place of eternal punishment: "neither wilt thou suffer thine Holy One to see corruption" (Psalm 16:10). As He repeatedly foretold, Jesus arose from the dead. This gave unquestionable evidence that He was the Christ (Romans 1:4) and made possible the completion of the work of man's redemption. He was "raised again for our justification" (4:25), which was completed by His appearing "in the presence of God for us. . . . to put away sin by the sacrifice of himself" (Hebrews 9:24, 26).

The women and disciples did not comprehend what had happened at the empty tomb. The women went to tell the disciples about the empty tomb. Nevertheless, the report "seemed to them as idle tales, and they believed them not" (Luke 24:11).

Later that day two disciples traveling to the village of Emmaus "talked together of all these things which had happened. And it came to pass, that, while they communed together and reasoned, Jesus himself drew near, and went with them. But their eyes were holden [restrained NKJV] that they should not know him" (Luke 24:14-16). He inquired about their conversation. They sadly asked,

> Art thou only a stranger in Jerusalem, and hast not known the things which are come to pass there in these days? And he said unto them, What things? And they said unto him, Concerning Jesus of Nazareth, which was

a prophet mighty in deed and word before God and all the people: And how the chief priests and our rulers delivered him to be condemned to death, and have crucified him. But we trusted that it had been he which should have redeemed Israel: and beside all this, to day is the third day since these things were done. Yea, and certain women also of our company made us astonished, which were early at the sepulchre; and when they found not his body, they came, saying, that they had also seen a vision of angels, which said that he was alive. And certain of them which were with us went to the sepulchre, and found it even so as the women had said: but him they saw not. Then he said unto them, O fools, and slow of heart to believe all that the prophets have spoken: Ought not Christ to have suffered these things, and to enter into his glory? And beginning at Moses and all the prophets, he expounded unto them in all the scriptures the things concerning himself. Luke 24:18-27

Later, when Jesus was with the two disciples at supper, "their eyes were opened, and they knew him" (Luke 24:31), but then He vanished. Quickly, the two disciples returned to Jerusalem and found the eleven apostles. They excitedly said, "The Lord is risen indeed, and hath appeared to Simon" (v. 34). As the two travelers told what had happened, Jesus came and stood among them. Being frightened, they were asked by Jesus, "Why are ye troubled? and why do thoughts arise in your hearts? Behold my hands and my feet, that it is I myself: handle me, and see; for a spirit hath not flesh and bones, as ye see me have" (vv. 38, 39; cf. Matthew 28:16, 17; Mark 16:14).

Jesus then explained to the band of disciples:

These are the words which I spake unto you, while I was yet with you, that all things must be fulfilled, which were written in the law of Moses, and in the prophets, and in the psalms, concerning me. Then opened he their understanding, that they might understand the scriptures, And said unto them, Thus it is written, and thus it behoved Christ to suffer, and to rise from the dead the third day: And that repentance and remission of sins should be preached in his name among all nations, beginning at Jerusalem. And ye are witnesses of these things. And, behold, I send the promise of my Father upon you: but tarry ye in the city of Jerusalem, until ye be endued with power from on high. Luke 24:44-49

As Jesus stated, "Christ [was] to suffer, and to rise from the dead the third day" (Luke 24:46). On the cross Jesus cried out at the end of His suffering, "It is finished" (John 19:30). His death finished the work of redemption. He was the Lamb of God, "without spot" (Hebrews 9:14), who shed His own blood to redeem sinful man. As the author of Hebrews wrote, "By his own blood he entered in once into the holy place, having obtained eternal redemption for us" (Hebrews 9:12; cf. vv. 26, 28). There was another part to Jesus' death, His resurrection. As Paul wrote, Jesus our Lord "was delivered [put to death] for our offences, and was raised again for our justification" (Romans 4:25; cf. II Corinthians 5:21). His resurrection is important: "If Christ be not raised, our faith is vain; ye are yet in your sins" (I Corinthians 15:17; cf. 14).

The Ascension

Jesus made many other appearances to His followers during the forty days after His crucifixion (Acts 1:3). Finally, as He and the apostles were together at the Mount of Olives near Bethany, the time approached for His ascension. He explained that the Holy Spirit would come to give them power to be His witnesses in Jerusalem, in Judea, in Samaria, and to the ends of the earth.

> When he had spoken these things, while they beheld, he was taken up; and a cloud received him out of their sight. And while they looked steadfastly toward heaven as he went up, behold, two men stood by them in white apparel; which also said, Ye men of Galilee, why stand ye gazing up into heaven? this same Jesus, which is taken up from you into heaven, shall so come in like manner as ye have seen him go into heaven. Acts 1:8-11

Chapter 4

Redemption Interpreted

Introduction

When Jesus Christ "was taken up; and a cloud received him out of their sight" (Acts 1:9), His personal earthly ministry ended after lasting about three years. This marked the beginning of the kingdom and the church. The disciples had received the Great Commission from Jesus. He had told them, "All power is given unto me in heaven and in earth. Go ye therefore, and teach all nations, baptizing them in the name of the Father, and of the Son, and of the Holy Ghost: Teaching them to observe all things whatsoever I have commanded you: and, lo, I am with you alway, even unto the end of the world" (Matthew 28:18-20).

Jesus did not leave His followers alone to face the task of evangelizing the world. He had earlier promised them the Counselor, "which is the Holy Ghost, whom the Father will send in my name, he shall teach you all things, and bring all things to your remembrance, whatsoever I have said unto you" (John 14:26). He repeated this promise just before His ascension. "But ye shall receive power, after that the Holy Ghost is come upon you: and ye shall be witnesses unto me both in Jerusalem, and in all Judaea, and in Samaria, and unto the uttermost part of the earth" (Acts 1:8). Let us look at some of the apostles' messages.

The Pentecost Sermon

After the disciples received the Holy Spirit at Pentecost, they spoke in several languages as the Spirit directed them. This bewildered the Jews who were visiting Jerusalem from various nations, since they heard the disciples speaking in their own languages. Some, amazed and perplexed, asked, "What does this mean?" (Acts 2:12 RSV; cf. Joel 2:28-32). Others reacted by thinking the disciples were drunk.

Peter preached the first sermon to explain what had happened. The disciples were not drunk, as some people thought, but had received what the prophet Joel had spoken of (Acts 2:16-21). Peter spoke of Jesus' life, suffering, and death, and of the responsibility of the Jewish people for His death. He also spoke of the resurrection and glorification of Jesus, showing what happened to Him was according to the Scriptures. Peter concluded his message with these words: "Let all the house of Israel know assuredly, that God hath made that same Jesus, whom ye have crucified, both Lord and Christ" (v. 36). Jesus was the long-awaited Messiah of Israel, that is, the Christ (*Christ* is the Greek term for the Hebrew *Messiah*).

Peter's message brought great conviction to the hearts of the Jewish hearers. In anguish they responded, "What shall we do?" (Acts 2:37). Peter told them, "Repent, and be baptized every one of you in the name of Jesus Christ for the remission of sins, and ye shall receive the gift of the Holy Ghost. For the promise is unto you, and to your children, and to all that are afar off, even as many as the Lord our God shall call" (vv. 38, 39).

This basic message of Christ's suffering and death on the cross was preached again and again; it was the central message of the early church. The crucifixion of Jesus was not the defeat it first appeared to be. His death was essential to bringing redemption to mankind. The following quotations from the Book of Acts show that the death and resurrection of Jesus Christ were the heart of the early church's message.

> [The Jewish people had] killed the Prince of life, whom God hath raised from the dead. Acts 3:15

> By the name of Jesus Christ of Nazareth, whom ye crucified, whom God raised from the dead.... This is the stone which was set at nought of you builders, which is become the head of the corner. Neither is there salvation in any other: for there is none other name under heaven given among men, whereby we must be saved. 4:10-12

> The God of our fathers raised up Jesus, whom ye slew and hanged on a tree. Him hath God exalted with his right hand to be a Prince and a Saviour, for to give repentance to Israel, and forgiveness of sins. 5:30, 31

He was led as a sheep to the slaughter; and like a lamb dumb before his shearer, so opened he not his mouth. . . . [explaining this] Philip opened his mouth, and began at the same scripture, and preached unto him Jesus. 8:32, 35

They slew and hanged [him] on a tree: Him God raised up the third day, and shewed him openly. . . . To him give all the prophets witness, that through his name whosoever believeth in him shall receive remission of sins. 10:39, 40, 43

And we declare unto you glad tidings, how that the promise which was made unto the fathers, God hath fulfilled the same unto us their children, in that he hath raised up Jesus again. . . . he, whom God raised again, saw no corruption. Be it known unto you therefore, men and brethren, that through this man is preached unto you the forgiveness of sins: And by him all that believe are justified from all things, from which ye could not be justified by the law of Moses. 13:32-39

Paul, as his manner was, went in unto them [Jews], and three sabbath days reasoned with them out of the scriptures, opening and alleging, that Christ must needs have suffered, and risen again from the dead. 17:2, 3

Certain philosophers . . . said, What will this [Paul] babbler say? other some, He seemeth to be a setter forth of strange gods: because he preached unto them Jesus, and the resurrection. 17:18

[God] hath appointed a day, in the which he will judge the world in righteousness by that man [Jesus] whom he hath ordained; whereof he hath given assurance unto all men, in that he hath raised him from the dead. 17:31

Saying none other things than those which the prophets and Moses did say should come: That Christ should suffer, and that he should be the first that should rise from the dead, and should shew light unto the people, and to the Gentiles. 26:22, 23

Redemption Through Christ

The above Scriptures make it clear that Christ's death was central to the gospel's message. Why was Christ's death so important?

Man's sin in the Garden of Eden broke the fellowship and communion between God and man. Since then man has refused to submit to the will of God and has set himself against God. God told His chosen people, "Ye shall do my judgments, and keep mine ordinances, to walk therein: I am the Lord your God. Ye shall therefore keep my statutes, and my judgments: which if a man do, he shall live in them: I am the Lord" (Leviticus 18:4, 5). Man's response was the "transgression of the law" (I John 3:4), which showed that he had become hostile to God and had "enmity against God" (Romans 8:7). God's holiness meant He could not tolerate sin and the presence of evil. God's holiness required Him to separate Himself from sin and thus from sinful man. The only way the two could be brought together again was by an act of God that would remove the enmity and cause a reconciliation of the two estranged parties.

Why would God want to remove the barrier between Him and man when it was man who refused to accept His Word through faith and listened to Satan in the Garden? The motivation for this reconciliation is love. The most prominent and familiar Scripture on this states, "For God so loved the world, that he gave his only begotten Son, that whosoever believeth in him should not perish, but have everlasting life" (John 3:16). John repeated this in his First Epistle: "In this was manifested the love of God toward us, because that God sent his only begotten Son into the world, that we might live through him. Herein is love, not that we loved God, but that he loved us, and sent his Son to be the propitiation for our sins" (I John 4:9, 10). God's love restores man to his original relationship: "Behold, what manner of love the Father hath bestowed upon us, that we should be called the sons of God" (I John 3:1). Christians "love him [God], because he first loved us" (4:19). Christians obey God "for this is the love of God, that we keep his commandments" (5:3).

Similarly, Paul wrote, "God commendeth his love toward us, in that, while we were yet sinners, Christ died for us" (Romans 5:8). "The love of Christ constraineth us; because we thus judge, that if one died for all, then were all dead: And that he died for all, that they which live should not henceforth live unto themselves, but unto him which died for them, and rose again" (II Corinthians 5:14, 15). "Walk in love, as Christ also hath loved us, and hath given himself for us an offering and a sacrifice to God for a sweet smelling savour" (Ephesians 5:2). And "the kindness and love of God our Saviour toward man appeared . . . according to his mercy he saved us" (Titus 3:4, 5). Christians should alway remember such love towards them.

Redemption Interpreted

Jesus Christ's shed blood is the basis of man's reconciliation to God. We have already seen that at Jesus' birth, an angel of the Lord foretold that "he shall save his people from their sins" (Matthew 1:21). Jesus also spoke of His mission when He said He came "to give his life a ransom for many" (Matthew 20:28; cf. Mark 10:45); "This is my body which is given for you" (Luke 22:19); and "I am the good shepherd: the good shepherd giveth his life for the sheep" (John 10:11; cf. vv. 15, 18).

Before considering some terms applied to Jesus' death, let us look at several Scriptures that speak of His death.

> He that spared not his own Son, but delivered him up for us all, how shall he not with him also freely give us all things? Romans 8:32

> Who is he that condemneth? It is Christ that died, yea rather, that is risen again, who is even at the right hand of God, who also maketh intercession for us. Romans. 8:34

> For whether we live, we live unto the Lord; and whether we die, we die unto the Lord: whether we live therefore, or die, we are the Lord's. For to this end Christ both died, and rose, and revived, that he might be Lord both of the dead and living. Romans 14:8, 9

> But if thy brother be grieved with thy meat, now walkest thou not charitably. Destroy not him with thy meat, for whom Christ died. Romans 14:15

> And through thy knowledge shall the weak brother perish, for whom Christ died? I Corinthians 8:11

> For I delivered unto you first of all that which I also received, how that Christ died for our sins according to the scriptures. I Corinthians 15:3

> Who gave himself for our sins, that he might deliver us from this present evil world, according to the will of God and our Father. Galatians 1:4

> But now in Christ Jesus ye who sometimes were far off are made nigh by the blood of Christ. Ephesians 2:13

> Let this mind be in you, which was also in Christ Jesus: Who, being in the form of God, thought it not robbery to be equal with God: But made himself of no reputation, and took upon him the form of a servant, and

was made in the likeness of men: And being found in fashion as a man, he humbled himself, and became obedient unto death, even the death of the cross. Philippians 2:5-8

For if we believe that Jesus died and rose again, even so them also which sleep in Jesus will God bring with him. I Thessalonians 4:14

For there is one God, and one mediator between God and men, the man Christ Jesus; who gave himself a ransom for all, to be testified in due time. I Timothy 2:5, 6

Looking for that blessed hope, and the glorious appearing of the great God and our Saviour Jesus Christ; Who gave himself for us, that he might redeem us from all iniquity, and purify unto himself a peculiar people, zealous of good works. Titus 2:13,14

But this man, after he had offered one sacrifice for sins for ever, sat down on the right hand of God. Hebrews 10:12

Wherefore Jesus also, that he might sanctify the people with his own blood, suffered without the gate. Hebrews 13:12

The blood of Jesus Christ his Son cleanseth us from all sin. I John 1:7

Hereby perceive we the love of God, because he laid down his life for us. I John 3:16

For thou wast slain, and hast redeemed us to God by thy blood out of every kindred, and tongue, and people, and nation. Revelation 5:9

The Scriptures use several technical terms to explain what Jesus Christ's death accomplished. These are redemption, ransom, propitiation, and reconciliation. Let us examine these terms.

Redemption

The term *redemption* is used to describe the effect of Christ's death. Its basic meaning is "to buy back." The Greek term *apolutrosis,* translated "redemption," signifies setting a captive free through a payment made by another. In a broader sense it involves deliverance from punishment, that is, redemption implies deliverance from the consequences of our sins. The Scripture uses price in the sense of having been "bought with a price" (I Corinthians 6:20; cf. 7:23) and "denying the Lord that bought them" (II Peter 2:1).

Several Scriptures denote redemption occurring through Christ's death. Paul wrote that we are "justified freely by his grace *through the redemption that is in Christ Jesus*: whom God has set forth . . . through faith *in his blood*" (Romans 3:24, 25); "In whom we have *redemption through his blood*, the forgiveness of sins, according to the riches of his grace; wherein he hath abounded toward us in all wisdom and prudence" (Ephesians 1:7, 8); "Who hath delivered us from the power of darkness, and hath translated us into the kingdom of his dear Son: In whom *we have redemption through his blood*, even the forgiveness of sins" (Colossians 1:13, 14).

The author of the Book of Hebrews wrote about Jesus Christ: "By his own blood he entered in once into the holy place, having *obtained eternal redemption* for us. . . . And for this cause he is the mediator of the new testament, that *by means of death, for the redemption of the transgressions* that were under the first testament, they which are called might receive the promises of eternal inheritance" (Hebrews 9:12, 15).

The verb *redeem* is also used in several passages to describe the concept of redemption: "Christ hath *redeemed* us from the curse of the law" (Galatians 3:13); "God sent forth his Son . . . to *redeem* them that were under the law, that we might receive the adoption of sons" (4:4, 5); "Our Saviour Jesus Christ; who gave himself for us, that he might *redeem* us from all iniquity, and purify unto himself a peculiar people, zealous of good works" (Titus 2:13, 14); and "Ye were not *redeemed* with corruptible things, . . . but with the precious blood of Christ, as of a lamb without blemish and without spot" (I Peter 1:18, 19). The Lamb "wast slain, and hast *redeemed us* to God *by thy blood*" (Revelation 5:9).

Ransom

Man has been brought back to God by means of a *ransom*. The term *ransom* means something of value paid to obtain the deliverance or release of a captive. Its usage may be observed in Exodus 21:30 and Proverbs 13:8. Jesus used the term in correcting two disciples who requested a place of prominence, telling all the disciples that "whosoever will be chief [great] among you, let him be your servant: Even as the Son of man came not to be ministered unto, but to minister, and to *give his life a ransom* for many" (Matthew 20:27, 28; Mark 10:45). The meaning of ransom is clarified later by Jesus, during the Last Supper. Concerning the cup, Jesus spoke, "This is my blood of the new testament, which is shed for many for the remission of sins" (Matthew 26:28; cf. Mark 14:24; Luke 22:20). The giving of His life, signified by the shedding of His blood, would ransom and result in remission of sins of all who meet the conditions of repentance and faith.

This concept of ransom was used by Paul when he wrote that we are "bought with a price" (I Corinthians 6:20, 7:23) and that "there is one God, and one mediator between God and men, the man Christ Jesus; Who *gave himself a ransom* for all" (I Timothy 2:5, 6). Peter wrote to exiled Christians that they were "not redeemed [ransomed, NASV, RSV] with corruptible things, as silver and gold, from your vain conversation received by tradition from your fathers [futile ways inherited from your fathers]; but with the precious blood of Christ, as a lamb without blemish and without spot" (I Peter 1:18, 19).

The concept of a ransom raises the question, To whom was the ransom paid? This question is hard to answer because the Scriptures do not give a direct answer. The New Testament writers and early church taught that *ransom* emphasized that someone other than man paid for his release from the consequences of sin, and that this release was very costly, requiring the highest possible price, the blood of God's only Son. This satisfied the government or justice of God and freed sinful man to enter into fellowship with Him.

Neither the New Testament or the early church formulated a theory to explain to whom the *ransom* and *redemption* "buy back" was paid. They were content to accept the fact of ransom and emphasized this fact without any thought to explain its operation. There are several theories that try to explain the meaning of the redemption and ransom process, but most are defective since the Bible is silent on this matter.

Propitiation

Another term used in the older English versions (KJV, ASV, et al.) that relates to Christ's death is *propitiation* or expiation. Webster's dictionary defines the term as "The act of making atonement," and "To make complete satisfaction for; atone for sin; as to expiate sin." The thought behind propitiation is that through Christ's death God's holy wrath against sin is satisfied so that God can again accept man.

Redemption Interpreted

Since "Christ died for our sins according to the scriptures" (I Corinthians 15:3), we should expect to find information on the coming Messiah's death in the Old Testament. We do find it there, for it was "witnessed by the law and the prophets" (Romans 3:21).

The term *propitiation* used in Romans 3:25, I John 2:2; 4:10, as many Old Testament terms, comes from the Greek translation of the Old Testament (the Septuagint) term for *mercy-seat* covering. The law demanded that sinners die for their sins. This demand was satisfied for the nation of Israel on the Day of Atonement, when the high priest took "two goats, and present[ed] them before the LORD at the door of the tabernacle of the congregation" (Leviticus 16:7). There lots were cast to determine which one was for "the LORD" and which one would be "the scapegoat" (v. 8). The one the LORD'S lot fell on would be offered as a sin-offering. The high priest would sprinkle its blood on the ark of the covenant's mercy seat, located in the Holy of Holies (Leviticus 16:13, 14; 17:11; Exodus 25:17-22; Hebrews 9:5). The blood symbolized the life of the body; when blood left the body, death occurred. This blood *covered* the sins of the people until the Messiah's suffering and sacrifice would take them away. The second goat was set free to symbolize the removal of sins by the sacrifice of the coming Christ.

The term *propitiation* is thus an Old Testament concept. The Book of Hebrews explains how the new covenant truths relate to the old covenant. After briefly describing the tabernacle regulations, the author of Hebrews described how the high priest once a year took "blood, which he offered for himself, and for the errors of the people" (Hebrews 9:7). Just as the high priest could enter into the Holiest Place only on the basis of the blood of the sacrifice, so Christ came into a heavenly tabernacle, where with "his own blood he entered in once into the holy place, having obtained eternal redemption for us" (v. 12). Christ's sacrifice was much more effective. If under the law "the blood of bulls and of goats, and the ashes of an heifer sprinking the unclean, sanctifieth to the purifying of the flesh: how much more shall the blood of Christ, who through the eternal Spirit offered himself without spot to God" (vv. 13, 14). Christ "put away sin by the sacrifice of himself. . . . So Christ was once offered to bear the sins of many" (vv. 26, 28). Christ did not enter into an earthly holy place, "but into heaven itself, now to appear in the presence of God for us" (v. 24).

As mentioned above, Christ's sacrifice "put away sin." Under the Old Testament, the sacrifice only *covered* the sins from the sight of God. This *covering* is the meaning of Old Testament atonement.[5]

In the next chapter the writer repeats that in the old covenant it was "the blood of bulls and of goats" that temporarily purified man (Hebrews 10:4). Christ became the Passover Lamb and "offered one sacrifice for sins for ever" (v. 12). "By one offering he hath perfected for ever them that are sanctified" (v. 14). Christ's suffering protects the repentant sinner from the wrath of God and purges his conscience so that he can serve God. Jesus, after His sacrifice, "sat down on the right hand of God" (v. 12).

Paul made the most elaborate statement on Christ's propitiatory death in the Book of Romans by writing, "Being justified freely by his grace through the redemption that is in *Christ Jesus: Whom God hath set forth to be a propitiation* through faith in his blood, to declare his righteousness for the remission of sins that are past, through the forbearance of God; To declare, I say, at this time his righteousness: that he might be just, and the justifer of him which believeth in Jesus" (Romans 3:24, 26). It was through the blood of Christ's sacrifice that God's righteousness was satisfied and that sinful man was again able to approach Him.

John also wrote of propitiation: *"Jesus Christ the righteous: And he is the propitiation for our sins*: and not for ours only, but also for the sins of the whole world" (I John 2:1, 2); and "Herein is love, not that we loved God, but that he loved us, and sent *his Son to be the propitiation for our sins"* (4:10).

The Greek term for *propitiation* in Romans 3:25 is translated *reconciliation* in Hebrews. Jesus "was made a little lower than the angels for the suffering of death . . . that he by the grace of God should taste death for every man. . . . the captain of their salvation [made] perfect through sufferings. . . . Wherefore in all things it behoved him to be made like unto his brethren, that he might be a merciful and faithful high priest in things pertaining to God, *to make reconciliation [propitiation] for the sins* of the people" (Hebrews 2:9, 10, 17).

---

[5] Atonement is an Old Testament term. Although the King James Version mistakenly uses the term in Romans 5:11, it should have been rendered "reconciliation."

Christ's Death as Suffering, Not Punishment

Christ's death was also *vicarious* (meaning Christ did something on behalf of us on Calvary) or *substitutionary*, that is, He suffered and died on behalf of sinners so they might receive eternal life. This substitutionary act was announced six hundred years before Christ was born in Bethlehem by the prophet Isaiah, who "saw [Christ's] glory, and spake of him" (John 12:41). Isaiah says,

> Surely he hath borne our griefs, and carried our sorrows: yet we did esteem him stricken, smitten of God, and afflicted. But he was wounded for our transgressions, he was bruised for our iniquities: the chastisement of our peace was upon him; and with his stripes we are healed. All we like sheep have gone astray; we have turned every one to his own way; and the LORD hath laid on him the iniquity of us all. Isaiah 53:4-6

After His resurrection, Jesus spoke to two disciples on the way to Emmaus about Old Testament prophecy, saying, "Thus it is written, and thus it behoved Christ to suffer, and to rise from the dead the third day" (Luke 24:46). Several times during His ministry Jesus spoke of His suffering: "Jesus ... shew unto his disciples, how he must go unto Jerusalem, and suffer many things ... and be killed" (Matthew 16:21; cf. Mark 8:31; Luke 9:22); "It is written of the Son of man, that he must suffer" (Mark 9:12; cf. Matthew 17:12); "must he [Jesus] suffer many things, and be rejected of this generation" (Luke 17:25); "I [Jesus] have desired to eat this passover with you before I suffer" (Luke 22:15). Jesus Christ's suffering is also emphasized in the following New Testament Scriptures:

> Those things, which God before had shewed by the mouth of all his prophets, that Christ should *suffer*, he hath so fulfilled. Acts 3:18

> I[Paul] witnessing both to small and great, saying none other things than those which the prophets and Moses did say should come: That Christ should *suffer*, and that he should be the first that should rise from the dead. Acts 26:22, 23

> But we see Jesus, who was made a little lower than the angels for the *suffering of death*, crowned with glory and honour; that he by the grace of God should taste death for every man. ... [being made] perfect *through sufferings*. Hebrews 2:9, 10

Though he were a Son, yet learned he obedience by the things which *he suffered*; and being made perfect, he became the author of eternal salvation unto all them that obey him. Hebrews 5:8, 9

Who his own self bare our sins in his own body on the tree, that we, being dead to sins, should live unto righteousness: *by whose stripes* ye were healed. I Peter 2:24

For Christ also hath once *suffered for sins*, the just for the unjust, that he might bring us to God, being put to death in the flesh, but quickened by the Spirit. I Peter 3:18

Twenty-eight times the KJV states that Christ suffered for us.[6] The Scriptures never speak of Christ being "punished" for sins or for sinners. The terms *punish* and *suffer* have significantly different meanings. Punish means "to cause to undergo pain, loss, or suffering for a crime or wrongdoing,"[7] whereas "suffer" does not involve guilt. Grider summarizes what John Miley wrote, "Since Christ was sinless, He was guiltless. When He died for us, therefore, He suffered but was not punished. And since there was a substitution of His suffering for the punishment that believers otherwise would have received in hell, the Father could actually forgive us. Punishment would have clearly satisfied God's justice. But since Christ suffered instead of being punished, the Father really could forgive those who repent and believe."[8] Grider wrote that Christ suffered in part "because God the Father really does forgive us—whereas, if He punished Christ instead of us, He could not then have forgiven us. In Christ's substitutionary punishment, justice would have been satisfied, precluding forgiveness. One cannot both punish and forgive, surely."[9]

---

[6] "Suffer" is referred to in Matthew 16:21; 17:12; Mark 8:31; 9:12; Luke 9:22; 17:25; 22:15; 24:46; Acts 3:18; 26:23; Romans 8:17; "suffered" in Luke 24:26; Acts 17:3; Hebrews 2:18; 5:8; 9:26; 13:12; I Peter 2:21, 23; 3:18; 4:1; and "suffering" in II Corinthians 5:21; Philippians 3:10; Hebrews 2:9, 10; I Peter 1:11; 4:13; 5:1.
[7] Webster, *op. cit.*
[8] J. Kenneth Grider, *A Wesleyan-Holiness Theology*, Kansas City: Beacon Hill of Kansas City, 1994, p. 330. Ref. John Miley, *The Atonement in Christ*, New York: Hunt and Eaton, 1889, pp. 167ff.
[9] Ibid., p. 331.

As Paul wrote, Jesus Christ "was delivered for our offences, and was raised again for our justification" (Romans 4:25) or "was put to death for our trespasses" (RSV). "Christ died for the ungodly. ... Christ died for us" (5:6, 8; cf. Galatians 1:4). There is disagreement on how to interpret the Greek term *huper* translated "for" here. Does it always mean "in behalf of," or can it mean the same as Greek term *anti*, translated "instead of?" In relation to Romans 5:6 and 8, in their newest Greek-English Lexicon (i.e., dictionary), Arndt and Gingrich wrote concerning *huper*, "after expressions of suffering, dying, devoting oneself, etc. ... die for someone or something .... So especially of the death of Christ ... *for, in behalf of* mankind, the world."[10] Vincent wrote, "It is much disputed whether [*huper*] *on behalf of*, is ever equivalent to [anti] *instead of*."

After giving several examples from the classical and church Fathers, Vincent writes, "None of these passages can be regarded as decisive. The most that can be said is that [huper] borders on the meaning of [anti]. *Instead of* is urged largely on dogmatic grounds. In the great majority of passages the sense is clearly *for the sake of, on behalf of*. The true explanation seems to be that, in the passages principally in question [Romans 5:6], those, namely, relating to Christ's death ... [*huper*] characterizes the more indefinite and general proposition—Christ died *on behalf of*—leaving the peculiar sense of *in behalf of* undetermined, and to be settled by other passages. The meaning *instead of* may be included in it, but only inferentially. Godet says, 'The preposition can signify only *in behalf of*. It refers to the *end*, not at all to the *mode* of the work of redemption.'"[11] It would seem Paul's statement would clearly mean Christ's death was *in behalf of* man, "so by the obedience of one shall many be made righteous" (Romans 5:19). As the writer of Hebrews wrote, Jesus by "the suffering of death ... he by the grace of God should taste death for every man" (Hebrews 2:9).

Surely He was "the Lamb of God, which taketh away the sin of the world" (John 1:29; I Peter 1:18, 19) and fulfilled Isaiah prophecies when he "saw [Christ's] glory, and spake of him" (John 12:41). As mentioned, Isaiah wrote, "Surely he hath borne our griefs ... was

---

[10] Arndt and Gingrich, *op. cit.*, p. 838.
[11] Marvin R. Vincent, *Word Studies in the New Testament*, Peabody, Mass.: Hendrickson, III:59, 60.

wounded for our transgressions . . . was bruised for our iniquities . . . with his stripes we are healed" (Isaiah 53:4-5). All these terms show His suffering. Christ came into the world to suffer according to the Father's will, who "laid on him the iniquity of us all. . . . It pleased the Lord to bruise him; he hath put him to grief: when thou shalt make his soul an offering for sin" (v. 10). When Christ died on the cross He "put away sin by the sacrifice of himself" (Hebrews 9:26; cf. 10:12).

Paul has one Scripture that some believe teaches that Christ took our sins and was punished for them by being our substitute, although it does not explicitly state that Christ took upon Himself man's sins. Paul wrote that God "made [Jesus] *to be sin* for us, who knew no sin" (II Corinthians 5:21). The statement that Jesus was made "to be sin for us" is difficult to understand. There are two interpretations of this verse. One interpretation holds that God made Christ to be "sin" by imputing man sin's to Him. The second interpretation is that "to be sin" refers to an alternate meaning of *hamartia* found in the Greek Old Testament the apostles and early church used, that means Christ's death was a "sin-offering." We will discuss the first interpretation below, and the second in the next section.

The first interpretation is held by those who hold to the Punishment Theory (also known as Penal Substitution) and is a legal-based theory advanced first by Augustine and made popular during the reformation by John Calvin. This theory holds that man, because of his sins, deserves the wrath and curse of God. Because of His holy and just nature, God must punish men as they deserve. To satisfy the righteous judgment of God, His Son assumed man's nature, lived under the law and fulfilled all righteousness. Man's sins were imputed to the otherwise sinless Christ (He was made "to be sin"), and He was punished for our sins when He died on the cross. His death fulfilled the demands of God's law, removing the death penalty man faced for his sins, so man could be redeemed.

This theory means that God made Jesus "sin." Obviously God the Father could not literally make His Son "sin." God is never portrayed as the source of sin. Because of this, some have softened this theory by saying that God did not literally make Jesus "sin," but Jesus can be considered as the personification of sin in a metaphorical way; namely, He became *sin* for us. In a symbolic sense and in a substitutionary way, sin was judged on the cross by being borne by and identified with Christ. Our sins were dealt with on the cross when Christ died for us, in our place.

There are several difficulties with the above "sin" interpretation. First it is not taught in the Greek New Testament or supported by the Hebrew Old Testament. The New Testament does not teach anything about the transfer of man's sins or guilt to Christ. As mentioned earlier, if He bore the guilt of man's sins, He would have been punished. Another difficulty is it distorts what Christ did on the cross. If all our sins (past, present, and future) were transferred to Christ and He was punished for them, man cannot be punished again for them. This leads either to all men being saved, which is contrary to Scripture (obviously not all are saved), or by some unknown reason, God chose only particular men to be saved. This means that some must be predestined to eternal life and some to damnation, and the elect are eternally secure regardless of what they do. Neither of these things are taught in Scripture.

How Was Christ's Suffering Treated

In what sense was Christ's suffering and death vicarious? Before we discuss this, let us remind ourselves that we should not get bogged down on this question since the Bible gives no formal statement on how God treated Christ's death on the cross. Many Christians try to develop a theory to explain Christ's work on the cross. This effort is of little benefit since the Bible had, as we have seen earlier in this chapter, to use several concepts to explain His work to men. Apparently there is no single term or simple theory that explains Christ's work; therefore let us be careful about imposing any theory on the Bible. But let us keep our eyes on everything the Bible says about Christ's death.

At least two Scriptures directly assert that Christ bore man's sins. Hebrews 9:28 states, "Christ was once offered to bear the sins of many." And Peter wrote similarly that Christ was "a lamb without blemish and without spot" (I Peter 1:19), "who did no sin . . . Who his own self bare our sins in his own body on the tree, that we, being dead to sins, should live unto righteousness: by whose stripes ye were healed" (2:22, 24). "Christ . . . hath once suffered for sins, the just for the unjust, that he might bring us to God, being put to death in the flesh" (3:18). By "the Just" (Christ) suffering physical death *for* "the unjust" (man), Christ becomes a sacrifice to redeem and ransom man so he would not have to suffer his due punishment in the lake of fire. The innocent and righteous can suffer. By Christ's self-sacrifice, He made intercession for man by pouring out His soul on the cross, thus making His blood an acceptable sacrifice for sin so God could forgive sinners instead of punishing them (see Leviticus 4:20, 26, 31, 35; et al.; Isaiah 53:6, 11, 12).

It should be mentioned that for Christ "to bear the sins of many" and that He in "his own self bare our sins" does not mean He was punished for our sins. Christ's sacrifice and sufferings as the "Lamb of God, [who took] taketh away the sin of the world" (John 1:29), fulfills the imagery of the scape-goat who bore "upon him all their inquities" into the wilderness (Leviticus 16:22). Christ gave His life publicly as a sacrifice to bear away or "carry up" the sins of many to the altar.[12]

In the author's opinion, the second interpretation of II Corinthians 5:21 mentioned in the preceding section, that Jesus was made "to be a sin-offering for us," is correct. *Sin-offering* is an alternate meaning of *hamartia* found in the Greek Old Testament. Since the apostles and the church at Corinth mainly used the Septuagint, they undoubtedly understood that *hamartia* could mean a sin-offering. This was not an ambiguous, obscure, or hard to understand passage for those Greek Christians who received this letter, or other early Christians who read it later.

Clarke supports the view that *hamartia* should be translated "sin-offering" here. He wrote that this "answers to the *chattach* and *chattath* of the Hebrew text; which signifies both sin and sin-offering in a great variety of places in the Pentateuch. The Septuagint translates the Hebrew by *hamartia* in ninety-four places in Exodus, Leviticus, and Numbers, where a sin-offering is meant; and where our version translates the word not *sin*, but an *offering for sin*" (see his comments in loc.).[13] This translation is supported by the Isaiah 53 prophecy: "he hath put him to grief: when thou shalt make his soul an offering for sin" (v. 10).

Others also support the *sin-offering* interpretation. Arndt and Gingrich wrote, "αμαρτια [*hamartia*] may equal *sin-offering* here,

---

[12] H. Orton Wiley, *The Epistle to The Hebews*, Kansas City: Beacon Hill, 1984, pp. 277, 78.

[13] Adam Clarke, *Clarke's Commentary*, New York: Abingdon, n.d., VI:338.

as Lev. 4:24."[14] A. A. Hodge, a Presbyterian and Calvinist theologian who taught at Princeton Theological Seminary, also supports the sin-offering interpretation. He wrote, "God 'hath made him [Christ], who knew no sin, to be a *sin-offering* for us that we might be made the righteousness of God in him.'"[15]

The sin offering translation is supported by Paul's use of *hamartia* in Romans 8:3: Christ came "for sin [*hamartias*], condemned sin in the flesh." "For sin" is translated in the NIV as "to be a sin offering" (cf. NAB, also ASV, NASV, and RSV footnotes); and in the NEB "as a sacrifice for sin." Arndt supports these translation,[16] as do several commentartors (cf. Wm. Black, F. F. Bruce, Adam Clarke, Wm. Newell, J. C. Wenger, et al.). It is also supported by Hebrews 9:28: Christ shall "appear the second time without sin [*hamartias*] unto salvation." Here *hamartias* implies sin-offering, otherwise it would imply Christ came the first time with sin, which of course is not true. This verse could read, "appear the second time without a sin-offering."

Obviously sin-offering is a metaphorical usage because Paul used a different Greek word in II Corinthians 5:21, *hamartia*. Jesus never literally became a lamb or a bullock. This interpretation places Christ's sacrificial death at the center of His work, as several other New Testament Scriptures do. As the author of Hebrews wrote, under the law, "without shedding of blood [there] is no remission" of sins (9:22). Because of this, Christ "appeared to put away sin by the sacrifice of himself" (v. 26; cf. v. 28; 10:12, 14). John the Baptist spoke of Jesus in the symbolism of the Old Testament's sacrifice, as "the Lamb of God, which taketh away the sin of the world" (John 1:29). Paul wrote that Christ gave "himself for us an offering and a sacrifice to God for a sweetsmelling savour" (Ephesians 5:2). Peter wrote that Christians were redeemed "with the precious blood of Christ, as of a lamb without blemish and without spot" (I Peter 1:19). Thus the sin-offering and sacrifice interpretation is not unusual as "made to be sin" would be.

The underlying idea behind the sin-offering interpretation is known as the Governmental theory. This theory was advanced by James Arminius and his student, Hugo Grotius, during the Reformation Period. It emphasizes that God brought judgment on sin when the

---

[14] Arndt and Gingrich, *op. cit.*, p. 43.
[15] A. A. Hodge, *Outline of Theology*, Grand Rapids: Zondervan, 1879, p. 409.
[16] Arndt and Gingrich, *op. cit.*, p. 644.

sinless Christ in love gave His life on the cross as a sacrifice or sin-offering so His suffering would satisfy the demands of a Holy God. This enabled God to forgive sins in a manner that would not just be over-looking them. "The central idea of this theory is, that God is not to be regarded merely as an offended party, but as the Moral Governor of the universe. He must therefore uphold the authority of His government in the interests of the general good. Consequently the sufferings of Christ are to be regarded, not as the exact equivalent of our punishment, but only in the sense that the dignity of the government was thereby upheld and vindicated as effectively as it would have been, if we had received the punishment we deserved."[17] Thus Christ's death was not only substitutional but also vicarious, that is, He did something *on behalf of* us as was mentioned earlier. Christ's work not only enabled God to forgive sin but also defeated the powers of evil and enables all who repent and believe to live a righteous life. "He died for all, that they which live should not henceforth live unto themselves, but unto him which died for them, and rose again" (II Corinthians 5:15).

A difficulty with the sin-offering interpretation is that the word "sin" would have to have two different meanings in one verse, separated by only two words in the Greek: God "made him [to be] *sin* for us, who knew no *sin*" (II Corinthians 5:21). This is not a major problem since we have an example of the same word having two different meanings in the same chapter. In the Septuagint there are many examples in the Law were *hamartia* is used in close proximity in sin and sin-offering senses. Another example is Christ's use of "sanctify" in two different senses in His prayer in John 17:17 and 19 (i.e., sanctification and consecration uses). Brunk wrote, "We have a similar example in the word *passover*—in Luke 22:1 the word means a *feast*, and in the 7th verse of the same chapter the same word means the *passover-offering*."[18]

In summary, let us keep in focus what Paul wrote before the "sin" statement. "All things are of God, who hath reconciled us to himself by Jesus Christ . . . God was in Christ, reconciling the world unto

---

[17] H. Orton Wiley and Paul T. Culbertson, *Introduction to Christian Theology*, Kansas City: Beacon Hill, 1946, p. 230.
[18] George R. Brunk I, *Rightly Dividing The Scriptures*, Harrisonburg, Va.: Sword and Trumpet, 1992, p. 49.

himself, not imputing their trespasses unto them . . . For he hath made him to be a [sin-offering], who knew no sin; that we might be made the righteousness of God in him" (II Corinthians 5:18, 19, 21).

Importance of Understanding the Work of Christ

It is important that we carefully look at Christ's work on the cross because the whole of redemption relates to the great sacrifice that took place at Calvary. An incorrect consideration of the extent and the meaning of the work of Christ could lead to unsound applications. For example, if one were to think that the extent of Christ's death was only to the degree required to satisfy the law for those who believe, and since obviously all men are not saved, then the value of Christ's death would have to be only sufficient to cover the sins of those who actually believe and persevere faithful to the end. But Scripture repeatedly affirms that Jesus died for the sins of the whole world (John 1:18, 29; I Timothy 2:6; 4:10; I John 2:2).

When Christ was crucified, Scripture says He took "away the sin of the world" (John 1:29). Christ's death affects all men (Romans 5:8, 18; II Corinthians 5:14, 15; I Timothy 2:4, 6; 4:10; Hebrews 2:9; I John 2:2; 4:14). The only ones who benefit from His death, however, are those who repent, believe, and remain faithful to Christ. The Bible does not teach that men will be saved who do not maintain a vital relationship with Christ and follow Him.

Christ's death was an infinite sacrifice of infinite value. It is of sufficient value to cover the sins of the world. Every person living or who has ever lived can draw upon the unlimited benefits of Christ's sacrifice. And even when the payment has been made for all the sins of the world, the value of His death is still nowhere near being exhausted or depleted. Yet there is a very definite way in which the benefits of Christ's death are limited. They are limited by man's choice.

God has determined that salvation would be available only through His Son. Only those who believe in Jesus, receive Him as their Lord and Savior, and continue in a vital, intimate relationship with Him will receive the benefits of His death on the cross. Salvation hinges on our being "in Christ." God can never be considered unjust for allowing anyone to spend eternity in the lake of fire. All necessary provisions have been made in Christ to redeem *whosoever will*. But those who are *whosoever won'ts* will experience the second death because they have rejected God's provision for everlasting life.

Another danger can arise if we wrongfully consider the extent of Christ's self-sacrifice in terms of legal punishment alone. Since Christ paid the ransom for the salvation of men, then we might be tempted to think that all men everywhere are saved and secure because the law has been satisfied. But God has made the reception of the benefits of Christ's death, including salvation, contingent on faith in Jesus Christ, who is the way, the truth, and the life. The sinner must come to God through Christ, and he must come to Christ in trusting and obedient faith. God does not apply salvation to man indiscriminately. John 3:18 speaks directly to this matter: "He that believeth on him is not condemned: but he that believeth not is condemned already, because he hath not believed in the name of the only begotten Son of God."

Salvation and condemnation are conditioned on faith in Christ, not on the law being satisfied or man being without sin. To be in Christ is to be in the Ark of Salvation. To be outside of Christ is to be engulfed in the sin of the world and without hope or assurance. Salvation thus depends upon our abiding relationship with Jesus Christ, being faithful to His words and to the ministry of His Holy Spirit to our spirits. Christians have assurance that they are the children of God (see I John 5:13), but there are many Scriptures that warn of the danger of falling away (Matthew 24:4, 5, 11-13; John 15:1-6; Acts 11:23; 14:21, 22; Colossians 1:23; 2:4-8, 18, 19; I Timothy 4:1, 16; II Timothy 3:14; 4:3, 4; James 5:19, 20; II Peter 1:8-11; 3:16-18; I John 2:23-25; Hebrews 2:1-3; 3:1-14; chap. 10; et al.)

Antinomianism, which is disregard for God's expressed will, is another danger of wrongly interpreting the extent of Christ's work. If salvation is strictly a legal matter, and if people are righteous in God's sight on the basis of what Christ did, then what difference does it make whether people follow God's will or not? Their salvation is a completed issue and not dependent upon their lifestyle. But this is precisely the attitude that the apostle Paul warns against in His discussion on justification in Romans (see 6:1, 2, 15).

A person who disregards the will of God and is insensitive to the Holy Spirit demonstrates by his lifestyle that he is not God's child. When a person is born of the Spirit of God and thus receives the new birth, he *wants* to follow Christ and do God's will. His new nature reflects the nature of Christ (I Corinthians 2:16). And Jesus always sought to do the will of the Father (Luke 22:42).

Then too, if we believe that Christ has paid for the sins of only those who will be saved, and surely they will be saved if Christ died specifically for them, then we might be less motivated to take the gospel to the lost. We might slip into an extreme predestination theology and think that those who are to be saved will be saved. Our evangelistic fervor might be quenched, and we might become caught up in religious activity without seeking to reach the lost (Luke 19:10).

One truth we must always keep in mind is God's love for the lost and His forgiveness of those who believe in Christ. God is a God of justice, but He is also a God of love and mercy. And we must always keep His attributes in balance. To look at the work of Christ strictly from either a legal aspect or a religious perspective is to only consider part of the character of God.

The most encompassing message the Bible has for man is that "God so loved the world, that he gave his only begotten Son, that whosoever believeth in him should not perish, but have everlasting life" (John 3:16). Also, "God commendeth his love toward us, in that, while we were yet sinners, Christ died for us.... when we were enemies, we were reconciled to God by the death of his Son, much more, being reconciled, we shall be saved by his life" (Romans 5:8, 10). The result of God's love is the forgiveness of sin: "We have redemption through his blood, the forgiveness of sins" (Ephesians 1:7; cf. Colossians 1:14; 2:13); "your sins are forgiven you for his name's sake" (I John 2:12). Let us look at the New Testament teachings on reconciliation in more detail.

Reconciliation

The effect of Christ's propitiation and suffering is our *reconciliation* to God. This term comes from a Greek verb *katallasso,* meaning "to change, exchange." In Scripture it is applied to man's relation to God; man is changed from a state of hostility or enmity towards God to being a son of God (John 1:12; Romans 8:14; I John 3:1). This exchange occurs because God's grace and love worked in Christ. Thus it is God who reconciles and who works the reconciliation of sinful man. This meaning can be observed in Paul's use of this term in the following Scriptures:

> For if, when we were enemies, we were reconciled to God by the death of his Son, much more, being reconciled, we shall be saved by his life. And

not only so, but we also joy in God through our Lord Jesus Christ, by whom we have now received the atonement [reconciliation]. Romans 5:10, 11

Therefore if any man be in Christ, he is a new creature: old things are passed away; behold, all things are become new. And all things are of God, who hath reconciled us to himself by Jesus Christ, and hath given to us the ministry of reconciliation. II Corinthians 5:17, 18

And that he might reconcile both unto God in one body by the cross, having slain the enmity thereby. Ephesians 2:16

For it pleased the Father that in him should all fulness dwell; and, having made peace through the blood of his cross, by him to reconcile all things unto himself; by him, I say, whether they be things in earth, or things in heaven. Colossians. 1:19, 20

The above Scriptures make it clear that Jesus Christ reconciled man to God. Thus Christ made it possible for man to be restored to the relationship he enjoyed with God before the Fall.

Effects of Redemption

Two major effects of Christ's redemption of man are the new nature he receives and the destruction of Satan's power over man.

Jesus Christ came to bring a new and better covenant. The Old Testament prophet Jeremiah spoke the word of the Lord: "This is the covenant that I will make with the house of Israel after those days, saith the Lord; I will put my laws into their mind, and write them in their hearts" (Hebrews 8:10; cf. 7:22; 10:16; John 6:45; Jeremiah 31:33). This was to be a "new and living way ... having our hearts sprinkled from an evil conscience, and our bodies washed with pure water" (Hebrews 10:20, 22). This is the teaching Jesus spoke to Nicodemus about: "Except a man be born again, he cannot see the kingdom of God" (John 3:3). Being "born again" means putting "on the new man, which after God is created in righteousness and true holiness" (Ephesians 4:24).

The point that the new man is "created after the likeness of God in true righteousness and holiness" (Ephesians 4:24 RSV) is mentioned in other Scriptures. Paul wrote to the Colossians about putting off various sins since we "have put off the old man with his deeds; and have put on the new man, which is renewed in *knowledge after the image of him that created him*" (Colossians 3:9, 10). The old man is abolished and is replaced by the new man. Being *new* means the Christian is renewed in the image of his Creator. This image restores what was lost in the Fall and renews man in spiritual knowledge. To the Corinthians Paul wrote that Christians "are *changed into the same image* from glory to glory; even as the Spirit of the Lord" (II Corinthians 3:18). Christians are to reflect as a mirror the glory of the Lord because His grace transforms and renews them. The goal is that "Christ be formed in you [in Christians]" (Galatians 4:19). Christians are "*partakers of the divine nature*, having escaped the corruption that is in the world through lust" (II Peter 1:4).

The second thing accomplished is Christ's destruction of Satan's power over men. At the time of the Fall, God told Satan, "I will put enmity between thee and the woman, and between thy seed and her seed: it shall bruise thy head, and thou shalt bruise his heel" (Genesis 3:15). This bruising of Satan's head was accomplished by the death and resurrection of Jesus Christ. The destruction of Satan's power by Jesus' death is emphasized several times in the New Testament. Jesus, speaking of His coming death, said, "Now shall the prince of this world be cast out" (John 12:31). Luke records Paul's defense before Agrippa, where Paul testified that Jesus told him "to open their eyes, and to turn them from darkness to light, and from the power of Satan unto God, that they may receive forgiveness" (Acts 26:18). The writer of Hebrews wrote "that through death he [Christ] might destroy him [Satan] that had the power of death, that is, the devil; And deliver them who through fear of death were all their lifetime subject to bondage" (Hebrews 2:14, 15). John wrote that "for this purpose the Son of God was manifested, that he might destroy the works of the devil" (I John 3:8). Jesus told the Pharisees, "If I cast out devils by the Spirit of God, then the kingdom of God is come unto you" (Matthew 12:28, 29).

Christ's destruction of Satan's power enables Christians to be victorious over the "old man," i.e., the lower nature. Paul emphasized this truth: "We are buried with him by baptism . . . raised up . . . so we also should walk in newness of life. . . . our old man is crucified with him, that the body of sin might be destroyed, that henceforth we should not serve sin" (Romans 6:4, 6), and "they that are Christ's have crucified the flesh with the affections and lusts" (Galatians 5:24).

Summary

Many theologians try to formulate precise statements as to the meaning of redemption. They are not very successful; it is difficult to explain the incomprehensible things that happened on the cross.

What was involved in Christ's death will doubtless remain somewhat a mystery until we reach heaven; yet many have attempted to explain it in terms men can understand. This has resulted in many theories about Christ's work of redemption. Most are incomplete since they attempt to explain something that has not been completely explained in the Scriptures. Because this book seeks to be a biblical study, the author will respect this silence of the Scriptures and will not attempt to make a formal statement on this subject. Although the Bible does not give a complete explanation of how the death of Jesus procured redemption and reconciliation, it does give us many insights. When we consider the several different biblical terms and statements together, they give a fuller meaning to the cross.

Jesus was born of a virgin and was called "Emmanuel, which being interpreted is, God with us" (Matthew 1:23). He was "tempted like as we are, yet without sin" (Hebrews 4:15). He was like a "lamb without blemish and without spot" (I Peter 1:19), in whom His critics could find "no cause" deserving death (Acts 13:28). He "suffered for sins, the just for the unjust, that he might bring us to God" (I Peter 3:18). "He is the propitiation for our sins" (I John 2:2), "who gave himself a ransom for all" (I Timothy 2:6), "in whom we have redemption through his blood, the forgiveness of sins, according to the riches of his grace" (Ephesians 1:7). He is the "one mediator between God and men" (I Timothy 2:5), who has made it possible for all men to "be renewed in the spirit of [their] mind; and that [they] put on the new man, which after God is created in righteousness and true holiness" (Ephesians 4:23, 24). "Behold, what manner of love the Father hath bestowed upon us, that we should be called the sons of God" (I John 3:1).

Chapter 5

Redemption Appropriated

Introduction

We have seen that Jesus Christ bridged the chasm between God and man caused by man's sin. God made it possible not only to redeem man from the consequences of his sin, but also to restore his spiritual nature. The question now is, "How do we receive the benefits of the redemption brought by Jesus Christ?"

John writes in the beginning of his gospel how "the Word [Jesus] was made flesh, and dwelt among us, . . . full of grace and truth. . . . And of his fulness have all we received, and grace for grace. For the law was given by Moses; but grace and truth came by Jesus Christ" (John 1:14-17). Through the Mosaic law, God had shown man his need of salvation. The old covenant brought condemnation and death. Under the new covenant, however, God deals with man on the basis of grace and truth.

The New Testament stresses that grace and truth brought by Jesus Christ supersedes the Mosaic law. Early in his ministry Paul emphasized this to a synagogue group in Antioch, saying, "Through this man [Jesus Christ] is preached unto you the forgiveness of sins: And by him all that believe are justified from all things, from which ye could not be justified by the law of Moses. . . . continue in the grace of God" (Acts 13:38, 39, 43). After Paul discussed justification by faith in his letter to the Roman church, he wrote that "sin shall not have dominion over you; for ye are not under the law, but under grace" (Romans 6:14). Later, writing about the covenant God made with Israel, Paul wrote that "there is a remnant according to the election of grace. And if by grace, then is it no more of works: otherwise grace is no more grace" (11:5, 6). Paul told the Galatians that he did "not frustrate the grace of God: for if righteousness come by the law, then Christ is dead in vain" (Galatians 2:21). Later he wrote concerning "every man that is circumcised, that he is a debtor to do the whole law. Christ is become of no effect unto you, whosoever of you are justified by the law; ye are fallen from grace" (5:3, 4). He wrote to Titus "that the kindness and love of God our Saviour towards man appeared. Not by works of righteousness which we have done, but according to his mercy he saved us.... Which he shed on us abundantly through Jesus Christ our Saviour; That being justified by his grace we should be made heirs" (Titus 3:4-7).

In Acts and the Epistles there is major emphasis on the redemption brought by Jesus Christ through grace. Let us look at grace closer.

Grace

The grace made available by Jesus Christ is one of the main differences between the two covenants. Grace is a central characteristic of the Gospel, and we must understand its meaning to understand the New Testament.

What is grace? The term has several meanings, but we will consider only those directly related to redemption. Arndt and Gingrich define grace as "a work of grace that grows from more to more.... Those who belong to him receive of the fulness of his grace ... the work of grace in conversion."[19] Strong defines it as "*the divine influence* upon the heart, and its reflections in the life."[20] Webster's definition reflects the biblical concept of grace: "unmerited *divine assistance* given man for his regeneration or sanctification."[21] The meaning of "grace" is best understood by its use in the New Testament.

Before we examine the use of the term *grace* in the New Testament, we need to mention an important aspect of grace. The New Testament always speaks of "the grace of God" (Acts 11:23; 13:43; 15:40; 20:24; Romans 5:15; I Corinthians 3:10; II Corinthians 8:1; 9:14; Galatians 2:21; Hebrews 2:9; 12:15; Jude 4; et al.) or "the grace of the Lord Jesus Christ" (Acts 15:11; Romans 16:20, 24; I Corinthians 16:23; Galatians 1:6; 6:18; Philippians 4:23; I

---

[19] Arndt, *op. cit.*, p. 878.
[20] James Strong, *Strong's Exhaustive Concordance of the Bible*, Greek Dictionary of the New Testament, New York: Abingdon Press, 1890, p. 77.
[21] *Webster's Ninth New Collegiate Dictionary.*

Thessalonians 5:28; II Thessalonians 3:18; I Timothy 1:14; Philemon 25; et al.) or both (II Thessalonians 1:12). Grace is not a man-made effort.

Grace plays the central part in *justification* of the sinner. Justification is the act whereby the sinner who believes in Jesus Christ is considered to have a perfect standing before God. The term is the positive act of God declaring the sinner *just* or *righteous*. "The term 'forgiveness' refers to what might be called the negative aspect of acceptance with God's, namely, the cancellation of guilt for one's sins."[22] Justification is by grace; salvation is the result of grace.

When Peter addressed the Jerusalem conference, he stated that "through the grace of the Lord Jesus Christ we shall be saved" (Acts 15:11). Apollos, a man well versed in the Scriptures and who taught accurately about Jesus, went to Achaia, where he greatly helped those who "had believed through grace" (Acts 18:27). Paul emphasised justification by grace, writing, "Being justified freely by his grace" (Romans 3:24); "Even when we were dead in sins, hath quickened us together with Christ (by grace ye are saved)" (Ephesians 2:5); "our Lord Jesus Christ . . . hath given us everlasting consolation and good hope through grace" (II Thessalonians 2:16); "Who hath saved us, and called us with an holy calling . . . according to his own purpose and grace" (II Timothy 1:9); "For the grace of God that bringeth salvation hath appeared to all men" (Titus 2:11); "Being justified by his grace" (Titus 3:7). From these Scriptures we see that grace plays the central part in man's redemption.

Today the justification aspect of grace is well-known and rightly receives much emphasis. However, grace is more. There are exceptional effects produced by grace. It bestows gifts and causes believers to do good works.

Paul emphasized this influence or power of grace in his epistles. One of the clearest statements on the operation of grace is found in his letter to Titus. There he wrote, "For the grace of God that bringeth salvation hath appeared to all men, teaching us that, denying ungodliness and worldly lust, we should live soberly, righteously, and godly, in this present world" (Titus 2:11, 12). As Paul stated, grace brings salvation, but it does not stop there. It continues to

---

[22]John C. Wenger, *Introduction to Theology*, Scottdale, Penn.: Herald Press, 1954, p. 284.

operate, teaching and training the Christian how to live a life that stands in sharp contrast to his former life. It teaches him to live a totally different life, "soberly, righteously, and godly."

Another passage showing grace's effect is found in Paul's letter to the Romans. He wrote that "where sin abounded, grace did much more abound: That as sin hath reigned unto death, even so might grace reign through righteousness unto eternal life by Jesus Christ our Lord" (Romans 5:20, 21). Paul, realizing that grace could be misunderstood, explained its implication in Romans 6. He began this explanation by asking, "Shall we continue in sin, that grace may abound?" (6:1). No! The Christian was raised from the dead as Christ was, "so we also should walk in newness of life" (v. 4). Later he again emphasised this death aspect,

> For in that he died, he died unto sin once: but in that he liveth, he liveth unto God. Likewise reckon ye also yourselves to be dead indeed unto sin, but alive unto God through Jesus Christ our Lord. Let not sin therefore reign in your mortal body. . . . For sin shall not have dominion over you; for ye are not under the law, but under grace. What then? shall we sin, because we are not under the law but under grace? God forbid. . . . ye became the servants of righteousness. vv. 10-15, 18

Ephesians 2 tells of what God had done for these Christians. Paul first wrote about the Ephesians' change in lifestyle, then emphasized God's mercy and love, and finally spoke of grace's operation. He wrote,

> You hath he quickened [made alive], who were dead in trespasses and sins: Wherein in time past ye walked according to the course of this world, according to the prince of the power of the air, the spirit that now worketh in the children of disobedience: Among whom also we all had our conversation in times past in the lusts of our flesh, fulfilling the desires of the flesh and of the mind; and were by nature the children of wrath, even as others. But God, who is rich in mercy, for his great love wherewith he loved us, even when we were dead in sins, hath quickened us together with Christ, (by grace ye are saved;) and hath raised us up together, and made us sit together in heavenly places in Christ Jesus. . . . For by grace are ye saved through faith; and that not of youselves: it is the gift of God: not of works, lest any man should boast. For we are his workmanship, created in Christ Jesus unto good works, which God hath before ordained that we should walk in them. Ephesians 2:1-10

The gift of grace saves repentant sinners, making them His workmanship, created to do good works, that is, the will of God.

To the Corthinthians Paul wrote he behaved "with holiness and godly sincerity, not by earthly wisdom but by the grace of God" (II Corinthians 1:12 RSV). God's grace enabled Paul to act in "holiness and godly sincerity."

To the Colossians Paul penned that "the word of the truth of the gospel; which is come unto you, as it is in all the world; and bringeth forth fruit, as it doth also in you, since the day ye heard of it, and knew the grace of God.... That ye might be filled with the knowledge of his will in all wisdom and spiritual understanding; that ye might walk worthy of the Lord unto all pleasing, being fruitful in every good work, and increasing in the knowledge of God" (Colossians 1:5, 6, 9, 10).

As Peter wrote in his second letter, Christians have "escaped the pollutions of the world through the knowledge of the Lord and Saviour Jesus Christ" (II Peter 2:20). At the end of this book, he wrote, "Grow in grace, and in the knowledge of our Lord and Saviour Jesus Christ" (3:18). It is through grace and knowledge that Christians grow and escape the pollutions of the world.

Grace is at the center of the redemptive process, and its "divine influence upon the heart" is extremely important in understanding redemption. In the New Testament this aspect is strongly emphasized. In the Book of Acts we see that Stephen's martyrdom resulted in a scattering of the disciples out of Jerusalem. Some went to Antioch and preached to the Greeks, and "a great number believed, and turned unto the Lord" (Acts 11:21). When the church at Jerusalem heard this, they had Barnabas investigate the matter since this was an early outreach to the Gentiles. There he saw "the grace of God" (v. 23); the grace of God produced a visible change in these Gentiles. Later Paul taught the Ephesian elders about "repentance toward God, and faith toward our Lord Jesus Christ" (20:21). His goal was to "finish [his] course" and fulfill "the ministry, which [he had] received of the Lord Jesus, to testify the gospel of the grace of God" in Jerusalem (v. 24). This good news of the grace of God was the power behind the repentance and faith he had earlier spoken about.

Scriptures teach that both grace and the Holy Spirit work to transform the sinner. Let us now look at several Scriptures that show the transforming influence of the Holy Spirit: "The Spirit ... that raised up Christ from the dead shall also quicken your mortal bodies by his Spirit that dwelleth in you.... if ye through the Spirit do mortify the deeds of the body, ye shall live" (Romans 8:11, 13); "The offering up of the Gentiles might be acceptable, being sanctified by the Holy Ghost" (15:16); "We all, with open face beholding as in a glass the glory of the Lord, are changed into the same image from glory to glory, even as by the Spirit of the Lord" (II Corinthians 3:18); "The washing of regeneration, and renewing of the Holy Ghost" (Titus 3:5). The work of the Holy Spirit does not contradict the work of God's grace. God's grace can work through the Holy Spirit: "We have received ... the spirit which is of God; that we might know the things that are freely given to us of God... the Holy Ghost teacheth" us (I Corinthians 2:12, 13).

There are many Scriptures that show how grace works. The apostles received "great power [to] witness of the resurrection of the Lord Jesus: and great grace was upon them all" (Acts 4:33). In Iconium Paul spoke to Jews and Gentiles, "speaking boldy in the Lord, who [the Lord] was bearing witness to the word of His grace" (Acts 14:3 NKJV). Paul testified, but it was the Lord who bore witness to the Word of His grace. When the apostles and their helpers went on their mission journeys, they were "recommended to the grace of God for the work which they fulfilled" (Acts 14:26; cf. 15:40).

Paul's life is an example of God's grace at work. He was a zealous Jew who intensely persecuted the church and by the grace of God became a prominent apostle and builder of the church. He "received grace and apostleship, for obedience to the faith" (Romans 1:5). Later in this book he twice referred to this grace: "Through the grace given unto me" (12:3), and "I have written the more boldly unto you ... because of the grace that is given to me of God" (15:15). Paul recognized that his part in building the church was not due to his own effort but was entirely of God's grace: "According to the grace of God which is given unto me, as a wise masterbuilder, I have laid the foundation" (I Corinthians 3:10).

Above all, Paul could say of himself, "By the grace of God I am what I am: and his grace which was bestowed upon me was not in vain; but I laboured more abundantly than they all: yet not I, but the grace of God which was with me" (I Corinthians 15:10). Paul knew "when it pleased God . . . [He] called me by his grace" (Galatians 1:15). Paul could write that "the dispensation of the grace of God. . . is given me" (Ephesians 3:2), and that he "was made a minister, according to the gift of the grace of God given unto me by the effectual working of his power. Unto me, who am less than the least of all saints, is this grace given, that I should preach" (vv. 7, 8). To Timothy Paul wrote that he was thankful that Jesus enabled him to be a minister though he was once "a blasphemer, and a persecutor, and injurious." He knew that "the grace of our Lord was exceeding abundant with faith and love" toward him (I Timothy 1:13, 14).

Grace is also a power in all Christians' lives. Paul wrote about Christians having "gifts differing according to the grace that is given to us" (Romans 12:6); during severe affliction and poverty "the grace of God [was] bestowed on the churches of Macedonia" (II Corinthians 8:1); and that "God is able to make all grace abound toward you; that ye, always having all sufficiency in all things, may abound to every good work. . . . By their prayer for you, which long after you for the exceeding grace of God in you" (9:8, 14). Christians through grace have rich blessings and experiences. The author of Hebrews wrote, "Let us therefore come boldly unto the throne of grace, that we may obtain mercy, and find grace to help in time of need" (Hebrews 4:16), and that "it is a good thing that the heart be established with grace" (13:9). God's grace will help us to hold fast when we are tempted, help us in our weaknesses, and is the power that establishes us in the faith. Also, the importance of grace is shown in most of the New Testament epistles' opening and closing remarks.

Since grace is so important, How does one receive grace? First, grace is "unmerited favor" because it offers salvation that we do not deserve instead of the eternal damnation we do deserve. No one receives grace by their own merit or righteousness. This unmerited aspect of grace means it is a *free gift*.[23]

The fact that grace is a free gift is emphasized in several New Testament Scriptures: We are "justified freely by his grace through the redemption that is in Christ Jesus" (Romans 3:24); "The free gift

---

[23]Many think the term *grace* means *free gift*. But since Scriptures speak of the "free gift" and "grace" in the same passages, these terms represent different concepts.

... the grace of God, and the gift by grace, which is by one man, Jesus Christ" (5:15; cf. 20, 21); "the grace of God which is given you by Jesus Christ" (I Corinthians 1:4); "the grace of God in you. Thanks be unto God for his unspeakable gift" (II Corinthians 9:14, 15); "To the praise of the glory of his grace, wherein he hath made us accepted in the beloved. In whom we have redemption through his blood, the forgiveness of sins, according to the riches of his grace" (Ephesians 1:6, 7); "by grace are ye saved . . . it is the gift of God" (2:8); "Now our Lord Jesus Christ . . . hath loved us, and hath given us everlasting consolation and good hope through grace" (II Thessalonians 2:16); "Who have saved us . . . according to his own purpose and grace, which was given us in Christ Jesus" (II Timothy 1:9); and "[God] giveth more grace . . . giveth grace unto the humble" (James 4:6). These Scriptures and others make it clear that grace and redemption are gifts.

In summary, the grace of God makes salvation available to us. The two aspects of grace—its influence upon men's hearts and its free gift—receive major emphasis throughout the New Testament. The question is now, How is grace made available to men? Several things—repentance, faith, and the new birth—work together to make grace available. The interaction of these will be discussed after reviewing each.

Repentance

One of the initial steps in realizing redemption brought by Jesus Christ is repentance. The message of John the Baptist, the forerunner of Jesus Christ, was, "Repent ye: for the kingdom of heaven is at hand" (Matthew 3:2). Jesus as well began His preaching and teaching with "Repent: for the kingdom of heaven is at hand" (Matthew 4:17; cf. Mark 1:15; Luke 13:3). Later He said, "They that are whole need not a physician; but they that are sick. I came not to call the righteous, but sinners to repentance" (Luke 5:32; cf. Matthew 9:13; Mark 2:17). The righteous do not need help. Those who are unrighteous sinners need help. The remedy to their condition is very simple; they need to repent.

Early in His ministry, Jesus sent out the twelve disciples and had them preach "that men should repent" (Mark 6:12). Just before sending them out, Jesus told the twelve that "whosoever shall not receive you, nor hear you, when ye depart thence, shake off the dust under your feet for a testimony against them. Verily I say unto you, It shall be more tolerable for Sodom and Gomorrha in the day of judgment, than for that city" (v. 11). They carried a serious message, with serious consequences if their call to repent was rejected.

Jesus often spoke of repentance throughout His ministry. He ended His earthly ministry with the commission "that repentance and remission of sins should be preached in his name among all nations" (Luke 24:47; cf. Acts 1:8), showing His continued interest in this message being available to all. This call for repentance was more than a message for the Jewish people; it was a call for all nations that still is going out today.

Repentance was a part of the apostles' preaching and teaching throughout their ministries. Many, after hearing Peter's first sermon in the newly born church at Jerusalem, asked, "What shall we do?" Peter replied, "Repent, and be baptized every one of you in the name of Jesus Christ for the remission of sins, and ye shall receive the gift of the Holy Ghost" (Acts 2:37, 38). In his second sermon, Peter urged, "Repent ye therefore, and be converted, that your sins may be blotted out, when the times of refreshing shall come from the presence of the Lord" (3:19). When the apostles were put in prison because of their message about Jesus, an angel soon released them after telling them to speak "in the temple to the people all the words of this life" (5:20). The Jewish leaders soon found the apostles there and brought them again before the council. Then Peter, after describing Jesus' death, said that "Him hath God exalted with his right hand to be a Prince and a Saviour, for to give repentance to Israel, and forgiveness of sins" (v. 31). Later, when Simon offered money for the apostle's power of laying on hands, Peter told him, "Repent therefore of this thy wickedness" (8:22).

Israel was not the only people called to repentance. "God also to the Gentiles granted repentance unto life" (Acts 11:18). Paul told the men at Athens that God "now commandeth all men every where to repent" (17:30). He spoke of testifying about "repentance toward God, and faith toward our Lord Jesus Christ" (20:21). And when he told King Agrippa about the Gentiles, Paul said that "they should repent and turn to God, and do works meet for repentance" (26:20).

What does it mean to *repent*? What is *repentance* all about? The Greek term *metanoeo*, often translated by the verb *repent*, according to Thayer means "to change one's mind for the better, heartily to amend with abhorrence of one's past sins,"[24] and according to Arndt and Gingrich it means to "change one's mind .... feel remorse, repent, be converted."[25] A second Greek term, *metanoia*, is a noun and corresponds to the above verb. It is translated *repentance*. It means "a change of mind." Another verb translated *repented* and *repent* (Greek term *metamellomai*) means "to change one's mind, turning about or conversion."

The meaning of these terms can be understood from their usage. John the Baptist was the one spoken of by the prophet Isaiah: "The voice of one crying in the wilderness, Prepare ye the way of the Lord, make his paths straight" (Matthew 3:3; cf. Mark 1:3; Luke 3:4; John 1:23; Isaiah 40:3). Eastern monarchs customarily sent a party ahead to prepare a road for them as they journeyed through desert country. John was to do the same thing for the coming King. John was to make the path straight by leveling spiritual mountains and filling up spiritual valleys, by calling for the people to repent. Repentance would remove sin's barriers to the King coming into men's hearts.

John told the Pharisees and Sadducees what the call for repentance involved: "O generation of vipers, who hath warned you to flee from the wrath to come? Bring forth therefore fruits meet for repentance. . . . every tree which bringeth not forth good fruit is hewn down, and cast into the fire" (Matthew 3:7, 10; cf. Luke 3:7, 8). John demanded true repentance that would bring a complete change of mind from the seeker that would result in "fruit." The "fruit" would be the doing of God's will (Matthew 3:1-10; Mark 1:1-6; Luke 3:1-14). John did not need to define repentance for his hearers; they knew from the Hebrew Scriptures that sinners had to repent of their sins (I Kings 8:46-48; II Chronicles 6:37-39; Isaiah 1:27-28; 55:7; Ezekiel 14:6; 18:21-32; Jonah 3:8-10; et al.).

John's call to repent was the call of the One whom he was preparing men for. When Jesus the Christ came, He proclaimed, "Repent ye, and believe the gospel" (Mark 1:15; cf. Acts 20:21). He called for a change of mind and purpose in the hearers' attitudes toward the gospel (good news); they were to change their minds from unbelief to belief in the gospel He brought.

---

[24] Joseph Henry Thayer, *A Greek-English Lexicon of the New Testament*, Grand Rapids: Baker Book House, 1977, p. 405.
[25] Arndt and Gingrich, *op. cit.*, p. 512.

Jesus spoke, "Repent: for the kingdom of heaven is at hand" (Matthew 4:17; cf. Luke 13:3). Repentance was also required because the kingdom of God, that is, His rule in the hearts of men, was to be established. Jesus would be the King, and seekers had to change their minds about God and sin and follow His will since the kingdom was near. No sinner who remains a sinner will enter God's kingdom because His holiness does not allow the presence of sin.

When the scribes and Pharisees murmured against Jesus for eating and drinking with sinners, He said, "They that are whole need not a physician; but they that are sick. I came not to call the righteous, but sinners to repentance" (Luke 5:31, 32; cf. Matthew 9:13; Mark 2:17). The righteous stand in sharp contrast to the sinners. The righteous stand cleansed before God, not because of anything they have earned or merited, but because of Jesus' blood and the grace He brought. Because God is holy, the sinners are the "sick" ones who need help. They need to repent or change their minds and hearts so they too can become righteous through Christ.

Jesus described the importance of repentance when He said there is joy "in heaven over one sinner that repenteth, more than over ninety and nine just persons, which need no repentance" (Luke 15:7; cf. v. 10). On one occasion, as He explained the Scriptures concerning His suffering, death, and resurrection to His disciples, He stressed its importance by stating "that repentance and remission of sins should be preached in his name among all nations" (24:47).

Earlier Jesus had spoken about those who "hunger and thirst after righteousness" (Matthew 5:6). They will find their hunger and thirst satisfied in Jesus Christ, and they will know this because they have fruits of righteousness in their lives. We know this change can happen because Jesus taught that His disciples will be "persecuted for righteousness' sake" (v. 10). He stated also that "except your righteousness shall exceed the righteousness of the scribes and Pharisees, ye shall in no case enter into the kingdom of heaven" (v. 20). They are to "seek ... first the kingdom of God, and his righteousness" (6:33). Sinners do not possess any righteousness produced by their own efforts but will find it present because of Christ's and the Holy Spirit's work in them.

When the scribes and Pharisees asked for a sign, Jesus told them the only sign they would have is that of the prophet Jonah. Jesus then mentioned that "the men of Nineveh shall rise in judgment with this generation, and shall condemn it: because they repented at the preaching of Jonas" (Matthew 12:41; cf. Luke 11:32). An illustration of repentance can be found in the story of Jonah and Nineveh. When Jonah told the men of Nineveh of the coming judgment, he told them to "cry mightily unto God: yea, let them turn every one from his evil way." They did this, and "God saw their works, that they turned from their evil way," and they were not destroyed (Jonah 3:8, 10). The men of Nineveh repented, turning from their evil ways.

In warning about "temptations to sin" (Luke 17:1 RSV), Jesus said, "If thy brother trespass [sin] against thee, rebuke him; and if he repent, forgive him" (v. 3). By speaking of repentance after sinning, Jesus shows that repentance involves turning from sin.

Jesus used the Greek term *metamelomia* in the parable of the two sons. When the father told his first son to go work in the vineyard, the son said, "I will not: but afterward he repented and went" (Matthew 21:29). The son changed his mind and went and worked in the vineyard. Jesus then explained that when John came, "ye [Jews] believed him not: but the publicans and the harlots believed him: and ye, when ye had seen it, repented not afterward, that ye might believe him" (v. 32).

The change brought by repentance is shown in Peter's second sermon. After telling what was done to the Prince of Life and how it fulfilled what was prophesied about His suffering, Peter told those who did those things to "Repent ye therefore, and be converted, that your sins may be blotted out" (Acts 3:19). By repenting sinners can experience conversion, and this results in their sins being forgiven and forgotten by God (cf. Hebrews 8:12; 10:17).

Paul spoke of testifying to the Jews and Gentiles about "repentance toward God, and faith toward our Lord Jesus Christ" (Acts 20:21). Repentance brings a change of mind about God and faith in His Son, the Lord Jesus Christ. When he appeared before King Agrippa, Paul said that he preached to the Gentiles "that they should repent and turn to God, and do works meet for *repentance*" (26:20), showing they had a changed attitude and mind. Here we see too that repenting involves both turning to God and a changed life that brings forth works that bear witness to the reality of that change.

Repentance involves changing one's attitude toward God. The author of Hebrews wrote about "repentance from dead works, and of faith toward God" (Hebrews 6:1). The writer did not go into details because he had just discussed the doctrine of Christ and Christian maturity and did not want to continue on foundational doctrines. Rather, he desired to go on to the subject of perfection. His readers already knew how repentance and faith worked together.

A third Greek term (*epistrepho*), although not translated repent or repentance, has a similar meaning. Jesus used this term in relation to the people's hearts being hardened, their ears being dull of hearing, and their eyes being closed, "lest at any time they should see with their eyes and hear with their ears, and should understand with their heart, and should be *converted*, and I should heal them" (Matthew 13:15; cf. Mark 4:12). Zacharias prophesied that John would be great and would be filled with the Holy Spirit, "and many of the children of Israel shall he *turn* to the Lord their God. . . . to *turn the hearts* of the fathers to the children, and the disobedient to the wisdom of the just" (Luke 1:16, 17). Jesus stated that Peter would deny Him and said, "I have prayed for thee, that thy faith fail not: and when thou art *converted*, strengthen thy brethren" (22:32).

The apostles used this term several times: "*turned to the Lord*" (Acts 9:35); "a great number believed, and *turned unto the Lord*" (11:21); "preach unto you that ye should *turn* from these vanities *unto the living God*" (14:15); "the Gentiles are *turned to God*" (15:19); "they should repent and *turn to God*, and do works meet for repentance" (26:20); "how ye *turned* to God from idols to serve the living and true God" (I Thessalonians 1:9).

Each person faces judgment. Everyone will have to face God and give an account for what he has done. This the Lord has promised (Matthew 25:32-46; John 5:25-29; cf. Acts 10:42; 17:31; Romans 14:10; I Corinthians 4:5; II Corinthians 5:10). People do not need to fear judgment if they prepare for it during their life. God's love and mercy has provided a way to avoid condemnation. Peter said, "The Lord is not slack concerning his promise, as some men count slackness; but is longsuffering [patient] to us-ward, not willing that any should perish, but that all should come to repentance" (II Peter 3:9). Sinners will not escape the judgment of God unless they repent. They should not count on God's kindness, forbearance, and patience to escape the consequences of their sins. They should realize that "the goodness of God leadeth [them] to repentance" (Romans 2:4).

Some other Scriptures that show God's gift of repentance are as follows: "a Saviour, for *to give* repentance to Israel, and forgiveness of sins" (Acts 5:31); "*God* also to the Gentiles *granted* repentance unto life" (11:18); and "God peradventure *will give them* repentance to the acknowledging of the truth" (II Timothy 2:25).

Seeing the kindness of God and recognizing one's own sinfulness, should lead the sinner to godly grief and repentance.

> Now I rejoice, not that ye were made sorry, but that ye sorrowed to repentance: for ye were made sorry after a godly manner.... For godly sorrow worketh repentance to salvation not to be repented of: but the sorrow of the world worketh death. For behold this selfsame thing, that ye sorrowed after a godly sort, what carefulness it wrought in you, yea, what clearing of yourselves, yea, what indignation, yea, what fear, yea, what vehement desire, yea, what zeal, yea, what revenge! II Corinthians 7:9-11

No one needs to fear judgment, because God is willing to grant repentance, but failure to repent will lead to judgment and condemnation. Jesus spoke out against Chorazin and Bethsaida, the cities where He did many mighty works, "because they repented not: ... if the mighty works, which were done in you, had been done in Tyre and Sidon, they would have repented long ago in sackcloth and ashes.... It shall be more tolerable for Tyre and Sidon at the day of judgment, than for you. And thou, Capernaum, which are exalted unto heaven, shalt be brought down to hell" (Matthew 11:20-23; cf. Luke 10:13). These cities did not turn from their sins and will be judged accordingly. Jesus spoke that theirs was an evil generation and that "the men of Nineveh shall rise in judgment with this generation, and shall condemn it: because they repented at the preaching of Jonas" (Matthew 12:41; cf. Luke 11:32). This same point was emphasized a third time when Jesus spoke about the Galileans that perished at Pilate's hand: "Except ye repent, ye shall all likewise perish" (Luke 13:3; cf. 13:5).

John in the Book of Revelation told five of the seven churches that they must repent to avoid judgment. The angel told the church at Ephesus, "I have somewhat against thee, because thou hast left thy first love. Remember therefore from whence thou art fallen, and repent, and do the first works; or else I will come unto thee quickly, and will remove thy candlestick out of his place, except thou repent" (Revelation 2:4, 5). He told the church in Pergamos that because they held the doctrines of Balaam and the Nicolaitanes, "which things I hate. Repent; or else I will come unto thee quickly, and will fight against them with the sword of my mouth" (vv. 15, 16). He told the church in Thyatira because they let "Jezebel, which calleth herself a prophetess, to teach and to seduce my servants to commit fornication, and to eat things sacrificed unto idols" (v. 20). She was given time to repent, but since she did not, the Lord said, "I will kill her children" (v. 23). He told the church at Sardis, "Remember therefore how thou hast received and heard, and hold fast, and repent" (3:3). He told the church of the Laodiceans, "I know thy works, that thou art neither cold not hot.... thou art lukewarm." (vv. 15, 16). They were counseled what to do, and "as many as I love, I rebuke and chasten: be zealous therefore, and repent" (v. 19). These Scriptures are clear that people and churches who fall away or become lukewarm must repent to avoid judgment.

Thus it is important that everyone repents. Because of this, Jesus desires "that repentance and remission of sins should be preached in his name among all nations" (Luke 24:47), showing that this condition of redemption should continue to go out to all.

Repentance, therefore, is a change of mind concerning man's sinful condition—that he is lost and bound for hell—and concerning who Jesus is and what He has done. The sinner needs to change his mind about Jesus' true identity—He is the divine Son of God, perfectly righteous and holy—and about Jesus' work of redemption. Jesus' suffering and death alone provide a propitiation for the sins of the world. The sinner needs to change his mind about following God's will and be determined to forsake his sins and follow Jesus. Both requirements were given to all men, from Jerusalem to the Gentiles: "They should repent and turn to God, and do works meet for repentance" (Acts 26:20). When a sinner acknowledges these truths and takes up his cross and follows Jesus Christ, he shows he has repented. This does not mean he has arrived at a state of perfection but that he does not continue sinning (I John 3:9). The Christian will continue to learn and grow, and "striving against sin" (Hebrews 12:4), he will run the race to maturity (v. 1), to win the incorruptible prize (I Corinthians 9:25).

Faith

Jesus Christ spoke about the need to believe in God, Him, and the gospel, showing that faith is important. Frequently, as the following

Scriptures show, Jesus linked eternal life to faith and belief. At the start of His ministry, He said, "Believe the gospel" (Mark 1:15). When a paralytic was lowered through the roof of a house in Capernaum to be healed, and "Jesus saw their faith, he said unto the sick of the palsy, Son, thy sins be forgiven thee" (2:5; cf. Luke 5:20). In the parable of the sower, Jesus explained that the seed was the word of God, and the seed that fell on the way side was trodden down because the devil took "away the word out of their hearts, lest they should believe and be saved" (Luke 8:12). Jesus told the disciples to go out into the world with the gospel and tell people that "he that believeth and is baptized shall be saved" (Mark 16:16). Jesus told Nicodemus that "whosoever believeth in him [the Son of man, Christ] should not perish, but have eternal life" (John 3:15; cf. vv. 16, 18). He told the Jews, "He that heareth my word, and believeth on him that sent me, hath everlasting life" (5:24). In the discourse on the bread of life, Jesus said, "He that believeth on me hath everlasting life" (6:47). At the Feast of Dedication in Jerusalem, Jesus told some Jews who asked Him if He was the Christ that "I told you, and ye believed not: . . . ye believe not, because ye are not of my sheep" (10:25, 26). He then explained, "My sheep hear my voice, and I know them, and they follow me: And I give unto them eternal life" (vv. 27, 28). Jesus told Martha after Lazarus' death, "I am the resurrection, and the life: he that believeth in me, though he were dead, yet shall he live" (11:25; cf. v. 26). Jesus told two of His disciples, "Believe in the light [Jesus Christ], that ye may be the children of light. . . . Jesus cried and said, He that believeth on me, believeth not on me, but on him that sent me. . . . I am come a light into the world, that whosoever believeth on me should not abide in darkness" (12:36, 44, 46). At His last Passover, Jesus said, "Let not your heart be troubled: ye believe in God, believe also in me. . . . I am the way, the truth, and the life; no man cometh unto the Father, but by me" (14:1, 6). These Scriptures show that the tie between belief and eternal life had a central place in Jesus' messages.

Paul wrote often on theological issues. One of these emphasized that faith appropriates grace, and grace brings justification. "It is of faith, that it might be by grace" that we are justified (Romans 4:16), and "We have access by faith into this grace" (5:2). Paul wrote to Titus that "according to his mercy he [Christ] saved us. . . . being justified by his grace" (Titus 3:5, 7). Faith is centered on Jesus

Christ; the Christian looks to Christ in faith for his deliverance. The believer's justification is not a matter of a "faith" work but solely rests on God's grace. This faith is not a work; our faith is due to grace. Luke wrote that the Ephesian brethren "believed through grace" (Acts 18:27). Paul wrote to the Ephesian church, that "by grace are ye saved through faith; and that not of yourselves: it is the gift of God" (Ephesians 2:8). Thus grace becomes available to the sinner through faith and not only results in the person having a just and righteous standing before God, but influences him to live an upright life.

Justification by faith is the theme of the Book of Romans. Paul wrote, "For I am not ashamed of the gospel of Christ: for it is the power of God unto salvation to every one that believeth; to the Jew first, and also to the Greek. For therein is the righteousness of God revealed from faith to faith: as it is written, The just shall live by faith" (Romans 1:16, 17). This last phrase translation has been influenced by Wycliffe's 1380 translation of the Latin text of Habakkuk 2:4. In Greek it literally reads "Now he who is righteous by faith shall live"[26] (cf. 1:17 RSV). Paul later explained how God works to make us *righteous by faith* so we can have eternal life (see see 10:2-13. esp. vv. 5, 6).

At the beginning of his discussion on justification, Paul wrote, "By the deeds of the law there shall no flesh be justified in his sight" (Romans 3:20). Under the new covenant the righteousness of God is manifested apart from the law, that is, the old covenant (v. 21). Now "the righteousness of God which is by faith of Jesus Christ [is] unto all and upon all them that believe" (v. 22). Man is justified, that is, declared righteous before God, by faith in Jesus Christ. Christ was sent to be the "propitiation through faith in his blood, to declare his righteousness for the remission of sins" (v. 25; cf. v. 26; 4:24, 25; 5:1). Propitiation, used in the older English versions, is the translation of the Greek term used in the Septuagint Old Testament for the mercy seat covering (Leviticus 16:13, 14). The sinner is justified by "his [Christ's] righteousness: that he might be just, and the justifier of him which believeth in Jesus" (Romans 3:26). It is Christ's self-offering on the cross that brings justification, not man's

---

[26] J. C. Wenger, *The Way to a New Life*, Scottdale, Penn.: Herald Press, 1977, p. 22.

efforts to keep the law. Christ's righteousness makes it possible for God to be just to His own character when He bestows a righteous standing on the believing convert. The Mosaic law did not justify. "Therefore it is of faith, that it might be by grace" that we are justified (4:16).

Justification by faith is emphasized later in Romans: "Therefore being justified by faith, we have peace with God through our Lord Jesus Christ" (5:1); "We have access by faith into this grace" (v. 2); "For Christ is the end [goal] of the law for righteousness to every one that believeth" (10:4); "Believe in thine heart that God hath raised him from the dead, [and] thou shalt be saved. For with the heart man believeth unto righteousness; and with the mouth confession is made unto salvation" (10:9, 10).

This theme of justification by faith also receives attention in Paul's other books. In these he emphasizes that man can again come into a right relationship with God, not by the works of the law, but by faith: "Man is not justified by the works of the law, but by the faith of Jesus Christ, even we have believed in Jesus Christ, that we might be justified by the faith of Christ, and not by the works of the law" (Galatians 2:16); they do not have their "own righteousness, which is of the law, but that which is through the faith of Christ, the righteousness which is of God by faith" (Philippians 3:9).

Paul wrote much on the theological importance of the new covenant replacing the old. By emphasizing faith in contrast to the works of the law, Paul was correcting a misunderstanding some first-century Christians with Jewish backgrounds had concerning justification. He contrasted the two terms to emphasize that the grace of God redeems man. This is brought out clearly in Ephesians 2:8, 9: "For by grace are ye saved through faith; and that not of yourselves: it is the gift of God: Not of works, lest any man should boast." Paul focuses on faith as a condition of salvation, in contrast to keeping the law, emphasizing that salvation is a gift of grace, not something to be earned. Faith becomes the means to emphasize that justification is "by his grace through the redemption that is in Christ Jesus: Whom God hath set forth to be a propitiation through faith in his blood" (Romans 3:24, 25). Paul's use of faith in contrast to the law (v. 21) shows it involves more than belief and trust; it involves commitment to Jesus Christ and the whole body of Christian truth He brought (John 1:17). To the Galatians he wrote, "Even we have believed in

Jesus Christ, that we might be justified by the faith of Christ, and not by the works of the law; for by the works of the law shall no flesh be justified" (Galatians 2:16). We will come back to this latter after discussing another concept that brings salvation to man.

Paul tied other spiritual truths to faith. He wrote "to the faithful in Christ Jesus" at Ephesus that in Christ "we have our redemption through his blood" (Ephesians 1:1, 7) and that God has "quickened us together with Christ" (2:5). Paul wrote to the "faithful brethren in Christ" at Colosse about hearing of their faith, that they "might walk worthy of the Lord ... being fruitful in every good work" (Colossians 1:2, 10), and that the Father "hath delivered us from the power of darkness, and hath translated us into the kingdom of his dear Son" (v. 13). To the Galatians he wrote about "faith which worketh by love" (5:6). Concerning his Christian experience, Paul said, "I am crucified with Christ: nevertheless I live; yet not I, but Christ liveth in me: and the life which I now live in the flesh I live by the faith of the Son of God" (2:20). Later Paul added that Christians "receive the promise of the Spirit through faith" (3:14).

What is this faith that gives man a just or righteous standing before God? Faith has several meanings: assurance or confidence in God, belief, trust. The New Testament uses faith in these senses.

The writer of Hebrews explained some of the elementary doctrines of Christ. Among them were repentance and "faith toward God" (Hebrews 6:1). Later in the book the author wrote to his readers of the need of endurance, so that after they had done the will of God, they might receive what was promised. "For yet a little while, and he that shall come will come, and will not tarry. Now the just shall live by faith. . . . But we are not of them who draw back unto perdition; but of them that believe to the saving of the soul" (10:37-39). Man must approach God in faith.

In chapter 11 the writer gives several examples of people who had a faith that produced works. This section opens with a definition of one aspect of God-pleasing faith.

> Now faith is the substance of things hoped for, the evidence of things not seen. . . . Through faith we understand that the worlds were framed by the word of God, so that things which are seen were not made of things which do appear. . . . But without faith it is impossible to please him: for he that cometh to God must believe that he is, and that he is a rewarder of them that diligently seek him. Hebrews 11:1, 3, 6

The Greek word translated *substance* here is translated *assurance* in the ASV, NASB, and RSV. Faith is the confidence or reality of things hoped for and the evidence or proof that God exists. Faith is not a blind acceptance of God's existence or Word. Faith is built upon Christian evidences, for God has given adequate reasons to assure men that Christianity is truth. Faith is an act of the mind that occurs because of the influence of grace and the work of the Holy Spirit. When man realizes his sinfulness and respects the evidence that shows God's reality, he then needs to turn to God in faith and trust that He will graciously help. This does not mean the mind is the grounds of faith. The grounds of faith are the evidences God has given in nature, in His Word, and through His Son.

The evidence God gives to man is an adequate basic for faith, so he can say, as did Paul, that "I know whom I have believed, and am persuaded that" Christ is able to keep me (II Timothy 1:12). John wrote that "we know that we are of God" (I John 5:19). Paul considered his worldly accomplishments as valueless in his pursuit of Christ, so "that I may know him" (Philippians 3:10). Paul pointed out to the Galatian church that there was a time when they did not know God, but now they "have known God" (Galatians 4:9). To the Ephesian church he expressed thanks when he heard of their faith, that "the Father of glory, may give unto you the spirit of wisdom," that they may be "enlightened; that ye may know what is the hope of his calling" (Ephesians 1:17, 18). He wrote that it was "good and acceptable in the sight of God our Saviour ... to come unto the knowledge of the truth" (I Timothy 2:3, 4). The grace of God was given by Jesus Christ so the Corinthians would be enriched "in all knowledge" (I Corinthians 1:5). Christians are able to know God because He gives grace and knowledge to them.

The writer of Hebrews is not giving in chapter 11 a formal definition of faith but is bringing out some of its characteristics. Hebrews 11:6 describes two ingredients of faith–that God exists, and that He will reward those who seek Him. The seeker must have faith or belief in God even though he has not seen Him. The seeker must also believe that God will judge all and reward those who diligently seek Him. If the seeker lacks these two ingredients of faith, he will make no effort to seek God's redemption. Hebrews 11 gives many illustrations of faith in action.

Another quality of faith is trust. The Greek term *pistis*, translated *faith*, means "to trust." Faith as we are considering it involves trust in God, Jesus Christ, and the Word of God. Trust is emphasised in the Old Testament, and one of its central figures, Abraham, is an outstanding example of faith and trust in God. For example, when Abraham was ninety-nine years old and still childless, God appeared to him and told him:

> I am the Almighty God; walk before me, and be thou perfect. And I will make my covenant between me and thee, and will multiply thee exceedingly.... Behold, my covenant is with thee, and thou shalt be a father of many nations. Genesis 17:1, 2, 4

Although it was difficult for Abraham to understand how God's promise could be fulfilled, he believed God, and God was faithful.

> Sarah conceived, and bare Abraham a son in his old age, at the set time of which God had spoken to him.... And Abraham was an hundred years old, when his son Isaac was born unto him. Genesis 21:1-7, 12

Abraham's faith in God was tested beyond any normal experience. He had believed the Lord that his descendants would be as numerous as the stars. Then God told him to take his "only son Isaac, whom thou lovest," to the land of Moriah; and there offer him as a burnt offering (Genesis 22:2). At the foot of Moriah, Abraham told two of his servants, "Abide ye here ... and I and the lad will go yonder and worship, and [we will] come again to you" (v. 5). He then went up in the mountain to offer Isaac. With complete confidence in God, Abraham bound him and laid him on the altar (Abraham expected God to raise Isaac after the sacrifice). Just as Abraham was ready to offer his son, an angel of the Lord appeared and said, "Lay not thine hand upon the lad, neither do thou any thing unto him: for now I know that thou fearest God, seeing thou hast not withheld thy son, thine only son from me" (v. 12). Paul used Abraham to show that he was justified by faith (Romans 4) and that the covenant God had made with Abraham was based on faith (Galatians 3).

Trust is not "faith" in something unknown. As Paul wrote, "I know whom I have believed, and am persuaded that he is able to keep that which I have committed unto him" (II Timothy 1:12). Trust is rooted in knowledge based on adequate evidence and signs (John 20:30, 31).

A second aspect of faith, that of self-surrender to God, can also be seen in Abraham. At God's first call, Abraham demonstrated his faith by leaving his country (Genesis 12:1); and throughout his life he had a family type relation to God that involved continuous self-surrender to His will. James comments, Abraham was "justified by works, when he had offered Isaac his son upon the altar. . . . Seest thou how faith wrought with his works, and by works was faith made perfect?" (James 2:21, 22). As Wenger wrote, "It is not sufficient to have been gloriously saved at the time of one's conversion; it is also necessary to maintain a life of holiness and obedience. This is an aspect of saving faith."[27]

Faith results in a life that seeks to please God and to obey the commands of Christ. Paul illustrates this in that he tried "to have always a conscience void of offence towards God" (Acts 24:16); he sought to run the race and "keep under my body, and bring it into subjection: lest that by any means, when I have preached to others, I myself should be a castaway" (I Corinthians 9:27).

Hebrews 11 is often called "the faith chapter." But since many of its examples of faith show that works followed faith, it could also be called "the works chapter." For example, the author wrote, "By faith Abel offered unto God a more excellent sacrifice" (v. 4); "By faith Enoch was translated that he should not see death" because "he pleased God" (v. 5); "by faith Noah. . . prepared an ark" (v. 7); "by faith Abraham . . . obeyed; and he went out. not knowing whither he went" (v. 8); "by faith Moses . . . [chose] to suffer affliction with the people of God" (vv. 24, 25).

Faith can also refer to the general body of Christian teaching or truth.[28] This usage is shown in the following verses: "stablished in the faith" (Colossians 2:7); "I have kept the faith" (II Timothy 4:7); many "of the priests were obedient to the faith" (Acts 6:7); "them who are of the household of faith" (Galatians 6:10); "One Lord, one faith, one baptism" (Ephesians 4:5); "unity of the faith" (v. 13); "some shall depart from the faith" (I Timothy 4:1); "he hath denied the faith" (5:8); "some have wandered away from the faith" (6:10 RSV); and "contend for the faith" (Jude 3). It is important to grasp

---

[27] Wenger, *Introduction to Theology*, op. cit., p. 274.
[28] Walter A. Elwell, Editor, *Baker Encyclopedia of the Bible*, Grand Rapids: Baker Book House, 1988, I:761.

this usage to avoid the danger of succumbing to "easy believism," an intellectual assent that shows no fruit or evidence of following Christ as Savior and Lord.

Reviewing the use of faith in other New Testament passages can help us better understand it. In the Sermon on the Mount, Jesus spoke against being anxious about life, drink, food, and clothing. He said, "If God so clothe the grass of the field, which to day is, and to morrow is cast into the oven, shall he not much more clothe you, O ye of little faith?" (Matthew 6:30; cf. Luke 12:28). Christians are to have faith, trusting God for their physical needs and not becoming unnecessarily worried about such things. When the disciples faced these difficulties, they were not to worry. It seems this quality of faith was hard for them to grasp. Once when they were in a boat and a great storm arose, they became fearful. Jesus rebuked them by asking, "Why are ye fearful, O ye of little faith?" (Matthew 8:23-27; cf. Mark 4:36-41; Luke 8:22-25). Again, when Peter saw Jesus walking on the water and tried it himself, he began to sink. Jesus challenged Peter, "O thou of little faith, wherefore didst thou doubt?" (Matthew 14:31). Jesus also rebuked the disciples for their lack of faith that the need for food for the multitudes would be supplied. "O ye of little faith, why reason ye among yourselves, because ye have brought no bread? Do ye not yet understand, neither remember the five loaves of the five thousand, and how many baskets ye took up? Neither the seven loaves of the four thousand, and how many baskets ye took up?" (Matthew 16:8-10). Jesus thus admonished and encouraged His disciples to trust God in everyday life.

Those who came to Jesus for healing often expressed explicit faith (trust). The centurion who came to Jesus to have his servant healed knew and trusted that if Jesus would "speak the word only," the servant would be healed. Jesus remarked, "Verily I say unto you, I have not found so great faith, no, not in Israel" (Matthew 8:8-10; cf. Luke 7:7-9). Another expression of faith in Jesus may be seen in the bringing of the paralytic on a bed to be healed. "Jesus seeing their faith" healed him (Matthew 9:2; cf. Mark 2:5; Luke 5:20). The woman who suffered from a hemorrhage for twelve years had such faith. She said, "If I may but touch his garment, I shall be whole." She did touch, and Jesus then turned to her saying, "Daughter, be of good comfort; thy faith hath made thee whole" (Matthew 9:20-22; cf. Mark 5:25-34; Luke 8:43-48). These seekers had heard of the miracles Jesus did and knew He could help them. They put their faith into action by asking for the Lord's help.

The verb *believe* and the noun *faith* are more closely related than the English spelling implies. In Greek the verb *pisteuo* is a cognate of the noun *pistis*. Before the late sixteenth century, the English language used faith as a noun and as a verb. Thus the Bible student should not think that believe and faith have different meanings. We can see the close connection of believe and faith in the following Scriptures. Jesus told the centurion, who had such great *faith*, "Go thy way; and as thou hast *believed*, so be it done unto thee" (Matthew 8:13). He said to the blind men who sought help from Him, "*Believe* ye that I am able to do this?" (9:28). They said they did, and He said, "According to your *faith* be it unto you" (v. 29). When the disciples marveled that the fig tree had withered because of Jesus' word, He told them, "Have *faith* in God. For verily I say unto you, That whosoever shall say unto this mountain, Be thou removed, and be thou cast into the sea; and shall not doubt in his heart, but shall believe that those things which he saith shall come to pass; he shall have whatsoever he saith. Therefore I say unto you, What things soever ye desire, when ye pray, *believe* that ye receive them, and ye shall have them" (Mark 11:22-24; cf. Matthew 21:18-22).

So faith is frequently used in the Bible to express trust and often is equivalent to "believe." Faith also expresses the means by which salvation becomes available to man. When Jesus began His ministry, He came preaching, "The kingdom of God is at hand: repent ye, and believe the gospel" (Mark 1:15). Later during His ministry, Jesus told the woman "which was a sinner" that it was her faith that had saved her (Luke 7:36-50).

In the Parable of the Sower, Jesus said, "The seed is the word of God. Those by the way side are they that hear; then cometh the devil, and taketh away the word out of their hearts, lest they should believe and be saved" (Luke 8:11, 12). Those who respond to the seed of the Word and believe will be saved. Those who believe for awhile and in the "time of temptation fall away" (v. 13) or those who are "choked with cares and riches and pleasures of this life, and bring no fruit to perfection" (v. 14), will not be saved (cf. Matthew 13:18-23; Mark 4:13-20). Faith (belief) is essential for salvation.

The fourth Gospel does not use the noun *faith* but the verb *believe*. In the statement of the theme John wrote, "But as many as received him, to them gave he power to become the sons of God, even to them that believe on His name: Which were born, not of blood, nor of the will of the flesh, nor of the will of man, but of God" (John 1:12, 13). At the close of his Gospel, John wrote, "Many other signs truly did Jesus in the presence of his disciples, which are not written in this book: But these are written, that ye might believe that Jesus is the Christ, the Son of God; and that believing ye might have life through his name" (20:30, 31).

John used the term *believe* to describe the means by which man obtains eternal life. This theme of "believing" is not something John developed but is based on Jesus' own words. Jesus said, "So must the Son of man be lifted up: That whosoever believeth in him should not perish, but have eternal life" (John 3:14, 15). "Verily, verily, I say unto you, He that heareth my word, and believeth on him that sent me, hath everlasting life, and shall not come into condemnation; but is passed from death unto life" (5:24). "This is the will of him that sent me, that every one which seeth the Son, and believeth on him, may have everlasting life: and I will raise him up at the last day" (6:40).

When John wrote of God's purpose for sending Jesus into the world, he connected belief with the carrying out of this purpose:

> God so loved the world, that he gave his only begotten Son, that whosoever believeth in him should not perish, but have everlasting life. For God sent not his Son into the world to condemn the world; but that the world through him might be saved. He that believeth on him is not condemned: but he that believeth not is condemned already, because he hath not believed in the name of the only begotten Son of God. John 3:16-18

In summary, saving Christian faith is believing and accepting that Jesus Christ is our Savior and Lord. It is trusting in Him and accepting His teachings. Thus salvation is both an immediate possession and a growth and learning process. Sincere faith (I Timothy 1:5 NKJV) is more than intellectual assent to Christianity based on one's cultural and educational heritage—redeeming faith is a deep-seated belief that moves one's innermost being to please God. Faith is centered in man's heart and mind: "with the heart man believeth unto righteousness" (Romans 10:10). Faith is a strong conviction and belief in God, Jesus Christ, and the Holy Spirit—and the revelation that is inspired of the Holy Spirit (II Peter 1:21; II

Timothy 3:16). Faith is not an isolated act of belief that saves a person by itself without creating an interest and desire to learn about Christian doctrine and practice.

Since there are warnings about false prophets and about brethren falling away, it is important to know whether one has *real* faith. The main evidence of faith is that it appropriates grace in the sinner because we are "justified by his grace . . . received by faith" (Romans 3:24, 25 RSV). Grace is attested to by the indwelling witness and work of the Holy Spirit (8:9, 10, 16; I John 3:24; 4:13) and by growth and obedience in the believer's life (I John 2:3, 5; 3:10, 14, 18, 19; 4:7 5:2). If there is no evidence of grace, there is no faith. "Faith" that does not affect one's life and walk is not saving faith. Saving faith will be accompanied by a life of reading the Bible, praying for Holy Spirit illumination, and seeking to obey all the light one receives from the Word.

The New Birth

Repentance involves, as noted earlier, a radical change of mind and heart. When man's repentance and faith are real, God's grace will create in him a "new birth." The new birth is an experience and fact associated with the redemption brought by Jesus Christ. He emphasized the importance of the new birth in a discussion He had with a Jewish leader and a member of the Sanhedrin. Nicodemus knew that Jesus was "a teacher come from God: for no man can do these miracles that thou doest, except God be with him" (John 3:2). He respected Jesus as a Master Teacher and apparently had come to learn from Him.

Since He was a Jew, and most first-century Jews opposed Roman rule and wished for the restoration of Israel's kingdom, Jesus often addressed the issue of the kingdom of God. He told Nicodemus, "Verily, verily, I say unto thee, Except a man be born again, he cannot see the kingdom of God" (John 3:3). Jesus tied a spiritual change to the reality of the kingdom of God. Because this spiritual connection puzzled Nicodemus, he asked, "How can a man be born when he is old? can he enter the second time into his mother's womb, and be born? Jesus answered, Verily, verily, I say unto thee, Except a man be born of water and of the Spirit, he cannot enter into the kingdom of God. That which is born of the flesh is flesh; and that which is born of the Spirit is spirit" (vv. 4-6). Jesus emphasized the spiritual nature of the new birth: a person had to be "born of water and of the Spirit," because that "born of the Spirit is spirit" (v. 6).

Although there is some disagreement among Bible teachers as to the meaning of being "born of water," the most logical meaning seems to relate to the issue at hand—the kingdom. Since John the Baptizer tied repentance and preparedness to enter the kingdom to water baptism, surely Jesus and Nicodemus must had this in mind. After all, even the King was baptized, not as an act of repentance, but as a sign of His identification with the prepared people and the kingdom message.

In Jewish theology, water baptism was required for a proselyte to be incorporated into the kingdom of Israel. It marked the change or "new birth" of the candidate, signifying his disassociation from his past life and identity and his acceptance of the new way of life. On occasion he was even given a new name.

To this day, when a Jewish person of orthodox background is converted to faith in Christ, the family will reluctantly tolerate this change. However, when the person is baptized, the Jewish family considers him as deceased and sometimes even has a funeral service declaring that "fact." The convert to Christianity has died to his old way of life and has been born into a new identity and life, and baptism symbolizes the demarcation point.

Jesus went on to tell Nicodemus, "Marvel not that I said unto thee, Ye must be born again. The wind bloweth where it listeth, and thou hearest the sound thereof, but canst not tell whence it cometh, and whither it goeth: so is every one that is born of the Spirit" (John 3:7, 8). There is a mystery involved in being "born again" as there is a mystery about the wind. Miraculously, the Holy Spirit operates on the soul, making a telling impact on a person's will, desires, and values, giving a new direction to his life. The person turns from his natural inclination to rebel against God to an earnest desire to obey God. How this occurs and what mixture there is of truth, intellect, and the Holy Spirit's operations is beyond human understanding. We know, however, that these work together to produce an effect clearly visible in an individual's life.

When Jesus was asked about who was the greatest in the kingdom, He said, "Verily, I say unto you, Except ye be converted, and become as little children, ye shall not enter into the kingdom of heaven" (Matthew 18:3; cf. John 3:3). The new birth results in a complete change in a person's life. "If any man be in Christ, he is a new creature: old things are passed away; behold, all things are become new" (II Corinthians 5:17). The Christian will continue in a childlike faith he began with because of the new birth, and his willingness to learn will continue throughout life. He will "set [his] affection on things above, not on things on the earth" (Colossians 3:2). The Christian will listen to the Word and the Holy Spirit will lead him to accept its teachings. The new birth will make him a "child of God" (Matthew 18:1-6; cf. Mark 10:13-16; Luke 18:17; I John 3:2, 10; etc.).

The necessity of the new birth is confirmed in other New Testament writings. Paul reveals how the Christian's old nature is affected by the new birth: "They that are Christ's have crucified the flesh with the affections and lusts" (Galatians 5:24). He wrote further to explain how the old covenant ritualism no longer was important, "For in Christ Jesus neither circumcision availeth any thing, nor uncircumcision, but a new creature" (6:15). Peter underscores this truth when he writes, "Being born again, not of corruptible seed, but of incorruptible, by the word of God, which liveth and abideth for ever" (I Peter 1:23).

The new birth is absolutely necessary because of man's sinful nature—"that which is born of the flesh is flesh" (John 3:6)—and because man is "dead in trespasses and sins" (Ephesians 2:1). Paul explains what this means: "The carnal mind is enmity against [or hostile towards] God: for it is not subject to the law of God, neither indeed can be. So then they that are in the flesh cannot please God" (Romans 8:7, 8). Those "in the flesh" are controlled by sinful passions that work in them and "bring forth fruit unto death" (7:5). These people will never see God unless something happens to the sin barrier created by man. God is holy and cannot permit sin in His presence. Only the "pure in heart" shall see God (Matthew 5:8). This sin barrier can only be removed by God's Son and the work of the Holy Spirit, which results in a radically changed human nature through a rebirth. The new birth begins a process that makes the sinner "pure in heart." Thus the new birth is central and crucial to restoring man to his original position of fellowship and sonship with God. This restored position results in Christians following the commandment of love (22:37, 39; cf. Luke 10:27; John 14:15; I John 4:7, 8, 11) that springs from a pure heart, a good consience, and a sincere faith (I Timothy 1:5 NKJV).

The restored position resulting from the new birth is accompanied by a desire to do God's will. This results in a life of discipleship. Jesus spoke of these results: "My sheep hear my voice, and I know them, and they follow me: And I give unto them eternal life" (John 10:27, 28); "If ye love me, keep my commandments. He that hath my commandments, and keepeth them, he it is that loveth me: and he that loveth me shall be loved of my Father, and I will love him, and will manifest myself to him" (14:15, 21; see vv. 15-24); "I am the true vine.... Abide in me, and I in you. As the branch cannot bear fruit of itself, except it abide in the vine; no more can ye, except ye abide in me.... Herein is my Father glorified, that ye bear much fruit; so shall ye be my disciples" (15:1-8).

The Relation of Repentance, Faith, and the New Birth

We have seen that realization of the redemption brought by Jesus involves repentance, faith, and rebirth. Although some Scriptures give faith primacy, repentance and the new birth cannot be overlooked. These three are all necessary to enter the kingdom and are interrelated.

The sinner must repent in order to believe. He has to change his mind about his rebellion against the Lord, which means he has to see his sinfulness and God's righteousness and realize that he is lost and heading for hell. He needs to see the necessity to walk in the light and change his mind about walking in sin. This change of mind is so radical that it requires or is called being "born again." Yet for repentance to bring about the new birth, the intellect must respond in faith to the facts of the Gospel. Faith and repentance cannot operate in a vacuum; they need the inner assurance that the Gospel is true. Then the repentant sinner must believe revealed truth. Yet this believing cannot occur unless there is a change of heart. So we see that these three—faith, repentance, and the new birth—are interrelated and go together. These three interrelated processes then work together to bring salvation, and their exact interactions cannot be separated or, for that matter, completely understood.

This does not change the fact that faith is the primary condition for salvation taught in the New Testament, but giving faith the primary position does not exclude repentance and the new birth. When Paul speaks of faith as the condition for salvation, he implies the necessity of repentance and the rebirth. For example, in Romans 6:2-4 he makes it clear that saving faith results in a changed life: "How shall we, that are dead to sin, live any longer therein? . . . We are buried with him by baptism into death: that like as Christ was raised up from the dead by the glory of the Father, even so we also should walk in newness of life" (Romans 6:2-4).

Other Conditions

Repentance, faith, and the new birth are accompanied by less frequently mentioned conditions. These are interrelated to the above mentioned truths and are motivated and implemented by grace and the power of the Holy Spirit. They are necessary conditions to salvation, not that they are separate works to earn it, but are the results of yielding to the Lord Jesus and the Holy Spirit.

One of these is confession. Jesus said, "Whosoever therefore shall confess me before men, him I will confess also before my Father which is in heaven. But whosoever shall deny me before men, him will I also deny before my Father which is in heaven" (Matthew 10:32, 33; cf. Luke 12:8, 9). This act of confession, along with belief, is one condition Paul gives: "If thou shalt confess with thy mouth the Lord Jesus, and shalt believe in thine heart that God hath raised him from the dead, thou shalt be saved. For with the heart man believeth unto righteousness; and with the mouth confession is made unto salvation" (Romans 10:9, 10). John also gives this as a condition. "Whosoever shall confess that Jesus is the Son of God, God dwelleth in him, and he in God" (I John 4:15).

Peter and Paul both give another condition for salvation through the words of the prophet Joel. "Whosoever shall call on the name of the Lord shall be saved" (Acts 2:21; Romans 10:13; cf. Joel 2:32). This message is simple to understand. Salvation is available to all who call on the name of the Lord. Before Paul's quotation of this passage, he makes the statement that "with the heart man believeth unto righteousness; and with the mouth confession is made unto salvation" (Romans 10:10). This calling upon the name of the Lord is interrelated to belief and confession, and to repentance, faith, and the new birth. In his opening remarks to the Corinthian church, Paul speaks of this call, also. He writes, "To them that are sanctified in Christ Jesus . . . with all that in every place call upon the name of

Jesus Christ our Lord" (I Corinthians 1:2). The sanctified, i.e., the saints, and those who "call" are one group.

The disciples from the very start of their preaching stressed the importance of baptism. Peter told those who responded on the Day of Pentecost, "Repent, and be baptized every one of you in the name of Jesus Christ for the remission of sins, and ye shall receive the gift of the Holy Ghost" (Acts 2:38). "They that gladly received his word were baptized" (v. 41).

Baptism is associated with the believer's new life in Christ (Romans 6:3, 4; Galatians 3:27; Colossians 2:12). This new life does not come through the physical act of water baptism; baptism symbolizes or illustrates what has already occurred. "Baptism doth also now save us (not the putting away of the filth of the flesh, but the answer of a good conscience toward God,) by the resurrection of Jesus Christ" (I Peter 3:21). Baptism does not put away the filth or sin in one's life. The sin issue is resolved before baptism occurs because the believer has a good conscience toward God. This good conscience is brought about by the Holy Spirit baptism, where the believer is made spiritually alive (new birth) and is added to the body of Christ, the Church: "By one Spirit are we all baptized into one body" (I Corinthians 12:13; see also John 3:5, 6; Titus 3:5).

A Life of Discipleship

Only those who have repented, exercised faith, experienced the new birth, and have received the indwelling of the Holy Spirit will obtain salvation. These believers will obey and be faithful disciples of Christ. Discipleship is necessarily a part of the Christian faith.

Discipleship is strongly emphasized by the Lord. He said that only those who obey and are faithful disciples will obtain redemption. Jesus said, "Not every one that saith unto me, Lord, Lord, shall enter into the kingdom of heaven; but he that doeth the will of my Father which is in heaven" (Matthew 7:21), and "He that taketh not his cross, and followeth after me is not worthy of me. He that findeth his life shall lose it: and he that loseth his life for my sake shall find it" (Matthew 10:38, 39; cf. Luke 9:23, 24). Likewise He says, "If any man will come after me, let him deny himself, and take up his cross, and follow me. For whosoever will save his life shall lose it: and whosoever will lose his life for my sake shall find it" (Matthew

16:24, 25; cf. Mark 8:34, 35). Jesus told His followers, "If ye continue in my word, then are ye my disciples indeed; and ye shall know the truth, and the truth shall make you free. If a man keep my saying, he shall never see death" (John 8:31, 32, 51).

This obedience Jesus calls for is possible only through the new birth and the empowering of the Holy Spirit. It results from being set free from sin and receiving a new love for Jesus (John 8:31-38). "He that hath my commandments, and keepeth them, he it is that loveth me: and he that loveth me shall be loved of my Father, and I will love him, and will manifest myself to him. . . . If a man love me, he will keep my words: and my Father will love him, and we will come unto him, and make our abode with him. He that loveth me not keepeth not my sayings: and the word which ye hear is not mine, but the Father's which sent me" (14:21-24; cf. 15:9, 10).

John explains this further in his first epistle.

> Whosoever believeth that Jesus is the Christ is born of God: and every one that loveth him that begat loveth him also that is begotten of him. By this we know that we love the children of God, when we love God, and keep His commandments. For this is the love of God, that we keep his commandments: and his commandments are not grievous. For whatsoever is born of God overcometh the world: and this is the victory that overcometh the world, even our faith. Who is he that overcometh the world, but he that believeth that Jesus is the Son of God? I John 5:1-5

Chapter 6

Redemption Clarified

Lessons From the Jews

The Jews, the chosen people, had a long history of rebellion against God; and they had a long, hard journey before they learned the importance of doing God's will. Finally, after Judah's seventy years in the Babylonian captivity, the Jews were cured of their idolatry. However, this cure did not solve their problems because their national life came to an end, and many of the people were scattered. The remnant that remained developed the Judaism religion. For them, the pendulum swung from rebellion to strict legalism based on the oral and literal interpretation of the law. God wanted the Jews to change, but their change to a zealous desire to keep the letter of the law caused them to miss the spirit and intent of it. Consequently, they built a whole system of traditions that was firmly grounded, not on the spirit and intent of the law, but on the letter.

This new emphasis on strict obedience to the letter of the law and to the elders' traditions was a source of the conflict that developed between the Jewish leaders and Jesus. It was a cause of the Pharisees and scribes' increasing opposition to Jesus that finally resulted in His crucifixion. Jesus tried to correct them when they accused His disciples of transgressing the tradition of the elders. He asked them, "Why do ye also transgress the commandment of God by your tradition?" (Matthew 15:3). He pointed out the fifth commandment to "Honour thy father and mother" (v. 4) and reminded them that they said, "It is a gift, by whatsoever thou mightest be profited by me. . . . he shall be free" (vv. 5, 6). By this they "made the commandment of God of none effect by [their] tradition" (v. 6). Jesus applied a prophecy from Isaiah to them: "This people draweth nigh unto me with their mouth, and honoureth me with their lips; but their heart is far from me. But in vain they do worship me, teaching for doctrines the commandments of men" (vv. 8, 9; cf. Mark 7:1-13; Isaiah 29:13).

The Church's First Outreach to the Jews Only

The legalism of the Jew carried over into the early church and threatened to pervert the Gospel message. This legalism not only confused some early Christians, but it also caused some of the apostles and other church leaders to fail to grasp the meaning of the law and its relation to the Gospel.

Many early church leaders failed to see that redemption is for all men, that Gentiles did not have to come under the Mosaic law to become Christians, and that Jewish Christians did not have to continue under it. Peter himself had this problem. It took an angel, a Gentile centurion named Cornelius, and a vision for Peter to see that the Gospel was for all men. Peter, having been on a long journey, desired something to eat. While his meal was being prepared, he fell into a trance. He saw an object like a great sheet coming down from heaven containing all kinds of four-footed animals, crawling creatures, and birds. "And there came a voice to him, Rise, Peter; kill, and eat. But Peter said, Not so, Lord; for I have never eaten any thing that is common or unclean" (Acts 10:13, 14). Then the voice said, "What God hath cleansed, that call not thou common" (v. 15).

"Peter doubted in himself what this vision which he had seen should mean" (Acts 10:17). Then three men came telling him that "Cornelius the centurion, a just man, and one that feareth God" (v. 22) was directed by a holy angel to seek and listen to what he had to say. Peter went to Cornelius and told him, "Ye know how that it is an unlawful thing for a man that is a Jew to keep company, or come unto one of another nation; but God hath shewed me that I should not call any man common or unclean. Therefore came I unto you without gainsaying, as soon as I was sent for" (vv. 28, 29). Peter explained later, "Of a truth I perceive that God is no respecter of persons: But in every nation he that feareth him, and worketh righteousness, is accepted with him" (vv. 34, 35). He then told them of Jesus Christ.

Making salvation available to Gentiles without them becoming Jews was something new to Peter and some of the other early church leaders. The apostles received the great commission to preach the Gospel to all nations (Matthew 28:19; Luke 24:47; Acts 1:8), but they were slow to realize this meant preaching to others besides the

Jews and their proselytes. Yet there was some preaching to others, as may be seen in Philip's preaching to the Samaritans (Acts 8). For the most part, however, the concept of the Jews being God's chosen people and the Gentiles being "common or unclean" was firmly grounded in the Jewish mind, and it influenced their outreach. The early Christians even failed to grasp the full meaning of Peter's experience with Cornelius. When they were scattered because of persecution after Stephen was stoned to death, they continued to speak the word "to none but unto the Jews" (11:19).

Christian Dissension Over Keeping the Law

Gradually, however, the word went beyond the Jews to the Gentiles. As more and more Gentiles came into the church, the question of their relation to the law became an issue. The church leaders now knew that God no longer showed partiality, but did this mean Gentile Christians could ignore the Mosaic law?

This issue came to a head when some men from Judea went out and told the Gentiles, "Except ye be circumcised after the manner of Moses, ye cannot be saved" (Acts 15:1). This caused "no small dissension and disputation" (v. 2). Finally to settle this issue, Paul and Barnabas (two who had labored much among the Gentiles) were appointed to go to Jerusalem with others to confer with the other apostles and elders. A conference was called at Jerusalem to find God's will on this matter.

One of the first to speak was Peter. He explained his earlier experience how that God "put no difference between us [the Jews] and them [the Gentiles], purifying their hearts by faith" (Acts 15:9). He continued, "Now therefore why tempt ye God, to put a yoke upon the neck of the disciples, which neither our fathers nor we were able to bear? But we believe that through the grace of the Lord Jesus Christ, we shall be saved, even as they" (vv. 10, 11).

The Holy Spirit led the apostles to the conclusion that Gentiles need not keep the Mosaic law but should abstain from idolatry, immorality, things strangled, and blood (Acts 15:20, 28, 29). These decisions were not the result of man's reasoning but involved revelation given to the Lord's chosen apostles.

This conference did not settle the question for all. Some still sought to make Christians live in obedience to the Mosaic law. The Judaizers (those who insisted that Christians must keep the Mosiac law) kept this issue alive during the last part of the first-century, and many of the New Testament books were written to explain the relation of the Mosaic Law to the Christian faith. Among these books are Galatians, Romans, and Hebrews.

Galatians—By Law or by Faith?

The earliest of Paul's letters dealing with the relationship of the Mosaic law to faith is Galatians. The churches in Galatia were composed mainly of Gentiles. Trouble came into these churches concerning the relation of Gentile Christians to the law because certain Jewish Christians (Judaizers) came and taught that Gentile Christians had to keep the law of Moses to be saved. Paul saw this as "another gospel," a perverted one, foreign to the one he had preached to them (Galatians 1:6).

Paul stressed that the Gospel he preached was "not after man," but that it came "by the revelation of Jesus Christ" (Galatians 1:11, 12). He told them of his relation to the other apostles and how the circumcision party had caused trouble before. Thus the trouble the Galatians were now facing was not new; others had faced it before.

To clarify the Gospel again for them, Paul wrote, "Knowing that a man is not justified by the works of the law, but by the faith of Jesus Christ, even we have believed in Jesus Christ, that we might be justified by the faith of Christ, and not by the works of the law: for by the works of the law shall no flesh be justified" (Galatians 2:16).

The question that probably came to the Galatian Christians' minds, put there by the circumcision party, was, "If salvation is now by faith, how were those who lived before Christ justified? Was Abraham justified by works? Is the basis now changed?" To answer this, Paul quoted from Genesis: "Abraham believed God, and it was accounted to him for righteousness" (Galatian 3:6; cf. Genesis 15:6; Romans 4:3). There was no mention of works of the law, and this basis of justification always remained in effect. It is, "They which are of faith, the same are the children of Abraham" (v. 7). Paul explained this by pointing out, "The scripture, foreseeing that God would justify the heathen through faith, preached before the gospel unto Abraham, saying, In thee shall all nations be blessed" (v. 8). Those who do not accept this basis but rely on works will not receive this blessing. They are "under the curse: for it is written, Cursed is every one that continueth not in all things which are written in the book of the law to do them" (v. 10). The law Paul refers to here is the Mosaic law, the Ten Commandments, the elaborate worship and offerings, the civil and social regulations, etc., found in the first five books of the Old Testament. The purpose of this law was never to justify man. The Old Testament states, "The just shall live by his faith" (Habakkuk 2:4). "And the law is not of faith: but, the man that doeth them shall live in them. Christ hath redeemed us from the curse of the law, being made a curse for us: for it is written, Cursed is every one that hangeth on a tree: That the blessing of Abraham might come on the Gentiles through Jesus Christ; that we might receive the promise of the Spirit through faith" (Galatians 3:12-14).

The circumcision party problems were caused by its failure to see that the promises spoken to Abraham and to his seed were not based on obedience to the law. The promises were made to his "seed," not "seeds" (Galatians 3:16). The promise thus referred to one, not to many. This One is Christ. The law did not annul or alter this promise: "The law, which was four hundred and thirty years after, cannot disannul, that it should make the promise of none effect" (v. 17). The law did not invalidate the covenant God made with Abraham. So if we claim the blessing promised to Abraham and his offspring, it is not on the basis of the law but of faith.

Paul, after refuting the idea that the law is connected to the promise, next answered the logical question that follows: "Wherefore then serveth the law?" (Galatians 3:19). He answered this by stating, "It was added because of transgressions, till the seed should come to whom the promise was made." It was needed to confine men or to keep men under restraint until the Seed came. The law was a "schoolmaster to bring us unto Christ" (v. 24). It was only a temporary thing, "but after that faith is come, we are no longer under a schoolmaster. For ye are all the children of God by faith in Christ Jesus" (vv. 25, 26). Since men are no longer under the schoolmaster, "there is neither Jew nor Greek" in Christ (v. 28). Christians "are all one in Christ Jesus. And if [they] be Christ's, then are [they] Abraham's seed, and heirs according to promise" (vv. 28, 29).

Paul warned his readers not to turn back "to the weak and beggarly elements" of the law (Galatians 4:9), from the promise they possessed through Christ. Paul was afraid some were doing this by observing "days, and months, and times [seasons], and years" (v. 10). By doing things to earn salvation or by saying that one must receive circumcision to be saved, a person is severed from Christ and "fallen from grace" (5:4). The point is that "neither circumcision availeth any thing, nor uncircumcision" (v. 6). What counts is "faith which worketh by love" and "a new creature" (6:15).

Romans and Justification

The relation of the Christian to the law of Moses was not a problem only in Galatia. Paul wrote to the Christians in Rome about this relationship. The theme of the Book of Romans is the same as Galatians, but Romans is a longer book, containing additional issues. Its theme is, "For I am not ashamed of the gospel of Christ: for it is the power of God unto salvation to every one that believeth; to the Jew first, and also to the Greek. For therein is the righteousness of God revealed from faith to faith: as it is written, The just shall live by faith" (Romans 1:16, 17).

The Jews thought they stood in favor with God because they were the children of Abraham. They did have a special relation to God as the chosen people; nevertheless they still needed salvation by faith. To bring this to their attention, Paul first wrote to them about the Gentiles' sins and drew the conclusion that "the wrath of God is revealed from heaven against all ungodliness and unrighteousness of men" (Romans 1:18). The Jews knew the Gentiles were exceedingly wicked. Paul portrayed this wickedness in Romans (1:18-31).

The Jews would have agreed with Paul's observation and conclusion that "God gave them [the wicked Gentiles] up" (Romans 1:24, 26, 28). In the Jews' minds, the Gentiles deserved spiritual death. As the Jews read Paul's letter to the Romans, they no doubt were glad they were separate from the Gentiles. But as they read on in the Book of Romans, they were in for a surprise. "Thou art inexcusable, O man, whosoever thou art that judgest: for wherein thou judgest another, thou condemnest thyself; for thou that judgest doest the same things" (2:1). The Jews had judged the Gentiles rightly, but the Jews were no better off since they were doing the same things. The Jews too refused to do God's will and were unrighteous and ungodly.

The Jews had misunderstood what God's kindness, forbearance, and patience meant for them. God would not overlook their sins because they were the chosen people. Paul asked them if they understood the sigificance of "the riches of his [God's] goodness and forbearance and longsuffering; not knowing that the goodness of God leadeth thee to repentance?" (Romans 2:4). Because the Jews had hard and impenitent hearts, they too were storing up unto themselves "wrath against the day of wrath and revelation of the righteous judgment of God; who will render to every man according to his deeds: To them who by patient continuance in well doing seek for glory and honour and immortality, eternal life: But unto them that are contentious, and do not obey the truth, but obey unrighteousness, indignation and wrath" (vv. 5-8). The important thing was not whether a person was a Jew or a Gentile, because there will be "tribulation and anguish" (v. 9) for all who do evil, and "glory, honour, and peace" for those who do good (v. 10), whether they are Jew or Gentile. "For there is no respect of persons with God" (v. 11).

All who "have sinned without law shall also perish without law: and as many as have sinned in the law shall be judged by the law" (Romans 2:12). It is not the hearers of the law but the doers who will be justified. The Gentiles who may not have the law yet "do by nature the things contained in the law" can be justified too (v. 14).

Paul explained that being circumcised may or may not have value. "Circumcision verily profiteth, if thou keep the law: but if thou be a breaker of the law, thy circumcision is made uncircumcision" (Romans 2:25). So the physical act of circumcision does not make one a real Jew. "He is a Jew, which is one inwardly; and circumcision is that of the heart, in the spirit, and not in the letter" (v. 29).

If this is the case, "What advantage then hath the Jew? or what profit is there of circumcision?" (Romans 3:1). If being one of the chosen people and being circumcised does not justify one before God, then what advantage does a Jew have? Paul answers this question. He says the Jew does have an advantage. It is "chiefly, because that unto them were committed the oracles of God" (v. 2). But the Jew is not better off in other ways. "Both Jews and Gentiles . . . are all under sin; as it is written, There is none righteous, no, not one: There is none that understandeth, there is none that seeketh after God. They are all gone out of the way, they are together become unprofitable; there is none that doeth good, no, not one" (vv. 9-12).

Everyone will be held "guilty before God. Therefore by the deeds of the law there shall no flesh be justified in his sight: for by the law is the knowledge of sin" (Romans 3:19, 20). The purpose of the law is to reveal sin, not to be a basis of righteousness before God. This righteousness "is by faith of Jesus Christ unto all and upon all them that believe: for there is no difference: For all have sinned, and come short of the glory of God; being justifed freely by his grace through the redemption that is in Christ Jesus: Whom God hath set forth to be a propitiation through faith in his blood" (vv. 21-25). The Law and the Prophets bore witness to Jesus Christ (v. 21).

Now, in the Christian era, "the righteousness of God which is by faith of Jesus Christ [is] unto all and upon all them that believe" (Romans 3:22). Man is justified, that is, declared righteous, acquitted, free from condemnation, set free, etc., by faith in Jesus Christ. He was sent to be a "propitiation through faith in his blood, to declare his righteousness for the remission of sins" (v. 25). Through Christ's blood the convert can find forgiveness and eternal life.

By contrasting the works of the law to faith, Paul shows that faith involves belief in whom Jesus Christ is and acceptance of the body of Christian truth. Faith is more than belief and trust; it represents the way God justifies men under the new covenant. Christian faith is more than faith *alone*, but, as we have seen earlier, it includes repentance, the new birth, and discipleship. Justifying grace creates in the sinner a new nature than is dead to sin but alive to righteousness. The sinner is justified by "his [Christ's] righteousness: that he might be just, and the justifier of him which believeth in Jesus" (Romans 3:26). By God accepting Christ's righteousness in place of the repentant sinner's sins, God is just to His own character when He declares the sinner righteous. It is Christ who works justification, not man's attempt at keeping the Old Testament law. Redemption through faith in Jesus means no one can boast because he is one of the chosen people or because of things he does. "A man is justifed by faith without the deeds of the law. . . . It is one God, which shall justify the circumcision by faith, and uncircumcision through faith" (vv. 28, 30).

Since this is the case, "What shall we say then that Abraham our father, as pertaining to the flesh, hath found?" (Romans 4:1). Was not he justified by works? No, he was not. The Scripture says, "Abraham believed God, and it was counted unto him for righteousness" (v. 3; cf. Genesis 15:6). Abraham was not counted righteous because of the works he performed, but because he believed God. "To him that worketh not, but believeth on him that justifieth the ungodly, his faith is counted for righteousness" (Romans 4:5). Paul then draws an important conclusion by comparing the time when Abraham's faith and circumcision occurred. "We say that faith was reckoned to Abraham for righteousness. How was it then reckoned? when he was in circumcision, or in uncircumcision? Not in circumcision, but in uncircumcision. And he received the sign of circumcision, a seal of the righteousness of the faith which he had yet being uncircumcised: that he might be the father of all them that believe, though they be not circumcised" (vv. 9-11).

Thus "the promise, that he should be the heir of the world, was not to Abraham, or to his seed, through the law, but through the righteousness of faith. For if they which are of the law be heirs, faith is made void, and the promise made of none effect: Because the law worketh wrath: for where no law is, there is no transgression" (Romans 4:13-15). The law does not make us heirs to the promise given to Abraham. The purpose of the law was not to bring salvation but the knowledge of sin. We become heirs through the righteousness of faith.

Since salvation comes by faith, it is by grace, and it is a gift given to those who are "of the faith of Abraham" (Romans 4:16). Abraham had a strong faith. When he was told, "I [God] have made thee a father of many nations" (v. 17), he did not have any children. Yet, "against hope [he] believed in hope. . . . And being not weak in faith, he considered not his own body now dead, when he was about a hundred years old, neither yet the deadness of Sarah's womb: He staggered not at the promise of God through unbelief; but was strong in faith, giving glory to God; and being fully persuaded that, what he had promised, he was able also to perform" (vv. 18-21). Abraham believed God's Word and was persuaded that God's promise would be fulfilled. His faith brought action and remains an example for men because of the written Word.

Righteousness and justification "shall be imputed [to us], if we believe on him that raised up Jesus our Lord from the dead; who was delivered for our offences, and was raised again for our justification" (Romans 4:24, 25). Jesus died for our sins that we "should live unto righteousness" (I Peter 2:24; cf. II Corinthians 5:21; I John 3:6-10).

The conclusion to the discussion of Romans chapter 4 is given in chapter 5. "Therefore being justifed by faith, we have peace with God through our Lord Jesus Christ: By whom also we have access by faith into this grace wherein we stand" (vv. 1, 2). This peace came about because "when we were yet without strength, in due time Christ died for the ungodly" (v. 6). We now have hope "because the love of God is shed abroad in our hearts by the Holy Ghost" (v. 5). Christ's death for the sinner is not what one would expect a man to do: "For scarcely for a righteous man will one die" (v. 7). Jesus Christ was different because of the love of God within Him. God showed "his love toward us, in that, while we were yet sinners, Christ died for us" (v. 8). Since He did this for us "when we were enemies" (v. 10), we can now expect "much more, being reconciled, we shall be saved by his life." Christ died for sinners when we were enemies of God, and now "much more" are we reconciled and saved by His resurrected life.

The benefit of Jesus' death—reconciliation to God—is a "free gift" to all men who will meet the necessary conditions. The transfer of this benefit is different from the transfer of the consequence of Adam's sin. The benefit of Jesus' death is much greater than Adam's trespass, which brought death to all men. Adam's one sin caused his sinful nature and death to be transmitted to all his descendants. Because of this we have a nature that leads each of us to sin, that is, to rebel and disobey God's Word. This depravity was transmitted to and inflicted on each of us through our fallen nature.

Adam brought sin to all through a natural transmission, but Christ's gift of grace has had a much greater effect: "Much more the grace of God, and the gift by grace, which is by one man, Jesus Christ, hath abounded unto many" (Romans 5:15). Grace far exceeds the effect of Adam's sin. It has the power to remove the rebellious nature of all who come under sin's influence and bring repentance, regeneration, and discipleship. Adam's sin brought death, but Christ brought life to the dead. Bringing life is a vastly greater achievement than bringing death.

Paul contrasts how one man's offense brought condemnation and how One's (Jesus Christ's) obedience made many righteous:

> by the offence of one judgment came upon all men to condemnation; even so by the righteousness of one the free gift came upon all men unto justification of life. For as by one man's disobedience many were made sinners, so by the obedience of one shall many be made righteous. Moreover the law entered, that the offence might abound. But where sin abounded, grace did much more abound: That as sin hath reigned unto death, even so might grace reign through righteousness unto eternal life by Jesus Christ our Lord. Romans 5:18-21

Romans 6—Faith and Obedience

As we have seen, Paul built a strong case for justification by faith and showed that no one is justified by the keeping of the law. The writer of Hebrews, we will see later, explained how Jesus brought in a much better way than that of following the law. When Paul explained the relationship of the new covenant's grace to the Mosaic law, he realized that some might misunderstand it and think they were now free to do as they pleased. He took up this potential problem by asking, "What shall we say then? Shall we continue in sin, that grace may abound?" (Romans 6:1).

The answer to this question was very simple to Paul: "God forbid. How shall we, that are dead to sin, live any longer therein?" (Romans 6:2). The Christian has been baptized into Christ's death and buried with Him to rise with Him so that he "should walk in newness of life" (v. 4). In this union "we have been planted together in the likeness of his death," and moreover we are united with him "in the likeness of his resurrection" (v. 5). The Christian's "old man is crucified with him, that the body of sin might be destroyed, that henceforth we should not serve sin" (v. 6). As Christ was raised from the dead and "liveth unto God" (v. 10), so also is the Christian. He is to realize that he is "dead indeed unto sin, but alive unto God through Jesus Christ our Lord" (v. 11). The natural result of this union with Christ is that the Christian will not "let sin . . . reign in [his] mortal" body or live in "unrighteousness" (vv. 12, 13).

The Christian's new life is no longer under the dominion of sin, since he is "not under the law, but under grace" (Romans 6:14). The goal of the plan of redemption is to deliver man from his sinful nature, which manifests itself in disobeying God, and return man to God so that he will again desire to do God's will. This was something the Mosaic law could never do. Reconciliation to God can occur only by the grace of God, which makes it possible for man to repent, to be born again, and to become a disciple of Jesus Christ.

Paul reinforces his argument by asking the same question again and giving the same answer. This time he explains his answer by a slavery illustration. A person is a slave to whom he obeys, "whether of sin unto death, or of obedience unto righteousness" (Romans 6:16). Paul says the Christian can thank God that though once you were a slave of sin; now "ye have obeyed from the heart that form of doctrine which was delivered you. Being then made free from sin, ye became the servants of righteousness" (vv. 17, 18).

This illustration from slavery is explained further. Paul says that the Christian has a new master. He writes, "For as ye have yielded your members servants to uncleanness and to iniquity unto iniquity; even so now yield your members servants to righteousness unto holiness" (Romans 6:19). Once they "were the servants of sin, . . . free from righteousness" (v. 20), but now they are "free from sin, and become servants to God" (v. 22). This brings with it "fruit unto holiness, and the end everlasting life."

The process of becoming a holy person is known as "sanctification." The term *sanctify* means to be made holy and is accomplished by the power of the Holy Spirit (Romans 15:16; II Thessalonians 2:13; I Peter 1:2). Justification and sanctification cannot be separated. Justification does not occur without sanctification or sanctification without justification. They are separate workings of grace occurring at the same time. Justification is the gracious act of God making the sinner righteous. Sanctification is the believer's initial setting apart and subsequent growth in holiness.

The theme of grace making us free from sin's power and enabling us to yield to Christ in Romans 6 is emphasized in Paul's other writings. He wrote to the Corinthians that the "love of Christ constraineth us" because "if one died for all, then were all dead: And that he died for all, that they which live should not henceforth live unto themselves, but unto him which died for them, and rose again" (II Corinthians 5:14, 15). He goes on to emphasize, "If any man be in Christ, he is a new creature: old things are passed away; behold, all things are become new" (v. 17). This is what Christ did for us. He reconciled the world to Himself so that "we might be made the righteousness of God in him" (v. 21).

In the Book of Galatians, Paul admonished his readers to "walk in the Spirit, and ye shall not fulfill the lust of the flesh" (5:16). Those who yield to the desires of the flesh are warned that "they which do such things shall not inherit the kingdom of God" (v. 21). Those who walk in the Spirit are those that belong to Christ Jesus and "have crucified the flesh with the affections and lusts" (v. 24).

Paul wrote to the saints at Ephesus that they were made alive after they had been "dead in [their] trespasses and sins" (Ephesians 2:1). They once followed the course of this world and lived "in the lusts of [their] flesh, fulfilling the desires of the flesh and of the mind.... But God, who is rich in mercy, for his great love wherewith he loved us, Even when we were dead in sins, hath quickened us together with Christ, (by grace ye are saved)" (vv. 3-5). By His grace God has saved us through faith and made us "his workmanship, created in Christ Jesus unto good works" (v. 10).

Paul wrote to the Colossian Christians that Christ's goal was that they "might walk worthy of the Lord unto all pleasing, being fruitful in every good work, and increasing in the knowledge of God" (Colossians 1:10). Christians are able to do this because the Father "hath delivered us from the power of darkness, and hath translated us into the kingdom of his dear Son" (v. 13). After extolling the preeminence of Christ (vv. 15-19), Paul emphasized Christ's reconciling work. The saints and faithful brethren in Christ at Colosse, who "were sometime alienated and enemies in [their] mind by wicked works ... hath he reconciled.... to present [them] holy" (vv. 21, 22). We "are circumcised with the circumcision made without hands, in putting off the body of the sins of the flesh by the circumcision of Christ: Buried with him in baptism, wherein also [we] are raisen with him through the faith" (2:11, 12). He has quickened us and blotted out "the handwriting of ordinances that was against us" (v. 14).

To the saints at Thessalonica Paul wrote that they had learned from him "how [they] ought to walk and to please God" (I Thessalonians 4:1). He then reminded them that he had given them the commandments by the authority of the Lord Jesus. Next he wrote, "For this is the will of God, even your sanctification, that ye should abstain from fornication.... For God hath not called us unto uncleanness, but unto holiness" (vv. 3, 7).

Paul wrote to Titus, who helped him establish churches on Crete and elsewhere, about the effect of God's grace on Christian living.

> For the grace of God that bringeth salvation hath appeared to all men, teaching us that, denying ungodliness and worldly lusts, we should live soberly, righteously, and godly, in this present world; looking for that blessed hope, and the glorious appearing of the great God and our Saviour Jesus Christ; who gave himself for us, that he might redeem us from all iniquity, and purify unto himself a peculiar people, zealous of good works. Titus 2:11-14

God's grace teaches us how to live a life of purity and good works, and enables us to do so.

Paul next wrote about what he and other Christians once were.

> For we ourselves also were sometimes foolish, disobedient, deceived, serving divers lusts and pleasures, living in malice and envy, hateful, and hating one another. But after that the kindness and love of God our Saviour toward men appeared, not by works of righteousness which we have done, but according to his mercy he saved us, by the washing of regeneration, and renewing of the Holy Ghost; which he shed on us abundantly through Jesus Christ our Saviour; that being justified by his grace, we should be made heirs according to the hope of eternal life. Titus 3:3-7

The above Scriptures emphasize that the grace of God that saves a person does not allow him to continue in rebellion against God's will. The grace that saves produces a new heart in the person so that he *wants* to do God's will.

Romans 7, 8—Why Obedience Is Possible

Paul explains in Romans 7 that the Christian is to live a fruitful life for God, the life he described in chapter 6. This is possible because the Christian is no longer under the Mosaic law. Paul explains that the law is binding on a person only during his life, and that death breaks its power. To show this is true, he asks his readers to think of marriage and points out that death breaks the marriage bond.

Christians have died "to the law by the body of Christ" (Romans 7:4). The law Paul is speaking of is the Mosaic law. Christians are in union with Christ and share in the benefits of His death so far as the law is concerned. The result is that we are now "married to another, even to him who is raised from the dead, that we should bring forth fruit unto God" (v. 4) This means believers are "delivered from the law, that being dead wherein we were held; that we should serve in newness of spirit, and not in the oldness of the letter" (v. 6). The old written code is gone; we now serve God with a new spirit.

Since Christians share in the benefits of Christ's death, what implications does this have for the law? Is the law sin? Paul answers this with a strong "God forbid" (Romans 7:7). The law isn't sin. It makes us aware of what sin is. He explains, "I had not known sin, but by the law: for I had not known lust, except the law had said, Thou shalt not covet" (v. 7). The law reveals God's will and makes us aware of sin. This sin then brings death.

Speaking of his own experience, Paul says, "But sin, taking occasion by the commandment, wrought in me all manner of concupiscence. For without the law sin was dead. For I was alive without the law once: but when the commandment came, sin revived, and I died. And the commandment, which was ordained to life, I found to be unto death. For sin, taking occasion by the commandment, deceived me, and by it slew me" (Romans 7:8-11). Sin is what brought death, so we can conclude that "the law is holy, and the commandment holy, and just, and good" (v. 12).

This is explained further: "Was then that which is good made death unto me? God forbid. But sin, that it might appear sin, working death in me by that which is good; that sin by the commandment might become exceeding sinful" (Romans 7:13). Using his own experience before he came to Christ, Paul described how sin and the law worked. He was "carnal, sold under sin" (v. 14). He did not understand his own actions. He said,

> For that which I do I allow not: for what I would, that do I not; but what I hate, that do I. If then I do that which I would not, I consent unto the law that it is good. Now then it is no more I that do it, but sin that dwelleth in me. For I know that in me (that is, in my flesh,) dwelleth no good thing: for to will is present with me; but how to perform that which is good I find not. For the good that I would I do not: but the evil which I would not, that I do. Now if I do that I would not, it is no more I that do it, but sin that dwelleth in me. Romans 7:15-20

Before coming to Christ, Paul was a Pharisee and had a deep desire to keep the law perfectly, but he could not because of his sinful nature. His flesh made him do the very opposite of what he wanted to do. Living under the law he had a desire to do good and delighted in the law of God, but something made him do the opposite (Romans 7:18-23). In despair he cried out, "O wretched man that I am! who shall deliver me from the body of this death?" (v. 24). He could not deliver himself. Could anyone? Yes, there was One who could, and Paul was thankful. He wrote that he thanked "God through Jesus Christ our Lord," implying that Christ delivered him (v. 25). Jesus brought grace that enabled Paul to finally do God's will. Paul then sums up his condition under the old covenant apart from Christ: "So then with the mind I myself serve the law of God; but with the flesh the law of sin" (v. 25).

The result of this deliverance is emphasized in Romans 8. Our deliverance means this: "There is therefore now no condemnation to them which are in Christ Jesus, who walk not after the flesh, but after the Spirit. For the law of the Spirit of life in Christ Jesus hath made me free from the law of sin and death" (vv. 1-2). Those in Christ walk not after the flesh because of the life they have in Him. They have been freed from the "law of sin," that is, they have been able to break away from the habit of sinning through the indwelling presence of the Holy Spirit, which was something the Mosaic law could not provide. God, by "sending his own Son in the likeness of sinful flesh, and for sin, condemned sin in the flesh" (v. 3). This occurred so that "the righteousness of the law might be fulfilled in us" (v. 4).

Paul describes Christians as those who "walk not after the flesh, but after the Spirit" (Romans 8:4). The term *flesh* describes the characteristics of fallen man, the sinful nature he inherited from Adam. Adam rebelled against God and subjected the whole human race to Satan's domination. The fleshly or carnal man cannot do good, even if he tries. He is the type of person pictured in Romans 7. Those who are controlled by "the flesh do mind the things of the flesh," and this brings death (vv. 5, 6). In contrast to this is the Christian characteristic of walking in the Spirit. The Christian sets his mind on "the things of the Spirit," and finds "to be spiritually minded is life and peace" (v. 6).

The reason for such a strong contrast between following the flesh and following the Spirit is that "to be carnally minded is death . . . the carnal mind is enmity against God: for it is not subject to the law of God, neither indeed can be" (Romans 8:7). The carnal mind is actively opposed to God and thus cannot please Him. But the Christian is different because he is "not in the flesh, but in the Spirit. . . . Now if any man have not the Spirit of Christ he is none of his" (v. 9). As mentioned above, "to be spiritually minded is life and peace" (v. 6). Paul concludes that the Christian is under obligation, "not to the flesh, to live after the flesh. For if ye live after the flesh, ye shall die: but if ye through the Spirit do mortify [put to death] the deeds of the body, ye shall live" (vv. 12, 13). The Christian wants to do God's will and is able by the power of the Holy Spirit to overcome his natural tendencies of seeking to do his own will.

Redemption Clarified 155

Those who live by the Spirit and "are led by the Spirit of God, they are the sons of God" (Romans 8:14). The children of God do not experience the "spirit of bondage again to fear," but they experience the "Spirit of adoption" and as sons cry out to God, "Abba, Father" (v. 15). As children of God, we are "heirs of God, and joint-heirs with Christ," and we will be glorified with Him (v. 17).

James - Faith and Works

The Book of James also deals with the relation of faith and works. James comes to the conclusion "that by works a man is justified, and not by faith only" (2:24). On the surface, this appears to conflict with the doctrine of justifcation by faith (Romans 3:28), but this is not the case. James's readers had a different view of faith than Paul's, and James sought to correct his readers' erroneous view. Paul also realized there was a danger of misunderstanding faith and attempted to deal with this in Romans 6.

James opens his discussion of justification by asking several questions. "What doth it profit, my brethren, though a man say he hath faith, and have not works? can [such] faith save him?" (James 2:14). To answer this question, James asks another question and then draws a conclusion from the answer he gives. James asks if a brother or sister is ill clad and lacks food, and someone tells them, "Depart in peace, be ye warmed and filled; notwithstanding ye give them not those things which are needful to the body; what doth it profit?" (vv. 15, 16). Obviously, it does no one any good.

James realized that some would object to his conclusion and claim that faith and works can exist apart from each other. He knew some would say, "Thou hast faith, and I have works" (James 2:18). He challenges those who say this to "shew me thy faith without thy works, and I will shew thee my faith by my works." Faith is known by the works it produces. True faith exists only if it produces good works. Faith and works are inseparable.

To those who try to separate faith and works, James warns them that their faith is invalid. He tells them, "Thou believest that there is one God; thou doest well: the devils [demons] also believe, and tremble" (James 2:19). Belief that is a mere acknowledgment of facts is not adequate. Such a belief shows the lack of regeneration.

James goes on to show from the Old Testament that faith apart from works is barren. He asks, "Was not Abraham our father justified by works, when he had offered Isaac his son upon the altar?" (James 2:21). Recall that when God tested Abraham, He told him, "Take now thy son, thine only son Isaac, whom thou lovest, and get thee into the land of Moriah; and offer him there for a burnt offering" (Genesis 22:2). When Abraham heard this call, he took God at His word and acted accordingly. Abraham took his son to the mountain, built an altar, bound Isaac, and placed him on the altar. Abraham did this because he had faith in God and was willing to do His will regardless of the cost. By this willingness to sacrifice Isaac, as shown by his action, Abraham's faith was tested and demonstrated to be genuine. Abraham was justifed by more than faith—"by works was faith made perfect.... Ye see then how that by works a man is justified, and not by faith only" (James 2:22, 24).

To further illustrate the relationship between faith and works, James reminds his readers about another Old Testament event. "Was not Rahab the harlot justifed by works, when she had received the messengers, and had sent them out another way?" (James 2:25; cf. Joshua 2). At the risk of her own life, Rahab hid the spies who entered Jericho and then sent them on their way. As a harlot of Canaan, Rahab had little opportunity of knowing God; but she had become convinced that the God of Israel was the living and true God. When the opportunity came to express that belief, she was ready to give everything—even her life—to serve Him. She was saved as a result of her works.

Both incidents point to the conclusion that faith and works are inseparable. "For as the body without the spirit is dead, so faith without works is dead also" (James 2:26). Faith must express itself in works to be faith. Without works there is no saving faith and consequently no justification. This is the message James wanted his readers to understand.

This emphasis of James is not in conflict with Paul's writings. The meaning the two gave to works is different, reflecting the changed atmosphere in which they wrote. Paul was faced with the problem of Jewish Christians perverting the Gospel by claiming that one needed to keep the Mosaic law to be saved, that is, justification by works. James wrote to show that Christian faith would be accompanied by a desire to do God's will as evidenced by godly works. To James works meant obeying God's will because one had faith in God. This agrees with Paul's teaching in Romans 6 and elsewhere.

Redemption Clarified

God's Will for the Christian

We have seen that God desires the Christian to be obedient. The question that must be asked is, To what is the Christian obedient? How does he know what God wants him to do?

First and foremost the answer is found in the reply Jesus gave to a lawyer, who asked, "Master, which is the great commandment in the law? Jesus said unto him, Thou shalt love the Lord thy God with all thy heart, and with all thy soul, and with all thy mind. This is the first and great commandment. And the second is like unto it, Thou shalt love thy neighbour as thyself. On these two commandments hang all the law and the prophets" (Matthew 22:36-40; cf. Luke 10:27, 28; Mark 12:30, 31; cf. Deuteronomy 6:5; 10:12, 13; Leviticus 19:18).

Love towards God finds its expression in keeping God's commandments brought by His Son. Jesus told His disciples, "If ye love me, keep my commandments" (John 14:15). The apostle John wrote, "By this we know that we love the children of God, when we love God, and keep his commandments. For this is the love of God, that we keep his commandments: and his commandments are not grievous" (I John 5:2, 3). Love is the foremost commandment Christians are to keep, but it is not the only one. Christians are to keep all the *commandments* given by Jesus Christ and His apostles for the church age.

The commandments of God for the most part are expressions of love. The apostles recognized that to love was to fulfill the law.

> Owe no man any thing, but to love one another: for he that loveth another hath fulfilled the law. For this, Thou shalt not commit adultery, Thou shalt not kill, Thou shalt not steal, Thou shalt not bear false witness, Thou shalt not covet; and if there be any other commandment, it is briefly comprehended in this saying, namely, Thou shalt love thy neighbour as thyself. Love worketh no ill to his neighbour: therefore love is the fulfilling of the law. Romans 13:8-10; cf. Galatians 5:14; Colossians 3:14; James 2:8

Second, one must realize that God's law or commandments do not originate within oneself, that is, one does not decide what he thinks is right and then does it. The source of right and wrong is from an outside authority, the Word of God, the Bible. Christians receive knowledge and power through the written Word to live a life of discipleship.

The Bible reveals God's will because it is inspired by Him. Paul emphasized this truth when he wrote, "All scripture is given by inspiration of God, and is profitable for doctrine, for reproof, for correction, for instruction in righteousness: That the man of God may be perfect, throughly furnished unto all good works" (II Timothy 3:16, 17). Scripture is the source of doctrine and is to be used for reproof, correction, and instruction in righteousness.[29] The Christian should be willing to literally follow the Word's teachings,[30] from such major issues as loving one's enemies (Matthew 5:38-45) to not wearing gold, and women wearing modest, inexpensive dresses (I Timothy 2:9; I Peter 3:3), etc. Scriptural teachings are not to be ignored; they are given for our benefit and compliance.

Another point to remember is that there are two kingdoms, the kingdom of God and the kingdom of the world (Satan). The message of the kingdom of God was central to Jesus' teaching and preaching. His very first message was, "The kingdom of God is at hand: repent ye, and believe the gospel" (Mark 1:15). Those who are part of this kingdom possess new values, of which the Sermon on the Mount (Matthew 5–7) is an example. These standards are markedly different from the standards of the kingdom of the world. The kingdom of the world is composed of the children of Satan (Matthew 13:38; John 8:44) and is ruled by Satan (Ephesians 2:2). The Christian is called to come "out of the world" (John 17:6) and not be a part of it (15:19; 17:14, 16).

The basic concept of the two kingdoms is also expressed in the Epistles. Paul introduced the third section of Romans (chapters 12–16) by giving practical instructions concerning the Christian life. He wrote, "And be not conformed to this world: but be ye transformed by the renewing of your mind, that ye may prove what is that good, and acceptable, and perfect, will of God" (12:2). The Christian is not to receive his code of conduct or system of values from the world. Since his mind has been transformed by being renewed, he no longer views things as the world does. His renewed mind makes it inconsistent for Him to look to the world for guidelines. Only by

---

[29]For a more complete treatment of Scripture, see the author's book, *The Authority of Scripture*.

[30]The reader should recognize that the common sense principle does not mean accepting figurative language literally.

turning from the world and being transformed by the renewed mind can he prove what is the will of God.

Peter similarity said: "As obedient children, not fashioning yourself according to the former lusts in your ignorance: But as he which hath called you is holy, so be ye holy in all manner of conversation [behavior]; because it is written, Be ye holy; for I am holy" (I Peter 1:14-16). "Be not conformed" expresses negatively the idea of holiness. The Christian's goal is to be holy because God is holy.

The apostle John wrote, "Love not the world, neither the things that are in the world. If any man love the world, the love of the Father is not in him. For all that is in the world, the lust of the flesh, and the lust of the eyes, and the pride of life, is not of the Father, but is of the world. And the world passeth away, and the lust thereof: but he that doeth the will of God abideth for ever" (I John 2:15-17). Again, a contrast is made between the world and God. The Christian is to turn his back to the lusts and pride of the world, since they are not of God. Rather, he is to turn to God, loving Him and doing His will. This turning is important because it carries the promise that those who do the will of God will abide forever. Christians often face situations where no direct word speaks to an issue. This does not mean Christians have nothing to guide them, because they always have the principle of love, i.e., love not the world, etc.

Christians will know God's will because they "walk in the Spirit, and . . . shall not fulfill the lust of the flesh" (Galatians 5:16). The Spirit contends with the flesh and motivates Christians not to do the works of the flesh. Paul wrote that "the works of the flesh are . . . adultery, fornication, uncleanness, lasciviousness, idolatry, witchcraft, hatred, variance, emulations, wrath, strife, seditions, heresies, envyings, murders, drunkeness, revellings, and such like" (vv. 19-21). Christians have no part in these activities. Christians have the fruit of the Spirit in their lives, which "is love, joy, peace, longsuffering, gentleness, goodness, faith, meekness, temperance," (vv. 22, 23). Paul concludes, "If we live in the Spirit, let us also walk in the Spirit" (v. 25). Godly brethren abstain from the works of the flesh and walk by the Spirit.

Christians also must remember that church leaders and other brethren can help them to understand scriptural principles and therefore know what is right for everyday situations. Both the brotherhood and the elders can share their thoughts and experiences on these situations.

The Book of Hebrews

We have discussed one of the major problems the Jewish Christian faced—the relation of the law to the Christian message. The Jewish believers also faced the question of the relation of the Old Testament's high priest, sacrificial system, etc., to the Christian faith.

The Book of Hebrews was written to answer these questions. Next to Romans, this is the most doctrinal book in the New Testament. Without a correct understanding of what Jesus Christ accomplished in His work of redemption, some early Jewish Christians were in danger of losing confidence in their new found faith. They were considering returning to their old ways of following the law. To prevent this, it was necessary to explain to them that the purpose of the old covenant (or Testament) had been fulfilled in Christ and the new covenant was now in effect.

The writer of Hebrews wanted to show how Jesus brought a *better* redemption than was available under the old covenant. The word *better* is a key word in the book.

After explaining Jesus' superiority to the angels, the author warns that "we ought to give the more earnest heed [much closer attention] to the things which we have heard, lest at any time we should let them slip. . . . How shall we escape, if we neglect so great salvation?" (Hebrews 2:1, 3). Other warnings, each more serious than those that preceded it, occur throughout the book. They are:

> To day if ye will hear his voice, harden not your hearts . . . . Take heed, brethren, lest there be in any of you an evil heart of unbelief, in departing from the living God. But exhort one another daily, while it is called To day; lest any of you be hardened through the deceitfulness of sin. For we are made partakers of Christ, if we hold the beginning of our confidence stedfast unto the end. Hebrews 3:7, 8, 12, 13

> For it is impossible for those who were once enlightened, and have tasted of the heavenly gift, and were made partakers of the Holy Ghost, and have tasted the good word of God, and the powers of the world to come, if they shall fall away, to renew them again unto repentance; seeing they crucify to themselves the Son of God afresh, and put him to an open shame. Hebrews 6:4-6

For if we sin wilfully after that we have received the knowledge of the truth, there remaineth no more sacrifice for sins, but a certain fearful looking for of judgment and fiery indignation, which shall devour the adversaries. Hebrews 10:26, 27

These verses remind us of Jesus' words: "No man, having put his hand to the plough, and looking back, is fit for the kingdom of God" (Luke 9:62). Clearly this is a warning to the Jewish Christians, as well as all Christians, not to "neglect so great salvation" and turn back from it.

Following this first warning about neglecting such a great salvation, the writer explains how this salvation came. Jesus came to the earth as a man, and now everything is in subjection to Him. Because of "the suffering of death," He is "crowned with glory and honour" (Hebrews 2:8, 9). He became man "that through death he might destroy him that had the power of death, that is, the devil; and deliver them who through fear of death were all their lifetime subject to bondage" (vv. 14, 15). The natural man rightly fears death. This can hold him in bondage throughout his life. But Jesus took the sting out of death for Christians (I Corinthians 15:54-57), so they no longer need to fear it. Jesus was "made like unto his brethren [man], that he might be a merciful and faithful high priest in things pertaining to God, to make reconciliation for the sins of the people" (Hebrews 2:17). By becoming a sinless man, Jesus was able to be both a high priest and a sacrifice; that is, He was able to suffer and die for man's sins and be a Mediator for man. His death and resurrection destroyed the power of death and enabled man to be saved.

The author explains the office of high priest in great detail. As to his function, he is "ordained for men in things pertaining to God, that he may offer both gifts and sacrifices for sins" (Hebrews 5:1). Jesus Christ was also appointed. He did not exalt Himself to a new position superior to any held by men before. He was designated a high priest after the order of Melchisedec (v. 6). Jesus learned "obedience by the things which he suffered; and being made perfect, he became the author of eternal salvation unto all them that obey him; called of God an high priest after the order of Melchisedec" (vv. 8-10).

Melchisedec was an Old Testament type of Jesus' priesthood. Melchisedec held a unique and exalted priesthood. His was unique since in the biblical record he is "without father, without mother, without descent, having neither beginning of days, nor end of life; but made like unto the Son of God; [he] abideth a priest continually" (Hebrews 7:3).

Melchisedec's position was exalted. "How great this man was, unto whom even the patriarch Abraham gave the tenth of the spoils" (Hebrews 7:4). Abraham was not required by custom or law to give Melchisedec a gift. Later there was a commandment for the people to pay tithes to the descendants of Levi, but this did not apply to Abraham, who lived some 500 years earlier. Abraham gave tithes to one in a higher position than Levi. Melchisedec also "blessed him that had the promises" (v. 6). Since the "less is blessed of the better" (v. 7), this shows Melchisedec's position was above Abraham's. Since these acts occurred before Levi, the father of the Jewish priests, was born, Levi "paid tithes in Abraham," showing that the position of the Levites was below that of Melchisedec (v. 9). Since Jesus' priesthood was after the order of Melchisedec, Christ's priesthood also is superior to the Levitical priesthood.

The necessity of the new priesthood was emphasized: "If therefore perfection were by the Levitical priesthood, ... what further need was there that another priest should rise after the order of Melchisedec, and not be called after the order of Aaron?" (Hebrews 7:11). Serving under the law, the Aaronic priesthood could not make men perfect, but could only offer sacrifices for their sins.

Since Jesus descended from Judah, a tribe never mentioned by Moses in connection with priests, it is evident there was a change in the priesthood. Jesus' priesthood was "not after the law of a carnal commandment, but after the power of an endless life" (Hebrews 7:16). This change in priesthood, which supersedes the Levitical priesthood, was necessary because the former was characterized by "weakness and unprofitableness" (v. 18). This weakness was because "the law made nothing perfect" (v. 19). It could not change the heart, that is, bring a new birth to any man. But now, with the new priesthood, there is a better hope through "which we draw nigh unto God."

This new priesthood differs from the old one in several ways. First, there are not many priests but only one. Death made it necessary to keep ordaining priests in the former economy, but since Jesus "continueth ever, [He] hath an unchangeable priesthood" (Hebrews 7:24). The result of His permanent priesthood is that "He is able also to save them to the uttermost that come unto God by him, seeing he ever liveth to make intercession for them" (v. 25).

Second, Jesus, our High Priest, is "holy, harmless, undefiled, separate from sinners, and made higher than the heavens" (Hebrews 7:26). This means He "needeth not daily, as those [Levitical] high priests, to offer up sacrifice, first for his own sins, and then for the people's: for this he did once, when he offered up himself" (v. 27). His single sacrifice was sufficient for man's sins once for all.

The conclusion of this argument is that "we have such an high priest, who is set on the right hand of the throne of the Majesty in the heavens; a minister of the sanctuary, and of the true tabernacle, which the Lord pitched, and not man" (Hebrews 8:1, 2). Thus Jewish Christians need not worry that the Christian faith lacks a high priest. There is One and His ministry is above the "example and shadow of heavenly things" contained in the law (v. 5). "He obtained a more excellent ministry, by how much also he is the mediator of a better covenant, which was established upon better promises" (v. 6). This better covenant was necessary because of the weakness of the old covenant. God told the Israelites through the prophet Jeremiah about its weakness and told them a new one was needed (Jeremiah 31:31-34). This new covenant made the first one obsolete and ready to disappear (Hebrews 8:13).

The author explains this further by discussing the first covenant's regulations for the sanctuary and worship. He points out that the high priest's offering of gifts and sacrifices made once a year in the tabernacle "could not make him that did the service perfect, as pertaining to the conscience, which stood only in meats and drinks, and divers washings, and carnal ordinances, imposed on them until the time of reformation" (Hebrews 9:9, 10). The people were to keep these regulations only until Christ appeared. Then there would be "a greater and more perfect tabernacle, not made with hands, that is to say, not of this building; neither by the blood of goats and calves, but by his own blood he entered in once into the holy place, having obtained eternal redemption for us" (vv. 11, 12). If the old covenant removed guilt, "how much more shall the blood of Christ, who through the eternal Spirit offered himself without spot to God, purge your conscience from dead works to serve the living God?" (v. 14).

How was it possible for this new covenant to replace the old? It was possible because Christ "is the mediator of the new testament, that by means of death, for the redemption of the transgressions that were under the first testament, they which are called might receive the promise of eternal inheritance" (Hebrews 9:15).

The first covenant was ratified with blood. The blood symbolized that a death occurred, thus putting the covenant in force. The importance of this blood is so great that Scripture says, "Almost all things are by the law purged with blood; and without shedding of blood is no remission" (Hebrews 9:22). The new covenant was also brought in by the shedding of blood. But this covenant was brought in by a better sacrifice, one that did not need to be repeated yearly.

> Christ is not entered into the holy places made with hands, which are the figures of the true; but into heaven itself, now to appear in the presence of God for us: Nor yet that he should offer himself often, as the high priest entereth into the holy place every year with blood of others; for then must he often have suffered since the foundation of the world: but now once in the end of the world hath he appeared to put away sin by the sacrifice of himself. And as it is appointed unto men once to die, but after this the judgment: So Christ was once offered to bear the sins of many; and unto them that look for him shall he appear the second time without sin unto salvation. Hebrews 9:24-28

In the next chapter the author continues to emphasize the relationship of the old and new covenants. First he points out a basic fact about the law and its sacrifices: "The law having a shadow of the good things to come, and not the very image of the things, can never with those sacrifices which they offered year by year continually make the comers thereunto perfect" (Hebrews 10:1). Those sacrifices were a "remembrance" of sins (v. 3). They could not take away sin or remove the consciousness of sin. "It is not possible that the blood of bulls and of goats should take away sins" (v. 4). God's foremost desire was not to have sacrifices and offerings—they gave Him no pleasure. He wanted One to "come to do [His] will" (v. 7) and thus take "away the first, that he may establish the second" (v. 9). This was accomplished when Jesus came and became a sacrifice: "By the which will we are sanctified through the offering of the body of Jesus Christ once for all" (v. 10). His all-effective sacrifice made sanctification (to be holy, perfect) possible. This one offering was the "one sacrifice for sins for ever.... For by one offering he hath perfected for ever them that are sanctified" (vv. 12-14).

As mentioned earlier, the need to change the covenant was spoken of in the first covenant. "This is the covenant that I will make with them after those days, saith the Lord, I will put my laws into their hearts, and in their minds will I write them" (Hebrews 10:16). Its effect was that "their sins and iniquities will I remember no more" (v. 17; cf. Jeremiah 31:33, 34).

In light of all this, we can have "boldness to enter into the holiest by the blood of Jesus, by a new and living way, which he hath consecrated for us, through the veil, that is to say, his flesh; and having an high priest over the house of God; let us draw near with a true heart in full assurance of faith, having our hearts sprinkled from an evil conscience, and our bodies washed with pure water. Let us hold fast the profession of our faith without wavering; (for he is faithful that promised)" (Hebrews 10:19-23).

The relation of the old covenant's offerings and sacrifices to the new covenant has been explained to the Jewish Christian. They can now have confidence in the new and better way through Jesus. The Jewish Christian will not want to neglect this better way. It is superior in all aspects to the old covenant.

To encourage the reader not to neglect this new way, the writer reminds these early Jewish Christians of the suffering they experienced when they "endured a great fight of afflictions; partly, whilst ye were made a gazingstock both by reproaches and afflictions" because they followed Jesus (Hebrews 10:32, 33). They joyfully accepted "the spoiling of [their] goods" because they knew they had found "in heaven a better and an enduring substance" (v. 34). Remembering this, they realized these experiences were not for naught. They would receive a great reward if they endured. "Ye have need of patience, that, after ye have done the will of God, ye might receive the promise. For yet a little while, and he that shall come will come, and will not tarry. Now the just shall live by faith: but if any man draw back, my soul shall have no pleasure in him. But we are not of them who draw back unto perdition; but of them that believe to the saving of the soul" (vv. 36-39).

Romans 9-11, The Jewish People

Most Jews failed to accept the Christian message and come under the new covenant. The next issue Paul addressed was, Why did the Jews reject Jesus as the Christ? Why would the Israelites, who had the benefits of "the adoption, and the glory, and the covenants, and the giving of the law, and the service of God, and the promises; whose are the fathers, and of whom as concerning the flesh Christ came," turn from their Messiah, their Christ (Romans 9:4, 5). This question is answered in Romans 9–11.

The failure of the Jewish people to come to Christ was "not as though the word of God hath taken none effect" (Romans 9:6). Rather, it is because "they are not all Israel, which are of Israel: Neither, because they are the seed of Abraham, are they all children" (vv. 6, 7). Abraham had two sons, but the promise was given to only one of them, Isaac. Abraham's first son, Ishmael, who was born to the slave Hagar, did not receive the promise (Genesis 16; 21:12; 25:1, 2). The same type of thing happened to Isaac's children. The promise was not given to his first son, Esau, but to the second son, Jacob. This shows that "they which are the children of the flesh, these are not the children of God: but the children of the promise are counted for the seed" (v. 8).

Next Paul explains the election of Jacob in more detail. Before Rebekah conceived the twins, before their "having done any good or evil, that the purpose of God according to election might stand, not of works, but of him [who] calleth; it was said unto her, The elder shall serve the younger. As it is written, Jacob have I loved, but Esau have I hated" (Romans 9:11-13). The honor of being the one through whom the promise given to Abraham would be fulfilled was determined by God and not by any man's works. This election does not concern the gift of eternal life but the honor and privilege of being the one through whom God would prepare mankind for His coming redemption. Esau and his descendants were not condemned because God called Jacob, and Jacob and his descendants did not receive eternal life because of their call. In fact, many of Jacob's descendants were rejected by God because of their wickedness. Nevertheless, a remnant was faithful, and God could work out His purpose among them to make salvation available to all men.

Knowing these facts, Paul thought the reader might ask, "Is there unrighteousness with God?" (Romans 9:14). So he asked it and gave an answer. Since God chose the persons through whom His redemption would come, does this imply He was unjust? Paul says, "God forbid." Injustice is against the very nature of God. His holiness and righteousness would never allow such a thing to occur.

Next Paul quotes God's words to Moses to show that God is not unjust. He told Moses, His faithful servant, "I will have mercy on whom I will have mercy, and I will have compassion on whom I will have compassion" (Romans 9:15; cf. Exodus 33:19). God's use of Moses was not due to anything he had done but because of God's mercy. God used Moses as He used Isaac and Jacob to fulfill His purposes. "It is not of him that willeth, nor of him that runneth, but of God that sheweth mercy" (Romans 9:16). Abraham may have willed that the promise would come through Ishmael, and Isaac may have willed that it would come through his oldest son, Esau, and Esau may have run for it; yet God, out of His mercy, gave the promise to Isaac and Jacob. These choices did not make God unjust but merciful in choosing the men through whom the promise would be fulfilled.

Paul again quotes Scripture to support his thesis. One cannot find fault with God because He used certain individuals to fulfill His purposes. "For the scripture saith unto Pharaoh, Even for this same purpose have I raised thee up, that I might shew my power in thee, and that my name might be declared throughout all the earth" (Romans 9:17). God used the events surrounding a cruel and oppressive Pharaoh rebelling against His will to show the Israelites that Moses was called by God to lead them from the land of Egypt and to strengthen their faith in God. The end result of this would be that His Name would be proclaimed throughout the whole world.

These verses are in that class of Paul's writings that Peter said contained "some things hard to be understood, which they that are unlearned and unstable wrest, as they do also the other scriptures, unto their own destruction" (II Peter 3:16). Some use these Scriptures in Romans 9 to support the view that God elects some men to be saved and hardens other hearts so they will be damned. But these Scriptures do not teach this.

In the first place, Romans 9 deals with Pharaoh's actions as a governmental leader and reveals how he was used to show God's power. These verses do not say anything about his election to eternal damnation. They show only that God used governmental acts to fulfill the promises given to Abraham, Isaac, and Jacob (Exodus 5:22–6:8).

In the second place, the question of how God used Pharaoh and how his heart was hardened must be considered. The Exodus account does state at the beginning that "the Lord said unto Moses, When thou goest to return into Egypt, see that thou do all those wonders before Pharaoh, which I have put in thine hand: but I will harden his heart, that he shall not let the people go" (Exodus 4:21). At first glance this appears to be a prophecy that God would force Pharaoh as a puppet to sin against the people. But this is not the case.

The reason Pharaoh's heart was hardened is evident from his first encounter with Moses and Aaron. Pharaoh's reaction to the request of Moses and Aaron was, "Who is the Lord, that I should obey his voice to let Israel go? I know not the Lord, neither will I let Israel go" (Exodus 5:2). Pharaoh would not listen and did things that hardened his own heart. This is reflected in later events: "He hardened his heart, and hearkened not unto them" (8:15; cf. v. 32). When a person is told to do something and refuses to do it after repeated requests, his heart becomes hardened even when he is forced to change his mind.

The Scriptures also state that God hardened his heart (Exodus 7:3; 9:12; 10:1, 20, 27; 11:10). The way God hardened Pharaoh's heart was to allow him to chose evil and then let him reap the fruits of his actions. This is how God works. In the first chapter of Romans Paul says, "God also gave them up" (Romans 1:24, 26, 28). This is what happened to Pharaoh. God gave Pharaoh signs, and when he chose not to believe and replied with cruel and oppressive acts, he started down a path that hardened his heart. One cannot resist God's Word without reaping serious consequences.

The conclusion Paul draws from what was said to Moses and Pharaoh is that God has "mercy on whom he will have mercy, and whom he will he hardeneth" (Romans 9:18). Pharaoh could not claim God's mercy because of the things he had done; nor could he protest against God because of how things turned out. Both Pharaoh and Moses were used by God to bring about His plan of redemption as He determined.

Some Jews might take these events as a basis that God elects some people to life and some to death and ask, "Why doth he yet find fault? For who hath resisted his will?" (Romans 9:19). Paul's first step to refute these implications is to remind them, "Nay but, O man, who art thou that repliest against God?" (v. 20). The potter has authority over the clay. And if God wants to choose a people and endure with them, "that he might make known the riches of his glory," we should not complain (v. 23).

Redemption Clarified

The riches made known to the Jews are now also made known to the Gentiles. This was planned long ago. Hosea said, "I will call them my people, which were not my people; and her beloved, which was not beloved. And it shall come to pass, that in the place where it was said unto them, Ye are not my people; there shall they be called the children of the living God" (Romans 9:25, 26; cf. Hosea 2:23; 1:10).

Isaiah also spoke concerning Israel. "Though the number of the children of Israel be as the sand of the sea, a remnant shall be saved" (Romans 9:27). This again emphasizes there is a difference between the children of the promise and the children after the flesh. This remnant was important to all Israel because, if it had not been for the remnant, Israel would have fared like Sodom and Gomorrah (v. 29; cf. Isaiah 10:22, 23).

As was prophesied long ago, the Gentiles came under the promise, and only a remnant of Israel obtained it. What can be said about this? "That the Gentiles, which followed not after righteousness, have attained to righteousness, even the righteousness which is of faith. But Israel, which followed after the law of righteousness, hath not attained to the law of righteousness. Wherefore? Because they sought it not by faith, but as it were by the works of the law" (Romans 9:30-32). No one can blame God for Israel's condition. It was their choice. They stumbled by rejecting Jesus as the Christ.

Israel's stumbling over Jesus is not final or permanent. This is shown in Paul's desire for them to be saved. He wrote, "Brethren, my heart's desire and prayer to God for Israel is, that they might be saved" (Romans 10:1). The rejection of Israel was due to their own faults and could not be blamed on God. When they turn around and meet God's conditions, they will be saved. If this were not the case, Paul could not have made the statement he did.

Paul realized where the Jews' problem lay. "They have a zeal of God, but not according to knowledge.... They being ignorant of God's righteousness, and going about to establish their own righteousness, have not submitted themselves unto the righteousness of God" (Romans 10:2, 3). The basic cause of this was their failure to see that "Christ is the end [goal] of the law for righteousness to every one that believeth" (v. 4).

Paul's Jewish brethren failed to understand the purpose of the law, and how it would lead to Christ. This should not have been the case since this message was given in the Old Testament. Moses warned,

"The man which doeth those things shall live by them" (Romans 10:5; cf. Leviticus 18:5). The righteousness spoken of here is that to be obtained by perfect obedience to the law. A man having this righteousness could not be condemned since he would meet the demands of the law. There would be no basis to condemn him.

After pointing to Moses' words about righteousness, Paul next points to another way to obtain the needed righteousness. "But the righteousness which is of faith speaketh on this wise, Say not in thine heart, Who shall ascend into heaven? (that is, to bring Christ down from above:) Or, Who shall descend into the deep? (that is, to bring up Christ again from the dead)" (Romans 10:6, 7). This alludes to Moses' words in Deuteronomy 30:12-14. Just before speaking to the people, Moses pointed out that the commandment he gave them "is not hidden from thee, neither is it far off" (v. 11). To Paul's readers these familiar words meant he was not requiring something impossible, but something really available.

The incarnation of Christ and His resurrection are central to the Gospel. One need not do impossible tasks to obtain salvation. This would contradict what the Scriptures say. "The word is nigh thee, even in thy mouth, and in thy heart: that is, the word of faith, which we preach; that if thou shalt confess with thy mouth the Lord Jesus, and shalt believe in thine heart that God hath raised him from the dead, thou shalt be saved. For with the heart man believeth unto righteousness; and with the mouth confession is made unto salvation" (Romans 10:8-10). Thus salvation is near and easy to obtain. Ignorance of this has caused many Jews to miss the Christ.

At the end of Romans 9, Paul showed how the Old Testament prophesied that the Gentiles would become a part of God's people. He now explains this further. Redemption is available universally to Jew and Gentile since "the scripture saith, Whosoever believeth on him shall not be ashamed" (Romans 10:11; cf. Isaiah 28:16). The word *whosoever* does not limit salvation to a certain nationality, i.e. the Jews. *Whosoever* includes the Gentiles. One can conclude from this that "there is no difference between the Jew and the Greek: for the same Lord over all is rich unto all that call upon him. For whosoever shall call upon the name of the Lord shall be saved" (Romans 10:12, 13). This quote is from the Old Testament prophet Joel. It is a prophecy concerning the coming Messiah (Joel 2:28, 32; cf. Acts 2:21) and implies no national limitations to salvation.

To call upon the Lord, one must have faith. To have faith, one must hear. To hear, there must be preachers. To have preachers, they must be sent. Isaiah prophesied of these preachers, which Paul quotes to support the preaching of the Gospel to all: "How beautiful are the feet of them that preach the gospel of peace, and bring glad tidings of good things!" (Romans 10:15; cf. Isaiah 52:7).

Paul realized that only a few who hear the Gospel respond. Isaiah also predicted this. "They have not all obeyed the gospel. For Esaias saith, Lord, who hath believed our report?" (Romans 10:16; cf. Isaiah 53:1). The report, the preaching, carries glad tidings, but so few believed Isaiah wondered whether any did. Jesus spoke of the rejection of the Gospel in the Parable of the Sower. Only a few seeds would bring forth fruit (Matthew 13).

Even though the response would be limited, the Word still went out to all. Some might object and ask, "Have they not heard?" Paul answers, "Yes verily, their sound went into all the earth, and their words unto the ends of the world" (Romans 10:18). The Gospel message was preached to all. Since it was preached to all, it must have been intended for the Gentile as well as the Jew.

But surely, "Did not Israel know?" Did they know that a time would come when the Gentiles would call upon the name of the Lord, and the Israelites would reject the same call? Yes, they knew. Moses spoke of it, "I will provoke you to jealousy by them that are no people, and by a foolish nation I will anger you" (Romans 10:19). And Isaiah spoke of it, "I was found of them that sought me not; I was made manifest unto them that asked not after me" (v. 20; cf. Deuteronomy 32:21; Isaiah 65:1). Thus the Jews were taught that the Gentiles would become a part of the people of God. The Jews had no excuse to stumble over the Gentiles' inclusion.

God was patient in dealing with Israel. Concerning Him, Isaiah wrote, "All day long I have stretched forth my hands unto a disobedient and gainsaying people" (Romans 10:21; cf. Isaiah 65:2). He did not cast them off but did everything possible to save them. Yet they disobeyed and rebelled against Him.

Because of Israel's rejection, Paul knew many Jews might wonder about God's dealing with them. The question that might come to some of them was: "Hath God cast away his people?" (Romans 11:1). Paul answers by explaining that Israel's rejection is neither complete nor final. Paul himself is evidence of this. "I also am an

Israelite, of the seed of Abraham, of the tribe of Benjamin. God hath not cast away his people which he foreknew" (vv. 1, 2).

Paul was not the only Jew who found Christ but was one of a remnant of Israel who found Him. This remnant existed just as seven thousand existed in Elijah's day. Elijah once pleaded to God against Israel, "Lord, they have killed thy prophets, and digged down thine altars; and I am left alone, and they seek my life" (Romans 11:3). God answered, "I have reserved to myself seven thousand men, who have not bowed the knee to the image of Baal" (v. 4). Those who felt that God rejected His people should realize that "even so then at this present time also there is a remnant according to the election of grace" (v. 5). Paul continues, "And if by grace, then is it no more of works: otherwise grace is no more grace" (v. 6). The remnant existed because some in Israel found Christ and did not stumble over works.

The main body of Israel was seeking God, but "Israel hath not obtained that which he seeketh for; but the election hath obtained it, and the rest were blinded" (Romans 11:7). This hardening was prophesied by the Old Testament prophets. "God hath given them the spirit of slumber.... [And] let their table be made a snare, and a trap, and a stumbling-block, and a recompence unto them. Let their eyes be darkened, that they may not see, and bow down their back alway" (vv. 8-10; cf. Psalm 69:22, 23; Isaiah 29:10). But some did obtain what Israel looked for—salvation through Christ. Others did not and perished because of their unbelief and rejection of Christ. They darkened their eyes and could not see Jesus as the Messiah.

The stumbling Israel experienced was not complete, as Paul pointed out, nor was it a final fall. "Have they stumbled that they should fall" never to rise again? Paul answered this, "God forbid" (Romans 11:11). The stumble was not a fall that would mean none of the Jews would ever accept Christ as their Messiah. Their rejection was not final.

One effect of the Jews' stumbling was that "through their fall salvation is come unto the Gentiles, for to provoke them to jealousy" (Romans 11:11). This does not mean the Gentiles would not have received the good news of the Gospel if Israel had not stumbled. They were included in the promise given to Abraham. It was because of this promise they received the good news. But Israel's rejection did have an effect on the Gentiles' receiving it. When the Jews rejected Jesus as Christ, the apostles increased their efforts to win the

Gentiles. Jesus pointed to this turning to the Gentiles in His parable of the marriage feast. He said, "The wedding is ready, but they which were bidden were not worthy. Go ye therefore into the highways, and as many as ye shall find, bid to the marriage" (Matthew 22:8, 9).

This turning from the Jews to the Gentiles can be seen at Corinth, where Paul "testified to the Jews that Jesus was Christ. And when they opposed themselves, and blasphemed, he shook his raiment, and said unto them, Your blood be upon your own heads; I am clean: from henceforth I will go unto the Gentiles" (Acts 18:5, 6).

Until this time Paul's greatest efforts were spent in trying to win the Jews to Christ. But because of their resistance and blasphemy, Paul placed greater effort toward winning the Gentiles. Nevertheless, he did not completely turn his back on the Jews. Part of his effort to win Gentiles was motivated by a desire to provoke the Jews to jealousy. He wanted them to become jealous of the Gentiles' accepting Jesus, hoping the Jews would want to share in the blessing Jesus brought. He wrote, "As I am the apostle of the Gentiles, I magnify mine office: If by any means I may provoke to emulation [to jealousy] them which are my flesh, and might save some of them" (Romans 11:13, 14).

Paul realized that the Jews' acceptance of Jesus would be an even greater blessing since their rejection meant the reconciliation of the Gentile world. "For if the casting away of them [the Jews] be the reconciling of the world, what shall the receiving of them be, but life from the dead?" (Romans 11:15).

The next basic principle is that "if the firstfruit be holy, the lump is also holy: and if the root be holy, so are the branches" (Romans 11:16). From the context "the firstfruit" apparently refers to the patriarchs, Abraham, Isaac, and Jacob. They were the first of God's chosen people. From them sprang the nation Israel. Because these patriarchs were holy, their true spiritual children should be holy too. Those who were not holy would be broken off.

From the above basic principle, Paul warns the Gentiles: "If some of the branches be broken off, and thou, being a wild olive tree, wert graffed in among them, and with them partakest of the root and fatness of the olive tree; boast not against the branches. But if thou boast, thou bearest not the root, but the root thee" (Romans 11:17, 18). The Jewish branches were broken off because they did not pursue righteousness on the correct basis (9:30ff.). The Gentiles, being as wild olives, were grafted in because they pursued righteousness on the basis of faith. These obtain their life from the rich root, the patriarch Abraham. The patriarchs were the ones through whom God chose to form the nation Israel. They were the chosen people to prepare man for the redemption brought by His Son. Thus they were the root through which He brought the life now available in Jesus. The Gentiles should not look down on the Jews. The Gentiles' roots are in the chosen people.

Paul realized that some Gentiles might become arrogant and argue, "The branches were broken off, that I might be graffed in" (Romans 11:19). But this is no basis for arrogance, "because of unbelief they were broken off, and thou standest by faith. Be not highminded, but fear: For if God spared not the natural branches, take heed lest he also spare not thee" (vv. 20, 21). Since the Gentiles stand only by faith, they should fear the possibility of being cut off too if they lose their faith. They should consider "the goodness and severity of God" (v. 22). God's severity was shown to those who fell. God's kindness was shown to those who obtained faith. To these God's kindness would continue, "if [they] continue in his goodness: otherwise [they] also [shall] be cut off" (v. 22). Those who fell, the unbelieving Jews, were also given a promise: "If they abide not still in unbelief, shall be graffed in: for God is able to graft them in again" (v. 23). Since God was able to graft in the wild olive branches (the pagan Gentiles), it will be easier for Him to graft in fallen Jews since they are natural branches and were once free from paganism (v. 24).

To help the Gentiles to continue in their faith, Paul explains to them a mystery. "Blindness in part is happened to Israel, until the fulness of the Gentiles be come in. And so all Israel shall be saved" (Romans 11:25, 26). Isaiah prophesied the same (Isaiah 59:20, 21; 27:9 LXX; cf. Zechariah 14 for more light on the Deliverer). Jesus also mentioned future events concerning Israel: "Jerusalem shall be trodden down of the Gentiles, until the times of the Gentiles be fulfilled" (Luke 21:24).

"All Israel shall be saved" means the Jewish people will accept Jesus as their Messiah in the future. They still are "beloved for the fathers' sakes. For the gifts and the calling of God are without repentance" (Romans 11:28, 29). God's promise given to the patriarchs still stands. (See Genesis 12:1-3, 7; 13:16; 15:5, 7, 18; 17:4ff.; 19; 21:12; 22:16ff.; 26:3, 4; 28:13; 35:12; Deuteronomy

Redemption Clarified

7:6ff.; 10:15.) These promises were unconditional and are therefore irrevocable. God's Word must stand; it cannot be changed.

Gentile believers are reminded that just as they were once disobedient and obtained mercy, so the Jews who are now disobedient can also obtain mercy (Romans 11:31, 32). Their rejection is neither final nor complete. Realizing how God's redemption has worked out for the good of both the Jew and Gentile, Paul writes, "O the depth of the riches both of the wisdom and knowledge of God! how unsearchable are his judgments, and his ways past finding out!" (v. 33). There is great depth to the wisdom and knowledge of God as He works out His plan of redemption. We cannot fully understand it; His wisdom is beyond us. Realizing this we can say with Paul, "To whom be glory for ever. Amen" (v. 36).

The Gentiles, Part of God's Chosen People

We have seen that the Book of Romans deals with the rejection of the Jews and the inclusion of the Gentiles into the family of God. In the Book of Ephesians, Paul wrote about how these two separate groups became one. This union is a major theme of the book.

At the beginning Paul wrote, "He hath chosen us in him before the foundation of the world, that we should be holy and without blame before him in love" (Ephesians 1:4). The *us* includes the Gentiles (2:11, 14, 16; 3:1, 6, 8; 4:17). God at the very beginning planned to make the Gentiles a part of His people.

Paul reminded his Gentile readers of their former condition and their present blessing of being "quickened [made alive] ... with Christ.... And hath raised us up together, and made us sit together in heavenly places in Christ Jesus" (Ephesians 2:5, 6).

The Gentiles did not always enjoy these benefits. Once they were separated from God (Ephesians 2:11, 12). Their inclusion into the kingdom of God was brought about by Christ Jesus. He brought them who "were far off" (v. 13) near to God by His blood. Jesus is our peace because He "hath made both one, and hath broken down the middle wall of partition between us" (v. 14). Jesus, by abolishing "the law of commandments contained in ordinances ... [made] in himself of twain one new man" [in place of two] (v. 15). He reconciled "both unto God in one body by the cross" (v. 16). It is now "through him we both have access by one Spirit unto the Father" (v. 18). Since Jesus did this, Paul could write:

> Now therefore ye are no more strangers and foreigners, but fellowcitizens with the saints, and of the household of God; and are built upon the foundation of the apostles and prophets, Jesus Christ himself being the chief corner stone; In whom all the building fitly framed together groweth unto an holy temple in the Lord: In whom ye also are builded together for an habitation of God through the Spirit. Ephesians 2:19-22

The bringing together of Jews and Gentiles was once a mystery, "which in other ages was not made known unto the sons of men, as it is now revealed unto his holy apostles and prophets by the Spirit; that the Gentiles should be fellowheirs, and of the same body, and partakers of his promise in Christ by the gospel" (Ephesians 3:5, 6). Paul was called as a minister "to make all men see what is the fellowship of the mystery, which from the beginning of the world hath been hid in God" (v. 9).

The uniting of Jews and Gentiles is mentioned in Galatians. "There is neither Jew nor Greek, . . . for ye are all one in Christ Jesus" (Galatians 3:28).

In Colossians Paul again mentions this oneness. "There is neither Greek nor Jew, circumcision nor uncircumcision, Barbarian, Scythian, bond nor free: but Christ is all, and in all" (Colossians 3:11).

The plan of redemption gradually unfolded. God chose to work out His plan through the Jews, but the means whereby the Gentiles would become a part of His people was a mystery to men. Now, however, this is no longer the case. Both Jewish and Gentile Christians know they can stand righteous before God only because of Jesus.

The Union of Believers With Christ

Let us review another aspect of redemption in Christ. In the discourse on the bread of life, Jesus spoke about Moses and manna and about "true bread from heaven . . . which . . . giveth life unto the world" (John 6:32, 33). Jesus is this "bread" from heaven (v. 41), and "he that believeth on me [Jesus] hath everlasting life" (v. 47). When Jesus, the Living Bread, said, "If any man eat of this bread, he shall live for ever: and the bread that I will give is my flesh, which I give for the life of the world" (v. 51), He was referring to giving His life on the cross. Jesus continued to speak figuratively when He said, "He that eateth my flesh, and drinketh my blood, dwelleth in me, and I in him" (v. 56). This eating is not like eating manna (v. 58) but is the union of two brought about by belief in Christ. Since the disciples thought this was a "hard saying," being impossible to follow, Jesus told them, "It is the spirit that quickeneth; the flesh profiteth nothing: the words that I speak unto you, they are spirit, and they are life" (v. 63). It is the indwelling Spirit that gives spiritual life (John 3:6; Romans 8:9-11). This partaking involves a union between Christ and the believer that brings life to the latter.

In a discourse involving branches and the vine, Jesus told His disciples to "abide in me, and I in you. As the branch cannot bear fruit of itself, except it abide in the vine; no more can ye, except ye abide in me.... If ye keep my commandments, ye shall abide in my love; even as I have kept my Father's commandments, and abide in his love" (John 15:4, 10). Abiding in Christ yields Christian growth: "Every branch in me that beareth not fruit he taketh away: and every branch that beareth fruit, he purgeth it, that it may bring forth more fruit" (v. 2; cf. vv. 5, 6). If there is no growth, the "branch" is taken away. Later, in His high priestly prayer, Jesus prayed that His disciples "may be one, even as we [Jesus and the Father] are one: I in them, and thou in me, that they may be made perfect in one; and that the world may know that thou hast sent me, and hast loved them, as thou hast loved me" (17:22, 23). This indwelling of Christ and abiding in Him is the basis of the union between believers and Christ.

Repeatedly Paul wrote of this union. When we surrender all to Christ, committing our lives to Him in faith, we become united to Him. Paul used several Greek compound words with the prefix *su*, which means *with*, to describe this mystical relationship. In English these are *co*- compound words. These Greek words—which could be translated co-crucified, co-buried, co-quickened, co-raised, and co-seated—are used in three of Paul's epistles to express the union of Christians with Christ.

The first word—co-crucified—involves the believers' union with Christ in death. Paul wrote, "We have been planted together in the likeness of his death.... our old man is *crucified with* him [Christ]" (Romans 6:5, 6). This co-crucifixion renders the old nature powerless. Paul used the Greek term meaning *rendered powerless* thirty-five times to show that Satan can no longer enslave those united with Christ. This union does not destroy Satan but liberates Christians from the bondage of the flesh, that is, from the sinful nature due to original sin. As Paul wrote to the Galatians, "They that are Christ's have crucified the flesh with the affections and lusts" (Galatians 5:24; cf. 6:14). In Philippian 3:10 Paul spoke of his own goals, "that I may know him, and the power of his resurrection, and the fellowship of his suffering, being made conformable unto his death; If by any means I might attain unto the resurrection of the dead."

The Greek conditional particle *ei,* translated *if* in "If we be dead with Christ" (Romans 6:8), is used in the sense that this statement is true. Thus Christians are to reckon themselves "to be dead indeed unto sin" (v. 11). This being dead to sin is a fact and therefore "sin [should not] reign in [a Christian's] mortal body, that [he] should obey it in the lusts thereof" (v. 12). Having died with Christ, Christians are co-buried with Him: "We are *buried with* him by baptism into death" (Romans 6:4) and are "buried with him in baptism" (Colossians 2:12). This spiritual burial of Christians in baptism shows they have died and that the power of sin in their lives has come to an end. Having been buried with Christ, Christians do not lie in the grave; they "are *risen with* him through faith of the operation of God" (v. 12). "If ye then be *risen with* Christ, seek those things which are above, where Christ sitteth on the right hand of God" (3:1). "As Christ was raised up from the dead ... so [Christians] also should walk in newness of life" (Romans 6:4; cf. Ephesians 2:5).

As Christ was quickened, that is, made alive, so God has "*quickened* us together *with* Christ" (Ephesians 2:5; cf. Colossians 2:13), so that we "live with him" (Romans 6:8). Those who died with Christ receive life because of their union with Him. God makes those in Christ dead to sin and alive to God; in other words, they receive a new life (v. 11).

Wenger wrote about some important aspects of union with Christ.

> Union with Christ does not blur the integrity and distinction between the personality of Christ and that of the believer. Christ remains the Lord of glory, while the believer continues as a creature on earth. Union with Christ does not involve irresponsibility on the part of the Christian for holiness or for one's decisions. Christ remains Christ and the Christian remains Christ's disciple. Union with Christ is rather the attachment of faith. Becoming a believer is turning to the Lord. A large number of people at Antioch, upon hearing preaching about the Lord Jesus Christ,

"turned to the Lord" (Acts 11:21). Having faith in Christ is one of the conditions for divine indwelling: "Whoever confesses that Jesus is the Son of God, God abides in him, and he in God" (I John 4:15). Union with Christ also involves the devotion of love, for John also states: "God is love, and he who abides in love abides in God, and God abides in him" (4:16). . . .
To be united with Christ is not only to exercise faith in Him, and to love Him: it also involves an identity of will and intention, the rendering to Him of full obedience. "By this we may be sure that we are in him: he who says he abides in him ought to walk in the same way in which he walked" (I John 2:5). John also wrote: "And this is his commandment, that we should believe in the name of his Son Jesus Christ and love one another, just as he has commanded us. All who keep his commandments abide in him, and he in them" (3:23, 24). To be in Christ is therefore to be His disciple, His bond servant, completely united with Him in will and purpose: "If you keep my commandments, you will abide in my love, just as I have kept my Father's commandments and abide in his love" (John 15:10).[31]

The end result of being united with Christ is that we "*sit with him* in the heavenly places in Christ Jesus, that in the coming ages he might show unmeasurable riches of his grace in his kindness toward us in Christ Jesus" (Ephesians 2:6, 7 RSV). Let us next look at the coming age in more detail.

---

[31]*Introduction to Theology,* pp. 299, 300

Chapter 7

The Completion of Redemption

Jesus' Second Coming

This book on redemption began with the creation of Adam and Eve and the fall of man. We have seen how God redeemed man from the consequence of his sins. Then we considered the call of Abraham and Israel and marveled at the life, death, and resurrection of Jesus Christ. Next we dwelt on the apostles' interpretation of the redemption brought by Jesus. The story of redemption, however, did not stop at the end of the first century. There is more to follow.

After His resurrection, Jesus remained on this earth for forty days with His apostles, showing "himself alive . . . by many infallible proofs, being seen of them . . . and speaking of the things pertaining to the kingdom of God" (Acts 1:3).

After this period of forty days, Jesus returned to His Father in heaven. Just before His departure, Jesus commissioned His disciples to witness

> both in Jerusalem, and in all Judaea, and in Samaria, and unto the uttermost part of the earth. And when he had spoken these things, while they beheld, he was taken up; and a cloud received him out of their sight. And while they looked stedfastly toward heaven as he went up, behold, two men stood by them in white apparel; Which also said, Ye men of Galilee, why stand ye gazing up into heaven? this same Jesus, which is taken up from you into heaven, shall so come in like manner as ye have seen him go into heaven. Acts 1:8-11

This message—"this same Jesus . . . shall so come" (Acts 1:11)—has been proclaimed repeatedly by the disciples. The return to earth of Jesus Christ stands at the very center of the New Testament message. This truth was not made up by the apostles but was proclaimed to them by Jesus Himself.

Jesus told His disciples about His second coming when He announced to them that He was going away to prepare a place for them. "In my Father's house are many mansions: if it were not so, I would have told you. I go to prepare a place for you. And if I go and prepare a place for you, I will come again, and receive you unto myself; that where I am, there ye may be also" (John 14:2, 3). Later on He told them, "Peace I leave with you, my peace I give unto you: not as the world giveth, give I unto you. Let not your heart be troubled, neither let it be afraid. Ye have heard how I said unto you, I go away, and come again unto you" (vv. 27, 28).

The disciples quickly grasped the meaning of His promise. During Jesus' last days in Jerusalem, they asked Him more about this second coming: "Tell us, when shall these things be? and what shall be the sign of thy coming, and of the end of the world?" (Matthew 24:3; cf. Mark 13:4; Luke 21:7). In response to this question, Jesus gave the "Olivet Discourse," found in Matthew 24 and 25, Mark 13, and Luke 17 and 21. In it Jesus emphasized His coming: "The Son of man coming in the clouds of heaven with power and great glory" (Matthew 24:30). "As the days of Noe [Noah] were, so shall also the coming of the Son of man be" (Matthew 24:37; cf. Luke 17:26). "Watch therefore: for ye know not what hour your Lord doth come" (Matthew 24:42; cf. v. 44; Luke 21:36). "The Son of man shall come in his glory" (Matthew 25:31). Jesus also mentioned His coming at His trial before the high priest. "Hereafter shall ye see the Son of man sitting on the right hand of power, and coming in the clouds of heaven" (26:64). Jesus spoke often about His second coming, showing it is an important doctrine of the Christian faith.

The second coming of Jesus is proclaimed throughout the New Testament. It is found not only in the four Gospels but also in Acts 1:11; I Corinthians 1:7; 4:5; 11:26; 15:23; Colossians 3:4; I Thessalonians 1: 10; 2:19; 3:13; 4:15-17; 5:2; II Thessalonians 1:7, 10; 2:2, 8; I Timothy 6:14; Titus 2:13; James 5:7; I Peter 5:4; II Peter 1:16; 3:4, 8-12; I John 2:28; 3:2; and Revelation 1:7; 19:11ff.; 22:12, 20. Since the second coming receives such strong emphasis, Christians should study these teachings, especially in light of the promises at the end of the Book of Revelation.

Jesus Tells of His Coming

When Jesus spoke of His second coming in Matthew 24:2, His disciples pointed out to Him the splendor of the temple buildings. Since they had spent most of their time in Galilee and only occasionally visited Jerusalem, the buildings impressed them very much. Jesus took this opportunity to tell them of coming events. "See ye not all these things? verily I say unto you, There shall not be left here one stone upon another, that shall not be thrown down" (cf. Mark 13:2; Luke 21:6).

Later that day, when the group was at the Mount of Olives, these words of Jesus still puzzled them, causing them to ask Jesus a three-part question. "Tell us, when shall these things be? and what shall be the sign of thy coming, and of the end of the world?" (Matthew 24:3; cf. Mark 13:4; Luke 21:7). The first part of this question concerned the time of the destruction of the temple; the second and third parts concerned Jesus' second coming and the events of the end times. Jesus did not give clearly defined, separate answers to the various parts of this question. Apparently the prophecies Jesus gave were to be applied to both the sooner and the later events. This dual application of prophecy follows the general pattern of much Old Testament prophecy.

The first-century Christians took Jesus' words as applying to their times. They heard the words and were saved when Jerusalem was destroyed by the Romans in A.D. 70.

We are here concerned about how the things Jesus mentioned apply to His second coming. Before we look at what He said, let us consider what other prophetic sources exist and how prophetic Scripture should be interpreted.

Latter-Day Events Foretold

The events Jesus described in His Olivet Discourse are explained in greater detail in both the Old and New Testament prophecies. The major prophets, Isaiah, Jeremiah, Ezekiel, and Daniel, and one of the minor prophets, Zechariah, all gave prophecies that have not been fulfilled. Jesus stated, "Till heaven and earth pass, one jot or one tittle shall in no wise pass from the law, till all be fulfilled" (Matthew 5:18). As many Old Testament prophecies were fulfilled to the minutest detail at His first coming, so will the remaining ones be fulfilled in the latter days and at His second coming. Not "one jot or

The Completion of Redemption

one tittle," the smallest letter or stroke, "shall in no wise pass from the law, till all be fulfilled" (v. 18).

The New Testament also contains many prophecies about Jesus' second coming. One book of the New Testament, Revelation, is given almost solely to this theme, and other books contain numerous prophecies. In the Book of Revelation, the apostle John was shown things concerning both current and coming events. He was commanded, "Write the things which thou hast seen, and the things which are, and the things which shall be hereafter" (Revelation 1:19). John wrote about "the things which are" in the first three chapters. He wrote about "the things which shall be hereafter" from chapter 4 to the end of the book.

Many have found prophecy hard to understand, especially that in the Book of Daniel and the Book of Revelation, because of their extensive use of symbolic language. But this need not be. Daniel gave pictures of these coming events in symbolic language, but he also gave their interpretation. These interpretations are not a matter of his own reasoning or guesswork but were divinely inspired. Revelation may be different from the other New Testament books because of its symbolic language, but the symbols were not given to obscure the message. This book is a revelation of latter-day events. It is "the Revelation of Jesus Christ, which God gave unto him, to shew unto his servants things which must shortly come to pass" (Revelation 1:1). Thus the purpose of this book is to reveal, not to obscure. This book also contains a promise for the reader: "Blessed is he that keepeth the sayings of the prophecy of this book" (22:7; cf. 1:3). The reader must understand the book's sayings to keep them. It is not an apocryphal book with a hidden message obscured in symbolic language that is hard, if not impossible, to understand.

Interpretation of Prophecy

Since many of the prophecies related to the latter-day events and Jesus' second coming are presented in figurative and symbolic language, it is important to establish a sound principle of interpretation before a study of prophecy is begun.

The basic principle to follow is to interpret prophetic Scriptures by the same rules used to interpret other writings. The Bible is written in ordinary language as other books are. Therefore, it should be understood by the same common-sense process by which other writings are understood. The Christian also has additional help from God in interpreting Scripture. God has given us His Spirit to teach us the truths of His Word, and His Spirit certainly does not leave us when we read prophetic passages.

A common-sense principle used in interpreting any writing is to take the literal sense of a passage unless such an interpretation involves obvious absurdities or contradictions. Literal interpretation does not imply that symbolism cannot be used. If symbolism occurs, the reader should look for a divine interpretation of that symbolism. The interpretation may be found in the immediate context or elsewhere in the book or in other books. If a divine interpretation is not given, the symbolism may remain an unsolved mystery. In such a case we should simply acknowledge we do not presently know what it means. The reader must not interpret these according to his own reasoning or speculate as to their meaning.

To understand how this principle applies, read the book of Daniel to see how the divinely given dreams were interpreted by him. The application of this principle may also be seen in Revelation. Much of the symbolism used is explained right in the book. For example, the "seven stars" are explained to be "the angels of the seven churches"; the "seven golden candlesticks" are "the seven churches" (Revelation 1:20); "the great city, which spiritually is called Sodom and Egypt," is Jerusalem, where "our Lord was crucified" (11:8); "a great red dragon" is "the Devil, and Satan" (12:3, 9); the "seven heads" are "seven kings" (12:3; 17:9, 10); the "ten horns" are "ten kings" (12:3; 17:3, 12); and the "seven heads are seven mountains" and kingdoms (17:9; Daniel 2:35, 44). These candid explanations of some of the symbols remove much of the confusion that would otherwise arise in trying to understand biblical prophecy.

In the following pages we will attempt to follow this principle of interpretation in order to give a clear picture of latter-day events. As the Old Testament "prophets have inquired and searched diligently, who prophesied of the grace that should come unto you: Searching what, or what manner of time the Spirit of Christ which was in them did signify, when it testified beforehand the sufferings of Christ, and the glory that should follow" (I Peter 1:10, 11), we too must search. As they could not completely understand His first coming even though they prophesied of it, we may not understand everything about His second coming by reading the prophetic writings. We should freely admit this and say we do not understand some details instead of guessing and speculating as to their meaning.

The reader may not agree with everything presented in this chapter, especially if he disagrees with the basic principle of interpretation used. If he seeks to spiritualize the prophecies instead of taking them literally, he will end up with a quite different interpretation. Hopefully the reader will still study this material to see what these prophecies tell if they are interpreted literally. It is also hoped that the reader will be as the Bereans, who "received the word with all readiness of mind, and searched the scriptures daily, [to see] whether those things were so" (Acts 17:11).

The Jews Return to the Promised Land

One of the first events to occur in the latter days is the return of the Jews to the Promised Land. Jeremiah wrote about the return, "For, lo, the days come, saith the LORD, that I will bring again the captivity of my people Israel and Judah, saith the LORD: and I will cause them to return to the land that I gave to their fathers, and they shall possess it" (Jeremiah 30:3). Later he wrote, "I will cause the captivity of Judah and the captivity of Israel to return, and will build them, as at the first. And I will cleanse them. . . . I will pardon all their iniquities. . . . And it shall be to me a name of joy, a praise and an honour before all the nations" (33:7-9).

Ezekiel also tells of this return. He relates a vision of a valley of dry bones, and how life came to the dry bones. He then was told the meaning of this vision:

> These bones are the whole house of Israel: behold, they say, Our bones are dried, and our hope is lost: we are cut off for our parts. Therefore prophesy and say unto them, Thus saith the Lord God; Behold, O my people, I will open your graves, and cause you to come up out of your graves, and bring you into the land of Israel. Ezekiel 37:11, 12; cf. 33:10

This is a prediction that Israel's political life will be restored from an utterly hopeless situation.

Ezekiel then tells how "the word of the Lord" again came to him, and about being commanded to write on one stick Judah's name and on another stick Israel's, and to join the two sticks together. He was told, "They shall become one in thine hand" (Ezekiel 37:15, 17).

When the people asked about the meaning of his action, he was told to say:

> Thus saith the Lord God; Behold, I will take the children of Israel from among the heathen, whither they be gone, and will gather them on every side, and bring them into their own land: and I will make them one nation in the land upon the mountains of Israel; and one king shall be king to them all: and they shall be no more two nations, neither shall they be divided into two kingdoms any more at all: Neither shall they defile themselves any more with their idols. . . . I will save them out of all their dwellingplaces, wherein they have sinned, and will cleanse them: so shall they be my people, and I will be their God. Ezekiel 37:21-23

Ezekiel goes on to explain how "David my servant shall be king over them; and they all shall have one shepherd; they shall also walk in my judgments, and observe my statutes, and do them" (Ezekiel 37:24). This must refer to Christ's rule since one king has not ruled Judah and Israel since the book of Ezekiel was written, nor have they observed God's statutes. Nor have the nations known "that I the LORD do sanctify Israel, when my sanctuary shall be in the midst of them for evermore" (v. 28).

It is obvious these prophecies have never been fulfilled. Some of the people of Judah did return after the seventy years of Babylonian captivity. Ezra and Nehemiah describe this return, but this return did not involve the ten tribes of the northern kingdom. The New Testament also bears witness to the fact that the twelve tribes as a whole were still in dispersion many years later (James 1:1).

The Olivet Discourse Warnings

The Olivet Discourse, found in three of the four Gospels (Matthew 24, 25; Mark 13; Luke 17; 21), contains Jesus' major prophecies concerning His second coming. These prophecies must occupy a central place in any study of the second coming. It provides the chronological framework into which all other prophecies must fit and upon which they must be built.

Jesus began His answer to the disciples' questions by giving them a warning. "Take heed that no man deceive you. For many shall come in my name, saying, I am Christ; and shall deceive many" (Matthew 24:4, 5; cf. Mark 13:5, 6; Luke 21:8). Apparently, men will be expecting Christ's return because of conditions existing at the time. This will create a danger of false prophets misleading some of Jesus' disciples by claiming they are the Christ. Jesus warned His disciples of this danger so they can remain faithful throughout the trials they will face and the deception that will abound.

Jesus next pointed out: "Ye shall hear of wars and rumours of wars: see that ye be not troubled: for all these things must come to pass, but the end is not yet. For nation shall rise against nation, and kingdom against kingdom: and there shall be famines, and pestilences, and earthquakes, in divers places" (Matthew 24:6, 7). Luke records that Jesus spoke here of "fearful sights and great signs ... from heaven" (Luke 21:11). These conditions do not mean that the time of His coming has arrived. "All these things must come to pass, but the end is not yet." They are signs only of the beginning of end-time sufferings. "All these are the beginnings of sorrows" (Matthew 24:6, 8; cf. Mark 13:7, 8; Luke 21:9-11).

It is clear that many nations will be at war with one another in the latter days. We have seen that Jesus spoke of "wars and rumours of wars" (Matthew 24:6) and that "nation shall rise against nation, and kingdom against kingdom" (v. 7).

There are several major prophecies about latter-day wars. The Old Testament prophets Daniel, Ezekiel, and Zechariah referred to these. The New Testament Book of Revelation also contains prophecies of coming wars. Our understanding of how these events fit together may not be complete, but where possible we will show how the Old Testament prophecies fit into the New Testament prophecies.

A Warning and an Encouragement

Jesus explained what the beginning of sorrows will mean for His disciples: "Then shall they deliver you up to be afflicted, and shall kill you: and ye shall be hated of all nations for my name's sake" (Matthew 24:9). Mark records additional words: "But take heed to yourselves: for they shall deliver you up to councils; and in the synagogues ye shall be beaten: and ye shall be brought before rulers and kings for my sake, for a testimony against them" (Mark 13:9). When the disciples face these trials, they are not to be concerned about working out a defense beforehand. They are to speak "whatsoever shall be given you in that hour ... for it is not ye that speak, but the Holy Ghost" (v. 11). Their "adversaries shall not be able to gainsay nor resist" their words (Luke 21:15).

This persecution will be hard to avoid because many "shall betray one another, and shall hate one another" (Matthew 24:10). Brother will betray his brother, father his son, and children their parents, causing them to be put to death (Mark 13:12; Luke 21:16).

Jesus next repeated His warning about false prophets. He stated that "many false prophets shall rise, and shall deceive many" (Matthew 24:11). The reason many will be deceived is that "iniquity shall abound, the love of many shall wax cold" (v. 12). Not all, however, will be led astray or grow cold. Some will endure. Jesus encourages these by promising, "He that shall endure unto the end, the same shall be saved" (v. 13; cf. Mark 13:13). One purpose of prophecy is to leave Christians with a knowledge of what the future holds, so they can have confidence in the outcome and remain faithful and be encouraged to endure to the end.

The Christian and the Tribulation

This period of sorrows and suffering on earth is called *tribulation*. Since the Book of Revelation and the Book of Daniel contain major prophecies about the Tribulation, it will be discussed in great detail. But before doing this, let us consider the questions; Will Christians go through the Tribulation? Will Jesus Christ come and remove them before it begins? The answer to these questions is important since it will affect our understanding of several prophecies.

Before we can answer this issue, we must consider when the Rapture occurs. The term *rapture* is not found in the Bible but is a Latin word meaning "to be caught up." The rapture idea is biblical. In I Thessalonians, Paul wrote concerning those Christians who had died:

> that Jesus died and rose again, even so them also which sleep in Jesus will God bring with him. For this we say unto you by the word of the Lord, that we which are alive and remain unto the coming of the Lord shall not prevent [precede] them which are asleep. For the Lord himself shall descend from heaven with a shout, with the voice of the archangel, and with the trump of God: and the dead in Christ shall rise first: Then we which are alive and remain shall be caught up together with them in the clouds, to meet the Lord in the air: and so shall we ever be with the Lord.
> I Thessalonians 4:14-17

This act of being caught up at Jesus' coming is what the word *rapture* refers to. The words *caught up* are used only in this passage,

The Completion of Redemption

but this does not mean this event has not received emphasis elsewhere. Jesus promised, "If I go and prepare a place for you, I will come again, and receive you unto myself" (John 14:3; cf. vv. 23, 27, 28; I Thessalonians 4:14-17; et al.).

Christians are divided as to when the Rapture will occur. There are two major views concerning the timing of the Rapture of the saints. The identification of the saints John wrote about in Revelation depends on which view one holds. The two views are a pretribulation and a posttribulation Rapture. The pretribulation view holds that the Rapture will occur before the Tribulation John wrote about in Revelation. The posttribulation view holds that it will occur after it. The author will give the stronger arguments for both positions.

Those holding to the pretribulation view of the Rapture believe the following points support their view:

1. The term *church or churches* is not found in Revelation from chapters 4 through 21, a sharp contrast to its being found 18 times in the first three chapters. Something must have happened between chapters 3 and 4 to account for this difference. This change plus the fact that the vision of heaven found in chapters 4 and 5 tells of elders being present in heaven means that the Rapture of the church must have occurred between chapters 3 and 4, and thus before the tribulation period.
2. God promised the Philadelphia church that He would "keep thee from the hour of temptation, which shall come upon all the world, to try them that dwell upon the earth" (Revelation 3:10). This suggests the church is raptured before the tribulation begins.
3. Daniel's seventieth week, the seven-year tribulation period, follows the church age, which occurs between the sixty-ninth and seventieth week. This is the time of "Jacob's trouble" and not the church's troubles.
4. The Jews are seen as doing evangelization work in the tribulation period (Revelation 7:1-4). Evangelism was the responsibility given to the church in the Great Commission; thus a change must have occurred.
5. First Thessalonians 4:13-18 and Revelation 19:11-21 stand in sharp contrast to each other. Their wording and overall messages are different, and therefore must describe different events.
6. Jesus said, "Pray . . . that ye may . . . escape all these things" (Luke 21:36). Paul later adds concerning the time when "sudden destruction cometh" that Christians have "for an helmet, the hope of salvation [future]" because "God hath not appointed us to wrath, but to obtain salvation by our Lord Jesus Christ" (I Thessalonians 5:3, 9). These promises mean the Christian will be raptured before the Tribulation.

Those holding to the posttribulation view of the Rapture find support for their view in the following points:

1. Followers of Jesus Christ are found throughout the tribulation period (Revelation 6:9-11; 7:9, 14; 9:4; 12:17; 13:7; 14:9, 12; 17:6; 18:4), and there is no direct teaching in Revelation that a rapture occurred before the marriage of the Lamb described in Revelation 19.

2. In the Olivet Discourse, Jesus told His followers, "Immediately after the tribulation of those days . . . shall appear the sign of the Son of man in heaven: and then shall all the tribes of the earth mourn, and they shall see the Son of man coming in the clouds of heaven with power and great glory. And he shall send his angels with a great sound of a trumpet, and they shall gather together his elect from the four winds, from one end of heaven to the other" (Matthew 24:29-31; cf. Mark 13:24-27; Luke 21:25-28). There are no Scriptures that explicitly place the Rapture before the Tribulation. There is much similarity between the event Jesus described here and the one Paul described to the Thessalonians. This gathering together of the elect is the gathering together of the church since the term elect is used to describe the church (Romans 8:33; Colossians 3:12; II Timothy 2:10; Titus 1:1). The Matthew 24 passage, which gives a "time" relation between the Rapture and Tribulation, places the Rapture after the Tribulation.

3. "But as the days of Noe [Noah] were, so shall also the coming of the Son of man be. For as in the days that were before the flood they were eating and drinking, marrying and giving in marriage, until the day that Noe entered into the ark, and knew not until the flood came, and took them all away; so shall also the coming of the Son of man be" (Matthew 24:37-39; cf. Luke 17:26-30). Noah was not saved until the day God's wrath went forth (Genesis 6:5-8; 7:6-23). In the last day the righteous in Christ will not be saved until God's judgment comes on the wicked.

4. In the parable of the wheat and the tares, the separation of the "children of the kingdom" and "the children of the wicked one" did not occur until "the end of this world" (Matthew 13:24-30, 36-43).

5. The resurrection of the saints is "at the last day" (John 6:37-44).

6. Three times John places the "first resurrection" after the Tribulation in Revelation (20:4-6). There can be but one "first"; thus no resurrection or rapture can occur before this time.

7. The marriage of the Lamb occurs after the Tribulation. The words "the marriage of the Lamb is come, and his wife hath made herself ready" (Revelation 19:7) occur at the end of the tribulation period when at His second coming Christ defeats the wicked and establishes His kingdom.

8. Jesus will "bring with him" those who died, to meet those living as they are "caught up together with them in the clouds, to meet the Lord in the air: and so shall we ever be with the Lord" (I Thessalonians 4:17). As in the parable of the ten virgins, the time came when "the bridegroom cometh; go ye out to meet him" (Matthew 25:6), so the five saved virgins went out to meet him and "went in with him to the marriage" (v. 10). Similarly, as the brethren heard of Paul's coming, they "came to meet" him and returned with him (Acts 28:15). So too those living in the last day will "meet the Lord in the air" and return with Him.

The preceding points represent the major and stronger arguments for these two views of the time of the Rapture. When one attempts to answer the question of the "when," one should avoid coming to a hard and inflexible position. It would be sad if one missed the benefit these prophecies can have for those living in the last days. Those holding to a pretribulation view should be especially careful. If the Rapture is posttribulational, they may face additional hardships during the Tribulation if they fail to realize what lies ahead. These hardships are not the result of God's wrath but of Satan's turning against Christians. God would never turn His wrath against His children.

Whichever view one holds, one must be careful that it is based solely on Scripture and not the result of superimposing a view on the Scriptures. Too many fall into this danger, especially when it comes to prophecy. It may sometimes be difficult to be objective, but it must be our goal. As mentioned at the beginning of this section, the question of when the Rapture will occur will affect our understanding of several prophecies. These areas will be pointed out in the following discussion of the tribulation period.

Daniel Tells of the Tribulation Period

After Jesus spoke of coming wars, He said, "The end is not yet. . . . All these are the beginnings of sorrows" (Matthew 24:6, 8). Daniel, an Old Testament prophet, wrote much about this period of sorrows or tribulation. He foretold of latter-day events through visions and interpretations he had of them. In Daniel 7 he told of his dream and vision of "four great beasts"—a lion, a bear, a leopard, and a fourth beast different from the first three. The latter was "dreadful and terrible, and strong exceedingly." It broke in pieces. "It had ten horns." From among these came a little horn, "before whom there were three of the first horns plucked up." This horn had "a mouth speaking great things" (vv. 1-8).

Daniel was not left to wonder about the meaning of this vision but was given an interpretation of it. "These great beasts, which are four, are four kings" (Daniel 7:17). The fourth one, the only one not identified, "shall devour the whole earth, and shall tread it down, and break it in pieces" (v. 23). From this one kingdom came

> ten kings that shall arise: and another shall rise after them; and he shall be diverse from the first, and he shall subdue three kings. And he shall speak great words against the most High, and shall wear out the saints of the most High, and think to change times and laws: and they shall be given into his hand until a time and times and the dividing of time. vv. 24, 25

This king will not keep his kingdom. (Earlier, Daniel wrote that "the saints of the most High shall take the kingdom, and possess the kingdom for ever, even for ever and ever," v. 18). Daniel then told how this was to occur:

> The judgment shall sit, and they shall take away his dominion, to consume and to destroy it unto the end. And the kingdom and dominion, and the greatness of the kingdom under the whole heaven, shall be given to the people of the saints of the most High, whose kingdom is an everlasting kingdom, and all dominions shall serve and obey him. vv. 26, 27

In chapter 8 Daniel told of another vision he received two years later. In this one he learned more about the king that spoke "great words against the most High" and who wore "out the saints of the most High" (Daniel 7:25).

> In the latter time of their kingdom, when the transgressors are come to the full, a king of fierce countenance, and understanding dark sentences, shall stand up. And his power shall be mighty, but not by his own power: and he shall destroy wonderfully, and shall prosper, and practise, and shall destroy the mighty and the holy people. And through his policy also he shall cause craft to prosper in his hand; and he shall magnify himself in his heart, and by peace shall destroy many: he shall also stand up against the Prince of princes; but he shall be broken without hand. 8:23-25

This event is described in more detail later. Daniel spoke of "seventy weeks" of years, divided into periods of 7 weeks, 62 weeks, and 1 week (Daniel 9:24-27). The first two time periods have occurred. The 7 weeks concerned the rebuilding of Jerusalem after the return from the Babylonian captivity. The 62 weeks of years is the time from then to the time when the Messiah was cut off (crucified). The last week of years does not occur immediately following the first sixty-nine weeks, but it is interrupted by the church age, which forms a parenthesis between the sixty-ninth and seventieth weeks.

The seventieth week is very important, for it gives the time frame of some latter-day events. Daniel writes that while he was praying and confessing the people's sins, he had a vision of Gabriel who informed him that a leader will make a

> covenant with many for one week: and in the midst of the week he shall cause the sacrifice and the oblation to cease, and for the overspreading of abominations he shall make it desolate, even until the consummation, and that determined shall be poured upon the desolate. Daniel 9:27

This coming king, who came from the people who earlier destroyed the city (Jerusalem), will make a covenant with the remaining Jewish people.[32] Apparently, the covenant is a treaty that will guarantee Israel's existence and protection from foreign interference. This covenant will allow the sacrifices and offerings of the Law of Moses to be reinstated. When this covenant is signed, a week of years, or a seven-year period of time, will begin. In the middle of the week the king will break the covenant, causing abominations and desolation to occur (Daniel 12:1; Matthew 24:21; Mark 13:19). This time period is also found in the Book of Revelation (11:2, 3; 12:6; 13:5). It is the time of tribulation.[33]

---

[32] Daniel 9:26 describes a prince that "shall destroy the city and the sanctuary." This refers to the destruction of Jerusalem by the Romans in A.D. 70. The next verse begins, "And he shall confirm the covenant." Apparently there is a time interval between these two verses, although the wording does not make it evident. Many prophecies of earlier and later events appear next to one another, without an obvious separation. The prince of verse 26 is not the same person who makes the covenant in verse 27.

[33] In the Old Testament, Daniel spoke of "a time of troubles, such as never was since there was a nation even to that time" (Daniel 12:1 ASV), and Jeremiah spoke of "the time of Jacob's trouble" (Jeremiah 30:7). Both of these state that God's people will not go through this. "At that time thy

The Temple Rebuilt

Historically the temple held a central place in the Jewish religion. After the children of Israel settled in the Promised Land, they built a temple to replace the tabernacle. There have been three temples, and all three have been destroyed. Solomon built the first one (I Kings 6; II Chronicles 3-5.). His father David wanted to build it. God forbade him to do so, however, because he was a man of war; so his son built it (I Chronicles 22:3). The second temple was built by Zerubbabel after the return from the Babylonian exile (Ezra 3–6). The third one was built by Herod the Great. It was started sometime before Jesus' birth and completed only a few years before it was destroyed by the Romans in A.D. 70. During His last week on earth, Jesus predicted its destruction (Matthew 24:2; Mark 13:2; Luke 21:6).

There has not been a Jewish temple in Jerusalem for over 1900 years, but a temple will play a part in latter-day events. It apparently will be rebuilt and sacrifices will be reestablished. There are several Old Testament and New Testament Scriptures predicting this.

In Daniel's prophecies we have seen that a coming king would cause sacrifices to cease (Daniel 9:27). Daniel also wrote that some "shall pollute the sanctuary of strength, and shall take away the daily sacrifice, and they shall place the abomination that maketh desolate" (11:31). The length of time of this is "a thousand two hundred and ninety days," or the last half of the seventieth week of years (12:11).

Jesus spoke of this period of desolation: "When ye therefore shall see the abomination of desolation, spoken of by Daniel the prophet, stand in the holy place, (whoso readeth, let him understand)" (Matthew 24:15). Paul also wrote of this period and the temple. "The son of perdition; who opposeth and exalteth himself above all that is called God, or that is worshipped; so that he as God sitteth in the temple of God, shewing himself that he is God" (II Thessalonians 2:3, 4). John also wrote about the temple. In a vision he was told to measure the temple except for the court. The court was not included in the temple measurements since at that time it was "given unto the Gentiles: and the holy city shall they tread under foot forty and two

---

people shall be delivered, every one that shall be found written in the book" (Daniel 12:1), "but he shall be saved out of it" (Jeremiah 30:7). This "time of trouble" may be the tribulation period or come at the end of the tribulation period and be the events related to Revelation 19.

months" (Revelation 11:2). Notice that this time period is the same as that given by Daniel (Daniel 12:11).

The Tribulation Period in Revelation

Let us now turn our attention to Revelation 6—19, which prophesies of the sorrow and tribulation referred to by both Jesus and Daniel.

The second part of Revelation, which tells of "the things which shall be hereafter" (1:19), opens with a prologue (chaps. 4 and 5). In this section John is told, "Come up hither, and I will shew thee things which must be hereafter" (4:1). Beginning with chapter 4, the following things are revealed.

The first thing John saw and described in heaven was the throne of God (Revelation 4). Then he saw a book "sealed with seven seals" (5:1). An angel called out, "Who is worthy to open the book, and to loose the seals thereof?" (v. 2). No one was found worthy to open it except the Root of David, the Lamb. A song was then sung to Him: "Thou art worthy to take the book, and to open the seals thereof: for thou wast slain, and hast redeemed us to God by thy blood out of every kindred, and tongue, and people, and nation; and hast made us unto our God kings and priests: and we shall reign on the earth" (vv. 9, 10). And then the angels said, "Worthy is the Lamb that was slain to receive power, and riches, and wisdom, and strength and honour, and glory, and blessing" (v. 12).

The Lamb next took the book and opened the seals one after another, until all seven were broken. These seven seals revealed events closely following the chronological order of the Olivet Discourse (Matthew 24). They revealed a period of Great Tribulation coming to the earth, with divine judgment being poured out on an ungodly world (Revelation 6–8). This period of Great Tribulation is the seventieth week of years, a seven-year period, spoken of by Daniel (Daniel 12:1; cf. 9:24-27) and other Old Testament prophets (Isaiah 24–28; Ezekiel 39:24; Zechariah 12ff.). These chapters contain symbolism. We can only understand this symbolism if the symbols are explained in the Scriptures. We should not try to guess the meaning of unexplained symbols, for we can never know if we are right.

The first four seals concerned visions of horses and their riders. The first was a white horse with a rider who "went forth conquering, and to conquer" (Revelation 6:2). The second was a red horse whose rider was given power "to take peace from the earth" (v. 4); he was given power to wage war (cf. Matthew 24:6, 7). The third was a black horse carrying a rider with "a pair of balances in his hand" (v. 5). A voice "in the midst of the four beasts" (v. 6) told of the high price of wheat and barley, showing that famine followed the warfare. The fourth seal was a pale horse carrying a rider named "Death and Hell" (v. 8) who had power over a fourth of the earth, "to kill with sword, and with hunger, and with death, and with the beasts of the earth," showing the presence of pestilence. Jesus spoke of famines and pestilence in the Olivet Discourse (Matthew 24:7b).

This tribulation period is not only a time of suffering, when war, famine, and great loss of human life occur among sinful men, but it is also a time when saints are killed. The fifth seal pictures "the souls of them that were slain for the word of God, and for the testimony which they held: And they cried with a loud voice, saying, How long, O Lord, holy and true, dost thou not judge and avenge our blood on them that dwell on the earth?" (Revelation 6:9, 10). These were told "that they should rest yet for a little season, until their fellowservants also and their brethren, that should be killed as they were, should be fulfilled" (v. 11).

The sixth seal pictures great earthquakes and falling stars (i.e., meteors). These bring physical change to the earth and cause such fear among evil men that they wish they were dead when they realize that the "wrath of the Lamb" is coming (Revelation 6:16).

Then John saw four angels holding "the four winds" and another angel saying to them, "Hurt not the earth, neither the sea, nor the trees, till we have sealed the servants of our God in their foreheads" (Revelation 7:1, 3). The number of those sealed from each tribe of the sons of Israel was twelve thousand, "an hundred and forty and four thousand of all the tribes of the children of Israel" (v. 4).

After this John said, "I beheld, and, lo, a great multitude, which no man could number, of all nations, and kindreds, and people, and tongues, stood before the throne, and before the Lamb, clothed with white robes, and palms in their hands" (Revelation 7:9). Later John asked who these were. He was told, "These are they which came out of great tribulation, and have washed their robes, and made them white in the blood of the Lamb" (v. 14). These are the many saints that the fifth seal revealed would be killed by ungodly men.

The Completion of Redemption

The seventh seal reveals seven angels and seven trumpets and more tribulation to follow as the judgment of God continues to fall on the ungodly. The first trumpet reveals that about a third of the world will be burnt up (Revelation 8:7); the second reveals that a third of the sea will become blood, a third of living creatures in the sea will die, and a third of the ships will be destroyed (vv. 8, 9). The third trumpet reveals that a "great star" will fall on a third of the rivers and fountains, making their water bitter and fatal to all who drink it (vv. 10, 11). The fourth trumpet reveals that a third of the light from the sun and the moon will be darkened (v. 12). The fifth trumpet reveals locusts will torture men for five months (9:1-11), and the sixth reveals that a third of mankind will be killed (vv. 13-19).

With the death of this last third of mankind, a total of 50 percent of the world's population will have been killed during the first half of the tribulation period (25 percent were killed earlier, Revelation 6:8). These judgments do not affect all men. Those who have "the seal of God in their foreheads" will escape (9:4). But even after this terrible tribulation period, "the rest of the men which were not killed by these plagues yet repented not of the works of their hands, that they should not worship devils, and idols" (v. 20).

After these events an angel will come down to earth with a little book and reveal seven thunders, but John was told not to write down what was said (Revelation 10:1-4). Since their messages were not recorded, we assume the Lord will reveal them again if needed.

John was then told by an angel "that there should be time no longer," that is, there shall be no delay (Revelation 10:6). The mystery of God will now be completely revealed. John was then given a little book to eat. Although we are not told the meaning of this act, John was then told, "Thou must prophesy again before many peoples, and nations, and tongues, and kings" (v. 11).

Then John was given a measuring rod and told, "Rise, and measure the temple of God, and the altar, and them that worship therein" (Revelation 11:1). He was told not to measure the outside court since "it is given unto the Gentiles: and the holy city shall they tread under foot forty and two months" (v. 2). This forty-two month period starts in the middle of the seven-year tribulation and was foretold by Daniel (9:27). The one who made the covenant with the Jewish people at the beginning of the tribulation period will break it and bring abomination and desolation to the temple and the land.

As seen earlier, the Jews will rebuild the temple and will reinstitute sacrifices. This must occur before the middle of the tribulation period. This temple will not be built at the command of God to show the way man can approach Him as were the Old Testament temples. It will be rebuilt because the Jews have rejected the Way, Jesus Christ (Revelation 11:1, 2; cf. John 14:6).

Preaching the Gospel During the Tribulation

Although there will be a time of tribulation before Jesus returns to the earth to set up His kingdom, Jesus said, "This gospel of the kingdom shall be preached in all the world for a witness unto all nations; and then shall the end come" (Matthew 24:14). This preaching will occur during the tribulation period, after "the beginning of sorrows" (v. 8). While the preaching of the Gospel will surely occur throughout the tribulation period, in the middle of the period, two special witnesses will spread the message.

Following these remarks about preaching the Gospel to the whole world, Jesus tells of an event that will occur in Jerusalem during the tribulation period. He said, "When ye therefore shall see the abomination of desolation, spoken of by Daniel the prophet, stand in the holy place, (whoso readeth, let him understand:) Then let them which be in Judaea flee into the mountains" (Matthew 24:15, 16; cf. Mark 13:14; Luke 21:20, 21). Jesus here is referring to Daniel's prophecy about one who for a half of the week of years (3½ years) "shall cause the sacrifice and the oblation to cease, and for the overspreading of abominations he shall make it desolate, even until the consummation, and that determined shall be poured upon the desolate" (Daniel 9:27). Daniel later wrote that "they shall pollute the sanctuary of strength, and shall take away the daily sacrifice, and they shall place the abomination that maketh desolate" (11:31).

During this time, when the temple is under the control of the nations, or the Gentiles, God will empower two witnesses to prophesy for 1260 days, the second 3½ years of the Tribulation. These two will witness in Jerusalem. No one can harm them during this time. But after the 1260 days are past, "the beast that ascendeth out of the bottomless pit shall make war against them, and shall overcome them, and kill them" (Revelation 11:7). The people will rejoice at their death and will come to see their dead bodies in Jerusalem. "And they that dwell upon the earth shall rejoice over them, and make merry, and shall send gifts one to another; because these two prophets tormented them that dwelt on the earth" (v. 10). Their message will be hard for the ungodly to listen to, so they will be glad when the prophets are dead. "After three days and an half the spirit of life from God entered into them, and they stood upon their feet; and great fear fell upon them which saw them" (v. 11). They then ascended into heaven. Their enemies saw what happened to them. Then when a great earthquake occurred, destroying a tenth of the city and seven thousand people, "the remnant were affrighted, and gave glory to the God of heaven" (v. 13).

Christ Establishes His Kingdom

Next the seventh trumpet sounds, and voices in heaven are saying, "The kingdoms of this world are become the kingdoms of our Lord, and of his Christ; and he shall reign for ever and ever" (Revelation 11:15). This trumpet signifies the first step in Christ's taking charge of His kingdom. It brings a reaction from the nations, "because thou hast taken to thee thy great power, and hast reigned. And the nations were angry, and thy wrath is come, and the time of the dead, that they should be judged, and that thou shouldest give reward unto thy servants the prophets, and to the saints, and them that fear thy name, small and great; and shouldest destroy them which destroy the earth" (vv. 17, 18). The events related to Christ establishing His kingdom are unfolded in chapters 12 through 19. The events in this section are revealed in highly symbolic language, yet they can be understood because the symbols are interpreted. Some aspects of these events are foretold in Daniel 11:36–45 and Zechariah 12–14.

These events show a conflict between God and the forces of evil empowered by Satan. This conflict is introduced by a great sign that reveals a conflict of the past. This sign is a woman who signifies Israel. "She being with child cried, travailing in birth, and pained to be delivered" (Revelation 12:2). Another sign followed this one. "A great red dragon, having seven heads and ten horns, and seven crowns upon his heads" (v. 3), threw a third of the stars (symbolizing his angels), to the earth. This "dragon stood before the woman which was ready to be delivered, for to devour her child as soon as it was born" (v. 4).This refers to Satan's influence on Herod that caused him to try to destroy all the boys under two years of age at Bethlehem at the time of Jesus' birth (Matthew 2:12-18).

Jesus' birth is next mentioned, including the fact that He "was to rule all nations with a rod of iron" (Revelation 12:5). This further rule was told to Mary at Jesus' birth. "He shall be great, and shall be called the Son of the Highest: and the Lord God shall give unto him the throne of his father David: And he shall reign over the house of Jacob for ever; and of his kingdom there shall be no end" (Luke 1:32, 33).

The passage in Revelation does not go into the details of this Child's life and ministry but jumps over them and mentions only that He "was caught up unto God, and to his throne" (Revelation 12:5). This clearly refers to Jesus' ascension.

With this review of the past conflict, apparently Revelation jumps beyond the church age and the first half of the seven-year tribulation to events that will happen to Israel during the last half of the tribulation period. "And the woman fled into the wilderness, where she hath a place prepared of God, that they should feed her there a thousand two hundred and threescore days" (Revelation 12:6).

Israel had to flee to safety because "there was war in heaven: Michael and his angels fought against the dragon" (Revelation 12:7). Because of this war there was no longer any room for Satan and his angels in heaven. "And the great dragon was cast out, that old serpent, called the Devil, and Satan, which deceiveth the whole world: he was cast out into the earth, and his angels were cast out with him" (v. 9). After Satan's first rebellion, when he was thrown out of the presence of God, his operation was limited to the first heaven and the earth. He became "the prince of the power of the air" (Ephesians 2:2), the head of the "spiritual wickedness in high places [heavenly places]" (6:12). The "air" and "heavenly places" refer to the sky surrounding the earth. But now we see that Satan lost this sphere of influence, and his activities are limited to the earth.

This limitation of Satan's power brought "a loud voice saying in heaven, Now is come salvation, and strength, and the kingdom of our God, and the power of his Christ: for the accuser of our brethren is cast down" (Revelation 12:10). This proclamation is given because the last steps leading to the establishment of the kingdom were now ready to begin. "Therefore rejoice, ye heavens, and ye that dwell in them. Woe to the inhabiters of the earth and of the sea! for the devil is come down unto you, having great wrath, because he knoweth that he hath but a short time" (v. 12).

Those in heaven can rejoice, but sorrow faces the inhabitants of the earth. "When the dragon saw he was cast unto the earth, he persecuted the woman which brought forth the man child" (Revelation 12:13). Satan's first act is to try to destroy Israel, but God intervenes to protect her. She is taken to "the wilderness, into her place, where she is nourished for a time, and times, and half a time, from the face of the serpent" (v. 14). When Satan sees her fleeing, he tries to destroy her with a flood, but God again acts and saves her. This draws a strong reaction from Satan. "The dragon was wroth [enraged] with the woman, and went to make war with the remnant of her seed, which keep the commandments of God, and have the testimony of Jesus Christ" (v. 17). This is the second time God's people undergo great suffering. The first is described in 6:9-11.

The Wars of the Beast

Satan does not directly make war against "the remnant of her [Israel's] seed," but gives power to a beast to make the war. This beast is referred to in symbolic language as having "seven heads and ten horns" (Revelation 13:1). This expression is used later in the book, where these two terms are explained. The seven heads are seven mountains and seven kings. In prophecy *mountain* is a symbolic term that refers to a kingdom (notice Daniel 2:35, 44). The ten horns are explained as ten kings who receive power for only a very short time (Revelation 17:9-12).

The beast is also referred to as a king (Revelation 17:10, 11). The Bible often refers to a government or state as either a kingdom or a king. This beast is said to rise "out of the sea" (13:1). John explained this later: "The waters which thou sawest, where the whore sitteth, are peoples, and multitudes, and nations, and tongues" (17:15). Thus the sea is a mass of people.

Daniel was given a vision and was troubled as to the meaning of one part of it, so he asked for an interpretation. The part that troubled him dealt with the fourth kingdom. This kingdom would occur in the distant future, as can be seen in the interpretation given him. "I beheld, and the same horn made war with the saints, and prevailed against them; until the Ancient of days came, and judgment was given to the saints of the most High; and the time came that the saints possessed the kingdom" (Daniel 7:21, 22; cf. 18).

Daniel wrote more about this future kingdom.

Thus he said, The fourth beast shall be the fourth kingdom upon earth, which shall be diverse from all kingdoms, and shall devour the whole earth, and shall tread it down, and break it in pieces. And the ten horns out of this kingdom are ten kings that shall arise: and another shall rise after them; and he shall be diverse from the first, and he shall subdue three kings. And he shall speak great words against the most High, and shall wear out the saints of the most High, and think to change times and laws: and they shall be given into his hand until a time and times and the dividing of time. Daniel 7:23-25

Many believe this unidentified fourth kingdom is the Roman Empire. If so, it is a future revived empire, at least encompassing the geographical areas of the old Roman Empire, as the following events indicate. Judgment will come against it, and "the kingdom and dominion, and the greatness of the kingdom under the whole heaven, shall be given to the people of the saints of the most High, whose kingdom is an everlasting kingdom, and all dominions shall serve and obey him" (Daniel 7:27). This has not happened, so this prophecy is yet to be fulfilled. John was given more details of these events, and as we continue our study in Revelation these will unfold.

This beast is described in more detail later by Daniel.

And the king shall do according to his will; and he shall exalt himself, and magnify himself above every god, and shall speak marvelous things against the God of gods, and shall prosper till the indignation be accomplished: for that that is determined shall be done. Neither shall he regard the God of his fathers, nor the desire of women, nor regard any god: for he shall magnify himself above all. Daniel 11:36, 37

The statement that he will not regard the God of his fathers may indicate he is of Jewish background. If so, he would be a Jewish atheist. Daniel continues: "A god whom his fathers knew not shall he honour with gold, and silver, and with precious stones, and pleasant things" (v. 38). This god will be described a little later in Revelation as a second beast. The first beast will give power to those who acknowledge him, "and he shall cause them to rule over many, and shall divide the land for gain" (v. 39).

Daniel next described some events that will occur at "the time of the end" (Daniel 11:40ff.). These will be discussed later.

The Completion of Redemption

The first beast is also described by Paul. He wrote, "That Wicked [will] be revealed, whom the Lord shall consume with the spirit of his mouth, and shall destroy with the brightness of his coming: Even him, whose coming is after the working of Satan with all power and signs and lying wonders, and with all deceivableness of unrighteousness in them that perish; because they received not the love of the truth, that they might be saved" (II Thessalonians 2:8-10).

The beast John spoke of in Revelation had one of its heads, a king, "wounded to death; and his deadly wound was healed" (Revelation 13:3a). This miraculous healing gave this king new power. "All the world wondered after the beast. And they worshipped the dragon which gave power unto the beast: and they worshipped the beast, saying, Who is like unto the beast? who is able to make war with him?" (vv. 3b, 4).

Satan gave this beast the authority to do his work for forty-two months. During this time he spoke against God and waged war against the saints. He spoke "great things and blasphemies; . . . he opened his mouth in blasphemy against God, to blaspheme his name, and his tabernacle, and them that dwell in heaven. And it was given unto him to make war with the saints, and to overcome them: and power was given him over all kindreds, and tongues, and nations" (Revelation 13:5-7).

All people will worship the beast except those whose names are written in the book of life. The saints are warned not to resist him. "If any man have an ear, let him hear. He that leadeth into captivity shall go into captivity: he that killeth with the sword must be killed with the sword. Here is the patience and the faith of the saints" (Revelation 13:9, 10).

A second beast, "coming up out of the earth" (Revelation 13:11), arose during the reign of this first one. The purpose of this second beast is similar to that of the first one. He too is a tool of Satan, yet he comes from a different place. His coming out of the earth contrasts to the beast that rose out of the sea. Many believe "the earth" refers to Israel since the sea represents the multitudes and nations (see "waters" or sea interpretation in 13:1; 17:15).

The second beast will be a deceptive one. He appears as a lamb but will speak as a dragon. This is because he obtains his authority from the first beast. And he will use it to make "the earth and them which dwell therein to worship the first beast" (Revelation 13:12). To do this he will perform great signs, such as to make "fire come down from heaven" (v. 13). This sign will deceive the people to follow his wishes. One is to make an image to the beast. He will give power to this image so it can "speak, and cause that as many as would not worship the image of the beast should be killed" (v. 15).

This second beast will cause all to receive a mark on "their right hand, or in their foreheads," in order to buy or sell (Revelation 13:16). "No man might buy or sell, save he that had the mark, or the name of the beast, or the number of his name" (v. 17). This mark will show that one gives his allegiance to the beast. God's people are later warned not to receive it. Here they are told how to identify it. "Here is wisdom. Let him that hath understanding count the number of the beast: for it is the number of a man; and his number is Six hundred three score and six" (v. 18).

Today we do not know who this number 666 identifies. Many have come up with various suggestions. Their confusing interpretations only show that man cannot identify this mysterious number at this time. Apparently we do not know with certainty what this number means before the "beasts" arrive on the world scene. When they arrive, and there is a need for the followers of Jesus Christ to identify them, the meaning of the number 666 will be clear, and it will play an important part in identifying these "beasts."

Those who do not worship the beast will be slain (Revelation 13:15). These will number 144,000 (cf. 7:4). They will have had the "Father's name written in their foreheads" (v. 14:1). They will not bear the mark of the beast but rather the seal of God. "These are they which were not defiled with women; for they are virgins. These are they which follow the Lamb whithersoever he goeth. These were redeemed from among men, being the firstfruits unto God and to the Lamb. And in their mouth was found no guile: for they are without fault before the throne of God" (14:4, 5).

These believers are described as "virgins." This term probably does not mean they never married but that they abstained from spiritual fornication and adultery by remaining separate from the beast. Jesus, in the Parable of the Ten Virgins (Matthew 25:1-13), and Paul, in II Corinthians 11:2, used the term *virgins* to describe true believers. The Old Testament also frequently uses the term to describe the faithful (Isaiah 37:22; Jeremiah 31:4, 21; Lamentations 2:13; Amos 5:2). These firstfruits are the first of mankind to suffer martyrdom during the 3½ years of the tribulation. This is Old Testament terminology that describes the first of the ripe fruit or grain that was offered to God.

Following this three angels will proclaim that the time of judgment has arrived. The first one will proclaim to all men, "Fear God, and give glory to him; for the hour of his judgment is come: and worship him that made heaven, and earth, and the sea, and the fountains of waters" (Revelation 14:7). The second angel will proclaim that "Babylon is fallen, is fallen, that great city" (v. 8) because of the evil she brought to the nations. The third one warns, "If any man worship the beast and his image, and receive his mark in his forehead, or in his hand, the same shall drink of the wine of the wrath of God, which is poured out without mixture into the cup of his indignation; and he shall be tormented with fire and brimstone in the presence of the holy angels, and in the presence of the Lamb" (vv. 9, 10).

Not all of mankind will worship the beast. Some persevere and keep "the commandments of God, and the faith of Jesus" (Revelation 14:12). They are to be patient and endure. Some of the Christians will suffer and die because Satan will continue to make war against the saints (cf. 12:17). John was told of those who died because of their faithfulness, "Blessed are the dead which die in the Lord from henceforth: Yea, saith the Spirit, that they may rest from their labours; and their works do follow them" (14:13). Later we will learn that they will receive a particular blessing.

Then John saw "a white cloud, and upon the cloud one sat like unto the Son of man, having on his head a golden crown, and in his hand a sharp sickle" (Revelation 14:14). An angel told Him, "Thrust in thy sickle, and reap: for the time is come for thee to reap; for the harvest of the earth is ripe" (v. 15). This Son of man is the Lamb, Jesus Christ, who now comes as the Judge. The Father "committed all judgment unto the Son. . . . because he is the Son of man" (John 5:22, 27). The Son of man was mentioned being in the midst of the seven candlesticks, the seven churches discussed in chapters 2 and 3 (Revelation 1:13; cf. 1:20).

Then came another angel with a sharp sickle. He was told by yet another angel, "Thrust in thy sharp sickle, and gather the clusters of the vine of the earth; for her grapes are fully ripe" (Revelation 14:18). This he did, "and gathered the vine of the earth, and cast it into the great winepress of the wrath of God" (v. 19). Isaiah used the term *winepress* in relation to God's day of vengeance (Isaiah 63:3; cf. Jeremiah 25:30, 31). This was a time of great judgment.

In the next three chapters these events are described in fuller detail. They begin with "the seven last plagues; for in them is filled up the wrath of God" (Revelation 15:1). The seven plagues are described in chapter 16. Between the sixth and seventh plagues is inserted the announcement of a message from the dragon, the beast, and the false prophet "unto the kings of the earth and of the whole world, to gather them to the battle of that great day of God Almighty" (16:14). The place of this war is "called in the Hebrew tongue Armageddon" (v. 16). This war occurs later and ends with the beast and the false prophet being thrown into the lake of fire (19:11-20).

After the description of the first six plagues or bowls of wrath (Revelation 16), the angel that revealed the seventh and last one told John, "Come hither; I will shew unto thee the judgment of the great whore that sitteth upon many waters: With whom the kings of the earth have committed fornication, and the inhabitants of the earth have been made drunk with the wine of her fornication" (17:1, 2). John then saw "a woman sit upon a scarlet coloured beast, full of names of blasphemy, having seven heads and ten horns" (v. 3). On "her forehead was a name written, MYSTERY, BABYLON THE GREAT, THE MOTHER OF HARLOTS AND ABOMINATIONS OF THE EARTH" (v. 5). She was "drunken with the blood of the saints, and with the blood of the martyrs of Jesus" (v. 6).

This description is in mysterious terms, and John wondered what it meant. The "woman . . . full of names of blasphemy . . . Babylon the Great" is a "great city, which reigneth over the kings of the earth" (Revelation 17:3, 5, 18). The angel told him, "Wherefore didst thou marvel? I will tell thee the mystery of the woman, and of the beast that carrieth her, which hath the seven heads and ten horns" (v. 7). The interpretation of this picture is given in the rest of the chapter.

The beast John saw "was, and is not; and shall ascend out of the bottomless pit, and go into perdition" (Revelation 17:8). He is a king that "was" but has lost power; he "is not" (v. 11). He was mentioned earlier, in chapter 13. He again receives power and becomes the eighth king to reign.

"The seven heads are seven mountains, on which the woman sitteth" (Revelation 17:9, 10). Associated with them are seven kings. "Five are fallen, and one is, and the other is not yet come" (v. 10).

"The ten horns ... are ten kings, which have received no kingdom as yet; but receive power as kings one hour with the beast" (Revelation 17:12). These ten kings come to power later, and together with the beast that will come forth from the abyss, they will form a confederation with one purpose. "These shall make war with the Lamb, and the Lamb shall overcome them: for he is Lord of lords, and King of kings" (v. 14). This ten-nation confederation is also described by Daniel (see Daniel 2:41ff.; 7:7, 24).

"The waters ... are peoples, and multitudes, and nations, and tongues" over which the woman reigns (Revelation 17:15).

These ten kings and the beast will go against the woman, Babylon the Great, and destroy her (Revelation 17:16). This will be done because God desires it: "For God hath put in their hearts to fulfil his will, and to agree, and give their kingdom unto the beast, until the words of God shall be fulfilled" (v. 17). God uses them only to destroy Babylon, and later they are destroyed.

The destruction of Babylon is described in great detail in chapter 18. "Babylon the great is fallen, is fallen" (v. 2). She is "the habitation of devils, and the hold of every foul spirit, and a cage of every unclean and hateful bird." She is described as misleading the kings and making the merchants rich (v. 3).

Although Babylon misled many, there were still some faithful ones living in her. These were warned, "Come out of her, my people, that ye be not partakers of her sins, and that ye receive not of her plagues. For her sins have reached unto heaven, and God hath remembered her iniquities.... Therefore shall her plagues come in one day, death, and mourning, and famine; and she shall be utterly burned with fire: for strong is the Lord God who judgeth her" (Revelation 18:4, 5, 8).

Babylon's destruction is mourned by many. "The kings ... shall bewail her, and lament for her.... Alas, alas, that great city Babylon, that mighty city! for in one hour is thy judgment come.... The merchants of the earth shall weep and mourn over her" (Revelation 18:9-11). They lost their trade of luxurious and splendid things. "Every shipmaster, and all the company in ships, and sailors ... cried when they saw the smoke of her burning" (vv. 17, 18).

But not all will mourn. "Rejoice over her, thou heaven, and ye holy apostles and prophets; for God hath avenged you on her" (Revelation 18:20). After Babylon's destruction, John heard, "Alleluia; Salvation, and glory, and honour, and power, unto the Lord our God: For true and righteous are his judgments: for he hath judged the great whore, which did corrupt the earth with her fornication, and hath avenged the blood of his servants at her hand" (19:1, 2).

The Marriage Feast

Next John saw a great marriage feast. "Let us be glad and rejoice, and give honour to him: for the marriage of the Lamb is come, and his wife hath made herself ready" (Revelation 19:7). The wife, His bride, is the church. She is clothed "in fine linen, clean and white" (v. 8). This dress is defined as "the righteousness of saints." It is not Christ's imputed righteousness since John wrote it was "the righteousness of saints." The New American Standard translates it as "the righteous acts of the saints" (cf. RSV). Saints can have righteousness, as Paul wrote, "Yield yourselves unto God . . . your members as instruments of righteousness unto God" (Romans 6:13); that men servants, "to whom ye obey; whether of sin unto death, or of obedience unto righteousness" (v. 16); "became the servants of righteousness. . . . yield your members servants to righteousness unto holiness" (vv. 18, 19).

The marriage of the Lamb fulfills the promise Jesus made: "If a man love me, he will keep my words: and my Father will love him, and we will come unto him, and make our abode with him" (John 14:23). The "righteous acts" glorify the Father, as Jesus stated, "Herein is my Father glorified, that ye bear much fruit, so shall ye be my disciples" (15:8). Paul too, as mentioned above, associated righteousness with the believers.

Jesus expects the church to be ready for His coming and clothed in "the righteousness of saints." This is why He gave His life. Paul, when he wrote of the husband-wife relationship, stated that "Christ also loved the church, and gave himself for it; That he might sanctify and cleanse it with the washing of water by the word, that he might present it to himself a glorious church, not having spot, or wrinkle, or any such thing; but that it should be holy and without blemish" (Ephesians 5:25-27).

John was next told, "Write, Blessed are they which are called unto the marriage supper of the Lamb" (Revelation 19:9). Who are these blessed? They are not the church since the church is the bride.

These guests may be the Old Testament saints. John the Baptist called himself "the friend of the bridegroom" (John 3:29). John was a "friend" since he served before Jesus brought in the church age. Since John called himself a "friend," the term is taken to apply to other Old Testament saints.

Those holding to a pretribulation rapture could identify these "friends" as those who were told to be "glad and rejoice" earlier in the chapter (Revelation 19:7). These are seen as those who suffered earlier during the tribulation period–those who wore "white robes" (6:11; 7:13-17) and whom John heard: "The voice of harpers harping with their harps [who] . . . sung as it were a new song before the throne . . . redeemed from the earth" (14:2-4). According to the pretribulation view, these are not a part of the church but persons who were converted and suffered death during the tribulation period—tribulation saints.

The events surrounding the marriage feast are also mentioned elsewhere. Jesus in His Olivet Discourse said,

> Immediately after the tribulation of those days shall the sun be darkened, and the moon shall not give her light, and the stars shall fall from heaven, and the powers of the heavens shall be shaken: And then shall appear the sign of the Son of man in heaven: and then shall all the tribes of the earth mourn, and they shall see the Son of man coming in the clouds of heaven with power and great glory. And he shall send his angels with a great sound of a trumpet, and they shall gather together his elect from the four winds, from one end of heaven to the other. Matthew 24:29-31

The trumpet will sound, and His elect will be gathered from all over the earth. "The four winds" describe the four directions: north, south, east, and west. "From one end of heaven to the other" emphasizes the same point, the gathering of the elect from all the earth to be together with Jesus. Since this gathering of the elect occurs after the Tribulation, it must relate to the marriage feast. The final judgment occurs later. Those who do not share in this gathering will mourn when they see His sign and the gathering together of the elect. They will mourn out of fear of what will happen to them. They will realize who Jesus is, and that they rejected Him. It will then be too late for the Gentiles to take up their crosses and follow Him. The time of the Gentiles will be over. It will not be too late for many Jews. They will finally see that Jesus is the Christ, their long-awaited Messiah.

Let us now turn to other passages relating to the Rapture. This may or may not be the proper place for this consideration, depending on one's view of when the Rapture occurs. Those holding to a pretribulation rapture would place these events before the Scriptures describing the beginning of the Tribulation. Those holding to the posttribulation view believe this to be the natural place for these Scriptures since they believe the Rapture and the marriage feast occur at the same time.

Thessalonian Christians were concerned about the Rapture since they feared their dead brethren or sisters in Christ had missed His coming. Paul wrote,

> But I would not have you to be ignorant, brethren, concerning them which are asleep, that ye sorrow not, even as others which have no hope. For if we believe that Jesus died and rose again, even so them also which sleep in Jesus will God bring with him. For this we say unto you by the word of the Lord, that we which are alive and remain unto the coming of the Lord shall not prevent [precede] them which are asleep. For the Lord himself shall descend from heaven with a shout, with the voice of the archangel, and with the trump of God: and the dead in Christ shall rise first: Then we which are alive and remain shall be caught up together with them in the clouds, to meet the Lord in the air: and so shall we ever be with the Lord. I Thessalonians 4:13-17

At the sound of the trumpet, the dead in Christ will arise and go with the living in Christ to meet the Lord and to be with Him forever.

Paul had more to say about the order of these events when he wrote to the Corinthian Christians concerning the resurrection.

> So in Christ shall all be made alive. But every man in his own order: Christ the firstfruits; afterward they that are Christ's at his coming. Then cometh the end, when he shall have delivered up the kingdom to God, even the Father; when he shall have put down all rule and all authority and power. I Corinthians 15:22-24

A little later Paul explained further the miraculous raising of the dead:

> How are the dead raised up? and with what body do they come? Thou fool, that which thou sowest is not quickened, except it die: And that which thou sowest, thou sowest not that body that shall be, but bare grain, it may chance of wheat, or of some other grain. But God giveth it a body as it hath pleased him, and to every seed his own body. All flesh is not the

The Completion of Redemption

same flesh: but there is one kind of flesh of men, another flesh of beasts, another of fishes, and another of birds. There are also celestial bodies, and bodies terrestrial: but the glory of the celestial is one, and the glory of the terrestrial is another. There is one glory of the sun, and another glory of the moon, and another glory of the stars: for one star differeth from another star in glory. So also is the resurrection of the dead. It is sown in corruption; it is raised in incorruption: It is sown in dishonour; it is raised in glory: it is sown in weakness; it is raised in power: It is sown a natural body; it is raised a spiritual body. I Corinthians 15:35-44

A new spiritual body is needed to enter heaven since our natural bodies are corrupted. Paul continues:

Flesh and blood cannot inherit the kingdom of God; neither doth corruption inherit incorruption. Behold, I shew you a mystery; we shall not all sleep, but we shall all be changed, in a moment, in the twinkling of an eye, at the last trump: for the trumpet shall sound, and the dead shall be raised incorruptible, and we shall be changed. For this corruptible must put on incorruption, and this mortal must put on immortality. I Corinthians 15:50-53

Earlier it was mentioned that many will mourn when they see the sign of the Son of man. The time of the Gentiles will be past, but many Jews will finally see that Jesus is the Messiah. This mourning and conversion of the Jews was prophesied by Zechariah in the Old Testament. He said that God would

pour upon the house of David, and upon the inhabitants of Jerusalem, the spirit of grace and of supplications: and they shall look upon me whom they have pierced, and they shall mourn for him, as one mourneth for his only son, and shall be in bitterness for him, as one that is in bitterness for his firstborn. In that day shall there be a great mourning in Jerusalem. . . . In that day there shall be a fountain opened to the house of David and to the inhabitants of Jerusalem for sin and for uncleanness. 12:10-11;13:1

This mourning will begin when the Jews see their Christ returning to the earth with His saints. This mourning will turn into a blessing when they accept Him as their Messiah, and they repent and are cleansed from their sins and uncleanness. When this happens, their idols and false prophets will be removed from the land. Zechariah speaks of the coming reaction of the people toward the false prophets. The prophets themselves will be ashamed of what they have done in misleading the people and will try to hide the fact that they were prophets (Zechariah 13:2-6).

The Gathering of the Nations Against Jerusalem

There are several prophecies predicting that the latter-day events will end with the nations gathered against Jerusalem. These events will now be described, although chronologically some may begin before the Rapture.

Earlier in our discussion we saw that the antichrist king came to power halfway through the tribulation period. "At the time of the end" this king will come under attack from the south, then the north, and then from the other directions.

> The king of the south [shall] push at him: and the king of the north shall come against him like a whirlwind, with chariots, and with horsemen, and with many ships; and he shall enter into the countries, and shall overflow and pass over. He shall enter also into the glorious land, and many countries shall be overthrown: but these shall escape out of his hand, even Edom, and Moab, and the chief of the children of Ammon. He shall stretch forth his hand also upon the countries: and the land of Egypt shall not escape. But he shall have power over the treasures of gold and of silver, and over all the precious things of Egypt: and the Libyans and the Ethiopians shall be at his steps. But tidings out of the east and out of the north shall trouble him: therefore he shall go forth with great fury to destroy, and utterly to make away many. Daniel 11:40-44

A southern nation will first attack Israel and the antichrist king. But their success will be short because "the king from the north" (Daniel 11:40) will launch a full scale attack against Israel. This king will crush Israel and go on to crush the southern powers. "Tens of thousands will fall," but some will escape (v. 41 RSV).

Who is this northern king? The nations lying directly north of Israel in order are Lebanon, Syria, Turkey, and Russia. Which of these is this power? Ezekiel speaks about "Gog, the land of Magog, the chief prince of Meshech and Tubal" (Ezekiel 38:2). Some think Meshech refers to Moscow and Tubal to Tobolsk, a Siberian city. If this is true, this power would likely be Russia and her friends. The Book of Ezekiel states that the Lord said of them, "I am against thee, ... I will turn thee back and put hooks into thy jaws" (vv. 3, 4).

The Completion of Redemption

These terms describe destruction. This will come about because the nations will attack Israel. Speaking of them, the Lord said,

> In the latter years thou shalt come into the land that is brought back from the sword, and is gathered out of many people, against the mountains of Israel, which have been always waste: but it is brought forth out of the nations, and they shall dwell safely all of them. Thou shalt ascend and come like a storm, thou shalt be like a cloud to cover the land, thou, and all thy bands, and many people with thee. Ezekiel 38:8, 9

Later the Lord said,

> In that day when my people of Israel dwelleth safely, shalt thou not know it? And thou shalt come from thy place out of the north parts, thou, and many people with thee, all of them riding upon horses, a great company, and a mighty army: And thou shalt come up against my people of Israel, as a cloud to cover the land; it shall be in the latter days, and I will bring thee against my land, that the heathen may know me, when I shall be sanctified in thee, O Gog, before their eyes. Ezekiel 38:14-16

Daniel wrote that after this northern invasion, "tidings out of the east and out of the north shall trouble" these powers (Daniel 11:44). These unidentified nations become concerned over the northern king's success. The Book of Ezekiel gives light on the others: "Sheba, and Dedan, and the merchants of Tarshish, with all the young lions thereof, shall say unto thee [the northern powers], Art thou come to take a spoil? hast thou gathered thy company to take a prey? to carry away silver and gold, to take away cattle and goods, to take a great spoil?" (Ezekiel 38:13). These nations that are concerned that others are receiving great spoils may be the ten confederate nations of Revelation 17. *Tarshish* is an ancient name of Great Britain. The other names also are ancient and are hard to identify today. The children of Tarshish may mean the English-speaking nations. They will come against the northern powers that overran Israel, and "he shall come to his end, and none shall help him" (Daniel 11:45). Ezekiel wrote, "Surely in that day there shall be a great shaking in the land of Israel" (Ezekiel 38:19), and all creatures and men

> shall shake at my presence, and the mountains shall be thrown down, and the steep places shall fall, and every wall shall fall to the ground. And I

> will call for a sword against him throughout all my mountains, saith the Lord God: every man's sword shall be against his brother. And I will plead against him with pestilence and with blood; and I will rain upon him, and upon his bands, and upon the many people that are with him, an overflowing rain, and great hailstones, fire, and brimstone. Thus will I magnify myself, and sanctify myself; and I will be known in the eyes of many nations, and they shall know that I am the LORD. vv. 20-23

Zechariah also prophesied of latter day events connected with Jerusalem.

> The burden of the word of the LORD for Israel, saith the LORD.... Behold, I will make Jerusalem a cup of trembling unto all the people round about, when they shall be in the siege both against Judah and against Jerusalem. And in that day will I make Jerusalem a burdensome stone for all people: all that burden themselves with it shall be cut in pieces, though all the people of the earth be gathered together against it. Zechariah 12:1-3

Judah along with all nations will be gathered against Jerusalem in the last days. The Lord will strike those coming against Jerusalem, even Judah. This will result in Judah recognizing the Lord is with Jerusalem, and she will turn against the other nations and "devour all the people" (v. 6).

The Lord will come to the aid of Jerusalem, and the nations will find she is a strong fighter because of this help. The Lord will first give victory to Judah so Jerusalem will not be exulted above Judah.

> In that day shall the LORD defend the inhabitants of Jerusalem; and he that is feeble among them at that day shall be as David; and the house of David shall be as God, as the angel of the LORD before them. And it shall come to pass in that day, that I will seek to destroy all the nations that come against Jerusalem. Zechariah 12:8, 9

Jesus' first coming was to save the lost, but His second coming will be to judge the world. During His first time on the earth He stated,

> I am come a light into the world, that whosoever believeth on me should not abide in darkness. And if any man hear my words, and believe not, I judge him not: for I came not to judge the world, but to save the world. He that rejecteth me, and receiveth not my words, hath one that judgeth

him: the word that I have spoken, the same shall judge him in the last day. John 12:46-48

Paul told the Athenians about these last days. "He [God] hath appointed a day, in the which he will judge the world in righteousness by that man whom he hath ordained; whereof he hath given assurance unto all men, in that he hath raised him from the dead" (Acts 17:31). Jesus spoke of Himself as being the one to judge. "For the Father judgeth no man, but hath committed all judgment unto the Son" (John 5:22).

Let us now return to our study in Revelation. The next major event in God's program is the coming of the Lord with His armies to destroy the nations gathered against Jerusalem. John wrote that he "saw heaven opened, and behold a white horse; and he that sat upon him was called Faithful and True, and in righteousness he doth judge and make war" (Revelation 19:11). He then described His appearance. "The armies which were in heaven followed him upon white horses, clothed in fine linen, white and clean. And out of his mouth goeth a sharp sword, that with it he should smite the nations: and he shall rule them with a rod of iron: and he treadeth the winepress of the fierceness and wrath of Almighty God" (vv. 14, 15). On His robe and thigh will be written the name "KING OF KINGS, AND LORD OF LORDS" (v. 16), making His identity clear to all.

The gathering of the nations against Jerusalem will be a time of trouble, but apparently the people of God will not go through it. Daniel prophesied:

> At that time shall Michael stand up, the great prince which standeth for the children of thy people: and there shall be a time of trouble, such as never was since there was a nation even to that same time: and at that time thy people shall be delivered, every one that shall be found written in the book. And many of them that sleep in the dust of the earth shall awake, some to everlasting life, and some to shame and everlasting contempt. And they that be wise shall shine as the brightness of the firmament; and they that turn many to righteousness as the stars for ever and ever. Daniel 12:1-3

Jesus' return will not be welcomed by the kings and armies of the world, who will gather to challenge His authority: "The beast, and the kings of the earth, and their armies, gathered together to make war against him that sat on the horse, and against his army" (Revelation 19:19). The coming of this battle was mentioned earlier. The dragon, the beast, and the false prophet will turn the kings and their military forces against the new invader. They will go out "unto the kings of the earth and of the whole world, to gather them to the battle of that great day of God Almighty.... And he gathered them together into a place called in the Hebrew tongue Armageddon" (16:14, 16), but their war efforts will quickly fail. "The beast was taken, and with him the false prophet that wrought miracles before him, with which he deceived them that had received the mark of the beast, and them that worshipped his image. These both were cast alive into a lake of fire burning with brimstone" (19:20). Their armies will also be destroyed. This battle will have so many dead that the birds are called to come to the battlefield for a "great supper," and "the fowls were filled with their flesh" (v. 21).

Ezekiel prophesied of this event: "I will give thee unto the ravenous birds of every sort" (Ezekiel 39:4), and "Speak unto every feathered fowl, ... that ye may eat flesh" (v. 17). Gog and Magog will be destroyed. Israel will "go forth, and shall set on fire and burn the weapons, ... and they shall burn them with fire seven years" (v. 9). For seven months they will search for Magog's dead and bury them (v. 12).

The result of this judgment was foretold by God. The supernatural destruction of the invading armies will cause the Jews to see who God and the Messiah are. Ezekiel recorded: "Thus saith the Lord God.... I magnify myself, and sanctify myself; and I will be known in the eyes of many nations, and they shall know that I am the Lord" (Ezekiel 38:14, 23).

This message was repeated in the prophecy against Magog. Ezekiel continued to record the Lord's words: "They shall know that I am the LORD. So will I make my holy name known in the midst of my people Israel; and I will not let them pollute my holy name any more: and the heathen shall know that I am the LORD, the Holy One in Israel" (Ezekiel 39:6-8; cf. vv. 13, 21, 22, 25). The fuller conversion of the Jews will occur when God will "have gathered them unto their own land" and "poured out [His] spirit upon the house of Israel, saith the Lord God" (vv. 28, 29).

Throughout history God has allowed man to accept or reject Him. But this freedom to choose will come to an end. Man will not be able

The Completion of Redemption

to reject God. God will make Himself clearly known, and men will know that He is the Lord. God will stand visible over His creation.

The Thousand-Year Reign

Jesus' reign on earth will begin after the Battle of Armageddon. While on earth, Satan caused nothing but trouble for the saints. Not only will the armies Satan motivated be destroyed, but the power behind them will be put in bondage. An angel

> laid hold on the dragon, that old serpent, which is the Devil, and Satan, and bound him a thousand years, and cast him into the bottomless pit, and shut him up, and set a seal upon him, that he should deceive the nations no more, till the thousand years should be fulfilled. Revelation 20:2, 3

Satan will not be able to deceive the nations and cause trouble on earth during this time, and Jesus will reign with the saints.

Those "that were beheaded for the witness of Jesus, and for the word of God, and which had not worshipped the beast, neither his image, neither had received his mark upon their foreheads, or in their hands ... lived and reigned with Christ a thousand years" (Revelation 20:4). These martyrs who lose their lives during the Tribulation are mentioned earlier in the Book of Revelation (see 6:9-11; 13:7; 14:13; 17:6). The rest of the dead will not come to life until the thousand years are completed (20:4-6). This apparently includes those who rejected Jesus and those who lost their lives in the great battle around Jerusalem, but certainly all the ungodly dead are included in this general resurrection.

Many Old Testament prophets foretold of a kingdom ruled by the Messiah, Jesus Christ, the "KING OF KINGS, AND LORD OF LORDS" (Revelation 19:16). These prophets predicted the return of Israel and Judah from their worldwide dispersion to the Promised Land and the restoration of the Davidic kingdom. God promised David that his "kingdom shall be established for ever before thee: thy throne shall be established for ever" (II Samuel 7:16; cf. Psalm 89:35-37). This promise was given to David's successor, Solomon, but was made dependent on his faithfulness (II Samuel 7:14, 15, 17; I Kings 2:3, 4; 9:4-9). Since Solomon and his successors proved unfaithful, the perpetuity of David's throne did not continue through them (Jeremiah 13:13, 14; 22:2-5, 18, 24-30; 29:16-19; 36:3-8).

Their unfaithfulness however did not nullify the promise given to David. It remained in effect. But David's kingdom was taken from his descendants and held in reserve "until he come whose right it is; and I will give it him" (Ezekiel 21:27).

The Coming One who will reign on David's throne is foretold by the Old Testament prophets. Isaiah wrote, "The LORD of hosts shall reign in mount Zion, and in Jerusalem" (Isaiah 24:23; see also 9:6ff.; 32:1ff.), and "He shall not fail nor be discouraged, till he have set judgment in the earth" (42:4). Jeremiah wrote, "Behold, the days come, saith the LORD, that I will raise unto David a righteous Branch, and a King shall reign and prosper, and shall execute judgment and justice in the earth" (Jeremiah 23:5; cf. 33:15ff.). Ezekiel wrote, "I will set up one shepherd over them, and he shall feed them, even my servant David; he shall feed them, and he shall be their shepherd" (Ezekiel 34:23).

Daniel wrote, "And in the days of these kings shall the God of heaven set up a kingdom, which shall never be destroyed: and the kingdom shall not be left to other people. . . . It shall stand for ever" (Daniel 2:44; cf. 7:27).

Hosea wrote, "For the children of Israel shall abide many days without a king, and without a prince. . . . Afterward shall the children of Israel return, and seek the LORD their God, and David their king; and shall fear the LORD and his goodness in the latter days" (Hosea 3:4, 5).

Zechariah wrote,

> Rejoice greatly, O daughter of Zion; shout, O daughter of Jerusalem: behold, thy King cometh unto thee: he is just, and having salvation; lowly, and riding upon an ass, and upon a colt the foal of an ass. And I will cut off the chariot from Ephraim, and the horse from Jerusalem, and the battle bow shall be cut off: and he shall speak peace unto the heathen: and his dominion shall be from sea even to sea, and from the river even to the ends of the earth. Zechariah 9:9, 10

The first part of this prophecy was fulfilled in Jesus' triumphal entry into Jerusalem (Matthew 21:1-9; Mark 11:7-10; Luke 19:35-38; John 12:12-16). The latter part is yet to be fulfilled. The extent of this King's rule was described later: "And the Lord shall be king over all the earth" (Zechariah 14:9).

The expectancy of this kingdom ruled by the Messiah is also found in the New Testament. When Mary, the mother of Jesus, was told of being the "highly favoured" by the angel Gabriel, the angel told her of one part of Jesus' ministry: "He shall be great, and shall be called the Son of the Highest: and the Lord God shall give unto him the throne of his father David: And he shall reign over the house of Jacob for ever; and of his kingdom there shall be no end" (Luke 1:32, 33).

Later Zechariah, the father of John the Baptist, spoke:

> Blessed be the Lord God of Israel; for he hath visited and redeemed his people, and hath raised up an horn of salvation for us in the house of his servant David; as he spake by the mouth of his holy prophets, which have been since the world began: that we should be saved from our enemies, and from the hand of all that hate us; to perform the mercy promised to our fathers, and to remember his holy covenant; the oath which he sware to our father Abraham, that he would grant unto us, that we being delivered out of the hand of our enemies might serve him without fear, in holiness and righteousness before him, all the days of our life. Luke 1:68-75

Thus Jesus' ministry is linked to the deliverance set forth in the Old Testament prophecies.

Later Jesus said, "I appoint unto you a kingdom, as my Father hath appointed unto me; That ye may eat and drink at my table in my kingdom, and sit on thrones judging the twelve tribes of Israel" (Luke 22:29, 30; cf. Matthew 19:28ff.). These statements caused the apostles to ask Jesus at His ascension, "Lord, wilt thou at this time restore again the kingdom to Israel?" (Acts 1:6). When Jesus answered this question, He did not rebuke them for their fundamental assumption but only told them, "It is not for you to know the times or the seasons, which the Father hath put in his own power," and then He commissioned them to be His witnesses (v. 7). Jesus accepted the apostles' concept of His future rule over a kingdom and explained to the apostles that the time of its fulfillment was not for them to know.

In his second sermon, Peter spoke of "Jesus Christ, which before was preached unto you: Whom the heaven must receive until the times of restoration of all things, which God hath spoken by the mouth of all his holy prophets since the world began" (Acts 3:20, 21). Peter was referring to the Old Testament prophets speaking of a restored kingdom on earth, when Satan's power would be limited and righteousness would be established on earth.

The fulfillment of these promises will occur when Jesus Christ returns to earth as "KING OF KINGS, AND LORD OF LORDS" (Revelation 19:16), reigning with "a rod of iron" (v. 15) for a thousand years (20:4). Jesus Christ brought a spiritual kingdom during His first coming, and a glorious, earthly kingdom will be established at His second coming.

Prophets described the future kingdom's character. Isaiah's prophecies give the most complete description of the earthly character of the thousand-year reign.

> And it shall come to pass in the last days, that the mountain of the LORD'S house shall be established in the top of the mountains, and shall be exalted above the hills; and all nations shall flow unto it. And many people shall go and say, Come ye, and let us go up to the mountain of the LORD, to the house of the God of Jacob; and he will teach us of his ways, and we will walk in his paths: for out of Zion shall go forth the law, and the word of the LORD from Jerusalem. And he shall judge among the nations, and shall rebuke many people: and they shall beat their swords into plowshares, and their spears into pruninghooks: nation shall not lift up sword against nation, neither shall they learn war any more. Isaiah 2:2-4

> The wolf also shall dwell with the lamb, and the leopard shall lie down with the kid; and the calf and the young lion and the fatling together; and a little child shall lead them. And the cow and the bear shall feed; their young ones shall lie down together: and the lion shall eat straw like the ox. And the suckling child shall play on the hole of the asp, and the weaned child shall put his hand on the cockatrice den. They shall not hurt nor destroy in all my holy mountain: for the earth shall be full of the knowledge of the LORD, as the waters cover the sea. Isaiah 11:6-9

> The wilderness and the solitary place shall be glad for them; and the desert shall rejoice, and blossom as the rose. It shall blossom abundantly, and rejoice even with joy and singing: the glory of Lebanon shall be given unto it, the excellency of Carmel and Sharon, they shall see the glory of the LORD, and the excellency of our God. Isaiah 35:1, 2

> And I will rejoice in Jerusalem, and joy in my people: and the voice of weeping shall be no more heard in her, nor the voice of crying. There shall be no more thence an infant of days, nor an old man that hath not filled his days: for the child shall die an hundred years old; but the sinner being an hundred years old shall be accursed . . . . The wolf and the lamb shall feed together, and the lion shall eat straw like the bullock: and dust

The Completion of Redemption

shall be the serpent's meat. They shall not hurt nor destroy in all my holy mountain, saith the LORD. Isaiah 65:19, 20, 25

For other Old Testament prophecies, see Jeremiah 30; 31; 33; Ezekiel 36; and Micah 4 and 5.

During this thousand-year reign, Jerusalem will be the center of the kingdom. "Every one that is left of all the nations which came against Jerusalem shall even go up from year to year to worship the King, the LORD of hosts, and to keep the feast of tabernacles" (Zechariah 14:16).

In Revelation 21 John described two visions of holy cities. There is considerable difference of opinions about what cities he saw. Are these two visions of the same city? Or is one of the millennial Jerusalem and the other of the eternal city?

In the first vision John wrote, "I saw a new heaven and a new earth: for the first heaven and the first earth were passed away; and there was no more sea. And I John saw the holy city, new Jerusalem, coming down from God out of heaven, prepared as a bride adorned for her husband" (Revelation 21:1, 2). This is apparently a vision of heaven since "the first heaven and the first earth were passed away," and there were no seas and death. This vision will be discussed later.

Following the above vision an angel asked John to come and see a city. This seems to be a different city than the one John saw in the first part of the chapter. One reason is that the angel said, "I will shew thee the bride, the Lamb's wife" (Revelation 21:9), indicating John would see something different than he just saw. Another reason is John's statement that "kings of the earth do bring their glory and honour into it" (v. 24). John also wrote that "there shall in no wise enter into it any thing that defileth, neither whatsoever worketh abomination, or maketh a lie; but they which are written in the Lamb's book of life" (v. 27). This statement implies this city is on the present earth since evil would not exist near the eternal "holy city, the new Jerusalem." Thus these Scriptures indicate that John described the millennial Jerusalem, the same city Zechariah wrote of (Zechariah 14:16, 17).

The angel showed John "the bride, the Lamb's wife" (Revelation 21:9), which refers to the church. He was shown "that great city, the holy Jerusalem, descending out of heaven from God" (v. 10). John gave a description of this city, including details of its gates, walls, and size. He used terms such as jasper, pure gold, sapphire, agate, emerald, and onyx to describe it. These terms indicate that it will be a magnificent city, unlike anything that has ever been (vv. 9-21). This description gives Christians the hope of a glorious future with Jesus Christ here on the earth.

Satan's Final Defeat

After the thousand years have passed, "Satan shall be loosed out of his prison, and shall go out to deceive the nations which are in the four quarters of the earth, Gog and Magog, to gather them together to battle" (Revelation 20:7, 8). Apparently not all who live under Christ's rule will be strong believers. When Satan is loosened for a short period of time after the thousand-year reign, he will find many people who are ready to rebel against the kingdom of God, "the number of whom is as the sand of the sea" (v. 8).

In John's vision these rebels gather in a great army to come against and surround "the camp of the saints about, and the beloved city" (Revelation 20:9). But their efforts come to a quick end. "Fire came down from God out of heaven, and devoured them." Not only are their armies destroyed, but "the devil that deceived them was cast into the lake of fire and brimstone, where the beast and the false prophet are, and shall be tormented day and night for ever and ever" (v. 10). The one who deceived man in the garden and throughout history meets his end and will never deceive man again.

The Final Judgment

John next tells of seeing "a great white throne, and him that sat on it" (Revelation 20:11), and the dead standing before it. These dead are the dead not raised in the first resurrection. Earlier John told about them, "The rest of the dead lived not again until the thousand years were finished" (v. 5). These who did not share in the thousand-year reign and those who followed Satan's rebellion stand together before the throne to be judged (v. 11). None of "the dead, small and great" (v. 12), will miss this final judgment. John saw them all standing before the throne. The sea, death, and Hades "delivered up the dead which were in them" (v. 13).

The teaching concerning the resurrection of the dead to face judgment is not unique to the Book of Revelation. Jesus spoke of it during His earthly ministry:

The Completion of Redemption

> Verily, verily, I say unto you, The hour is coming, and now is, when the dead shall hear the voice of the Son of God: and they that hear shall live. For as the Father hath life in himself; so hath he given to the Son to have life in himself; and hath given him authority to execute judgment also, because he is the Son of man. Marvel not at this: for the hour is coming, in the which all that are in the graves shall hear his voice, and shall come forth. John 5:25-29

At another place Jesus spoke of this coming judgment in a parable and explained:

> The tares are gathered and burned in the fire; so shall it be in the end of this world. The Son of man shall send forth his angels, and they shall gather out of his kingdom all things that offend, and them which do iniquity; and shall cast them into a furnace of fire: there shall be wailing and gnashing of teeth. Then shall the righteous shine forth as the sun in the kingdom of their Father. Matthew 13:40-43

He explained this further: "At the end of the world: the angels shall come forth, and sever the wicked from among the just" (v. 49).

In the Gospel of John, Jesus spoke of the coming resurrection, but in terms of the believers only. He will "lose nothing, but should raise it up again at the last day.... Every one which seeth the Son, and believeth on him, may have everlasting life: and I will raise him up at the last day" (John 6:39, 40). This resurrection of the last day was spoken of at several other places (vv. 44, 54; 11:24).

In the Olivet Discourse Jesus spoke of a coming judgment, but there is disagreement as to when this will occur. Some view it as being the "great white throne" judgment. Others see it as a judgment associated with the Rapture since He comes "in his glory, and all the holy angels with him" (Matthew 25:31), and other details appear different from those of the great white throne judgment.

Perhaps we need not know when this judgment occurs. Since it occurs in our future, we can learn about a judgment many will face, no matter if it occurs at the time of the Rapture or if it is the same as the great white throne judgment. In this judgment, "before him shall be gathered all nations: and he shall separate them one from another, as a shepherd divideth his sheep from the goats: and he shall set the sheep on his right hand, but the goats on the left" (Matthew 25:32, 33). This great separation will be based on how the individuals treat those who are "the least of these my brethren" (v. 40) who are hungry, thirsty, sick, and in prison.

The Bases of Judgment

The great white throne judgment will be based on what is found in the "books" or "the book of life" (Revelation 20:12). "The dead were judged out of those things which were written in the books, according to their works. . . . and they were judged every man according to their works. . . . Whosoever was not found written in the book of life was cast into the lake of fire." (vv. 12, 13, 15).

It is a fact that only one book is required to name the righteous and books to name the wicked. This was implied in Jesus teaching, "wide is the gate, and broad is the way, that leadeth to destruction . . . strait is the gate, and narrow is the way, which leadeth unto life, and few there be that find it" (Matthew 7:13, 14). The basis of judgment given here is works. This basis is mentioned in other Scriptures.

> Many will say to me in that day, Lord, Lord. . . . And then will I profess unto them, I never knew you: depart from me, ye that work iniquity. Matthew 7:22, 23; cf. Luke 13:27

> The Son of man . . . shall reward every man according to his works. Matthew 16:27

> Who will render to every man according to his deeds: To them who by patient continuance in well doing seek for glory and honour and immortality, eternal life: But unto them that are contentious, and do not obey the truth, but obey unrighteousness, indignation, and wrath, tribulation and anguish, upon every soul of man that doeth evil. Romans 2:6-9

> We must all appear before the judgment seat of Christ; that every one may receive the things done in his body, according to that he hath done, whether it be good or bad. II Corinthians 5:10

> Be not deceived; God is not mocked: for whatsoever a man soweth, that shall he also reap. For he that soweth to his flesh shall of the flesh reap corruption; but he that soweth to the Spirit shall of the Spirit reap life everlasting. Galatians 6:7, 8

> He that doeth wrong shall receive for the wrong which he hath done: and there is no respect of persons. Colossians 3:25

The Completion of Redemption

> To execute judgment upon all, and to convince all that are ungodly among them of all their ungodly deeds which they have ungodly committed, and of all their hard speeches which ungodly sinners have spoken against him. Jude 15

> All the churches shall know that I am he which searcheth the reins and hearts: and I will give unto every one of you according to your works. Revelation 2:23

The Scripture not only speaks of works as being a basis of judgment, but tells us that man will also be judged according to how he responds to Jesus Christ and His Gospel.

> Whosoever therefore shall be ashamed of me and of my words in this adulterous and sinful generation; of him also shall the Son of man be ashamed, when he cometh in the glory of his Father with the holy angels. Mark 8:38; cf. Luke 9:26; Matthew 10:33

> Verily, verily, I say unto you, He that heareth my word, and believeth on him that sent me, hath everlasting life, and shall not come into condemnation; but is passed from death unto life. John 5:24

> I am come a light into the world, that whosoever believeth on me should not abide in darkness.... He that rejecteth me, and receiveth not my words, hath one that judgeth him: the word that I have spoken, the same shall judge him in the last day. John 12:46, 48

> The Lord Jesus shall be revealed from heaven with his mighty angels, In flaming fire taking vengeance on them that know not God, and that obey not the gospel of our Lord Jesus Christ. II Thessalonians 1:7, 8

Are these two bases of judgment in conflict? How can one be judged according to works and also according to his response to Jesus Christ and the Gospel? The answer to this question is that good works follow when one responds and believes the Gospel. When one repents and believes the Gospel and has faith in Jesus Christ, he is born anew and from then on seeks to do God's will. This doing of God's will results in the good works that are the basis of judgment. There is no conflict between looking for these works or one's response to Jesus Christ, since these works are the result of a positive response to the Gospel.

Christ, at the end of the parable on service, told what the Christian's response should be at judgment. He said, "When ye shall have done all those things which are commanded you, say, We are unprofitable servants: we have done that which was our duty to do" (Luke 17:10). The Christian did not earn anything but only did what the grace of God and the Holy Spirit worked in his life.

The Eternal Punishment

"Whosoever was not found written in the book of life was cast into the lake of fire" (Revelation 20:15). Fire is frequently used to describe the place where the wicked are punished. The term *Gehenna* is commonly used in the New Testament to describe this place of punishment. *Gehenna* is one of the Greek words translated "hell" in our English Bibles. Another Greek term, *Hades*, is also translated "hell," especially in the King James Version.

The Valley of Gehenna, just south of the city, was where Jerusalem's garbage and the dead bodies of criminals were burnt. Because of wickedness associated with the valley, its name was used for the place of final punishment of the wicked. Hell is often associated with fire, as the following Scriptures show: "He will burn up the chaff with unquenchable fire" (Matthew 3:12); "hell fire" (5:22); "shall cast them into a furnace of fire" (13:42; cf. v. 50); "to be cast into hell fire" (18:9); "Depart from me, ye cursed, into everlasting fire, prepared for the devil and his angels" (25:41); "hell, into the fire that never shall be quenched" (Mark 9:43; cf. v. 48); "and in hell he lift up his eyes, being in torments. . . . I am tormented in this flame" (Luke 16:23, 24); "if a man abide not in me, he is cast forth as a branch, and is withered; and men gather them, and cast them into the fire, and they are burned" (John 15:6); and "the vengeance of eternal fire" (Jude 7).

One of the most awful aspects of the punishment of the wicked is their eternal separation from God the Father and Jesus Christ. On judgment day many will hear the words, "Depart from me, ye that work iniquity" (Matthew 7:23; cf. Luke 13:27), and "Depart from me, ye cursed, into everlasting fire, prepared for the devil and his angels" (Matthew 25:41). On that day there will be a great separation: "And these shall go away into everlasting punishment" (v. 46); "Between us and you there is a great gulf fixed" (Luke 16:26); "Who shall be punished with everlasting destruction from the presence of the Lord, and from the glory of his power" (II Thessalonians 1:9).

Other passages describe this separation in terms of being cast into darkness. Since God is described as light, darkness would describe a complete and total separation from Him. Scriptures using the term darkness are: "shall be cast out into the outer darkness" (Matthew 8:12; cf. 22:13; 25:30); "God spared not the angels that sinned, but cast them down to hell, and delivered them into chains of darkness, to be reserved unto judgment" (II Peter 2:4); "mist of darkness" (II Peter 2:17); "blackness of darkness for ever" (Jude 13).

Those in the lake of fire will remember for eternity their banishment from the presence of God. They will have seen the Judge, Jesus Christ, whom they rejected at their judgment. They will be haunted by the memory that they rejected Jesus Christ as their Savior. Perhaps too the thought of the glories of God and heaven that they will be missing will haunt them for eternity. They will remember the opportunities they had to respond to the truth, but they will realize they turned from their opportunities to follow their own sinful desires.

Other Scriptures show hell will be a place of great suffering. Scriptures showing this are: "to be cast into hell, into the fire that never shall be quenched: Where their worm dieth not" (Mark 9:45, 46), and "There shall be weeping and gnashing of teeth" (Matthew 8:12; cf. 13:42; 22:13; 24:51; 25:30; Luke 13:28). The fire conveys the idea of external suffering, and the worm the idea of internal suffering. The weeping is due to the sorrow, grief, and anguish of being in hell. Those in hell will experience a complete loss of happiness and will weep bitterly when they think of their condition. The gnashing of teeth and the grinding of the teeth together suggest mental anguish.

These terms *darkness, fire, worm, weeping, gnashing of teeth,* etc., used to express the great suffering in hell, should not be tampered with. No interpretation of them should take away from the awfulness of hell. Hell is a dreadful place, and these words describe its awfulness only in part.

Those in hell will not all suffer the same; there are degrees of punishment in hell. The punishment the wicked suffer depends on the opportunities they had to know the truth and how they responded. When Jesus sent out His disciples to preach the good news, He said, concerning those who rejected them, "It shall be more tolerable for the land of Sodom and Gomorrha in the day of judgment, than for that city" (Matthew 10:15). A little later Jesus condemned the Jewish leaders' unbelief: "Woe unto thee, Chorazin! woe unto thee, Bethsaida! for if the mighty works, which were done in you, had been done in Tyre and Sidon, they would have repented long ago in sackcloth and ashes" (Matthew 11:21, 22; cf. Luke 10:13, 14).

Jesus warned the scribes and Pharisees that the results of their missionary efforts were not what they expected. "Ye compass sea and land to make one proselyte, and when he is made, ye make him twofold more the child of hell than yourselves" (Matthew 23:15). In a parable Jesus told about a faithful steward and an unfaithful steward and said, "That servant, which knew his lord's will, and prepared not himself, neither did according to his will, shall be beaten with many stripes. But he that knew not, and did commit things worthy of stripes, shall be beaten with few stripes. For unto whomsoever much is given, of him shall be much required: and to whom men have committed much, of him they will ask the more" (Luke 12:47, 48).

These Scriptures all show there will be degrees of punishment in hell. God is just, and even unbelievers will be treated justly. Those who had little opportunity will receive lighter punishment than those who had great opportunity to accept redemption but refused.

The Eternal Reward

Following the scene of the great white throne, John described a vision of "a new heaven and a new earth: for the first heaven and the first earth were passed away; and there was no more sea" (Revelation 21:1). God will dwell with His people, and they will be together. John saw the coming of God to dwell with His people. "I John saw the holy city, new Jerusalem, coming down from God out of heaven, prepared as a bride adorned for her husband. And I heard a great voice out of heaven saying, Behold, the tabernacle of God is with men, and he will dwell with them, and they shall be his people, and God himself shall be with them, and be their God" (vv. 2, 3). This city was mentioned near the beginning of this book, "the city of my God, which is new Jerusalem, which cometh down out of heaven from my God" (3:12).

John wrote that he "heard a great voice out of heaven saying, Behold, the tabernacle of God is with men, and he will dwell with

The Completion of Redemption

them, and they shall be his people, and God himself shall be with them, and be their God" (Revelation 21:3). Being with God is incomprehensible to us, but we know His dwelling with His children will bring righteousness and joy to man. "God shall wipe away all tears from their eyes; and there shall be no more death, neither sorrow, nor crying, neither shall there be any more pain" (v. 4). These things are part of the fallen world, and since "the former things are passed away" (v. 4), they will not be in heaven. God promised that He would "make all things new" (v. 5). We have this hope because "he [God] that sat upon throne" told John, "Write: for these words are true and faithful" (v. 5).

God promised to "give unto him that is athirst of the fountain of the water of life freely" (Revelation 21:6). Not everyone will drink from this fountain. Unbelievers, murderers, whoremongers, sorcerers, idolaters, and liars "shall have their part in the lake which burneth with fire and brimstone: which is the second death" (v. 8).

The present heaven and earth were corrupted by Satan, sin, and evil. It is an unfit place for the eternal kingdom of God. The old heaven and earth will pass away, and a new heaven and earth without sin and evil will replace it. The passing of the present creation is found in several Scriptures (Psalm 102:25, 26; Matthew 5:18; Mark 13:31; II Peter 3:12). The statement that there will be "no more sea" (Revelation 21:1) shows the new earth is drastically different from the present one. We are not told why there is no sea. Because the sea is symbolic of the nations in turmoil and unsettledness, perhaps its absence shows in the new earth there will be no disunity or ethnic distinctions.

This new heaven and earth are described by the Old Testament prophet Isaiah. Speaking for the Lord God, Isaiah wrote, "For, behold, I create new heavens and a new earth: and the former shall not be remembered, nor come into mind. But be ye glad and rejoice for ever in that which I create: for, behold, I create Jerusalem a rejoicing, and her people a joy. And I will rejoice in Jerusalem, and joy in my people: and the voice of weeping shall be no more heard in her, nor the voice of crying" (Isaiah 65:17-19). Later he wrote, "For as the new heavens and the new earth, which I will make, shall remain before me, saith the Lord, so shall your seed and your name remain" (66:22). God's children in heaven will live in joy and have no recollection of the present evil world.

In the New Testament Peter wrote about the coming of the Lord. He wrote that after the Lord's delay to give time for men to repent:

> The day of the Lord will come as a thief in the night; in which the heavens shall pass away with a great noise, and the elements shall melt with fervent heat, the earth also and the works that are therein shall be burned up. Seeing then that all these things shall be dissolved, what manner of persons ought ye to be in all holy conversation and godliness, looking for and hasting unto the coming of the day of God, wherein the heavens being on fire shall be dissolved, and the elements shall melt with fervent heat? Nevertheless we, according to his promise, look for new heavens and a new earth, wherein dwelleth righteousness. II Peter 3:10-13

What will this new heaven and earth be like? We do not have a complete picture but are given glimpses of it. Paul, although not writing about heaven, told of our incomplete view: "For now we see through a glass, darkly; but then face to face: now I know in part; but then shall I know" (I Corinthians 13:12). John gives a similar view: "Beloved, now are we the sons of God, and it doth not yet appear what we shall be: but we know that, when he shall appear, we shall be like him; for we shall see him as he is" (I John 3:2, 3).

The Scriptures quoted from Peter's writing about the new heaven and earth reveal one aspect of heaven. Righteousness dwells there. The sin and evil so prevalent in our present world will be replaced by an atmosphere of righteousness. Thus God will no longer need to be separated from His people but can again dwell with them as He did in the beginning. This explains creation's waiting for "the times of restitution of all things" (Acts 3:21). Paul had this in mind when he wrote, "The creature itself also shall be delivered from the bondage of corruption into the glorious liberty of the children of God. For we know that the whole creation groaneth and travaileth in pain together until now" (Romans 8:21, 22). This deliverance will mean that "the righteous [shall] shine forth as the sun in the kingdom of their Father" (Matthew 13:43).

The Book of Revelation gives us another glimpse of heaven—it will be a place of joy. "God shall wipe away all tears from their eyes; and there shall be no more death, neither sorrow, nor crying, neither shall there be any more pain: for the former things are passed away" (Revelation 21:4). Isaiah wrote similarly that death shall be swallowed up in victory and that "the Lord GOD will wipe away tears from off all faces; and the rebuke of his people shall he take away from off all the earth: for the Lord hath spoken it" (Isaiah 25:8). Later he said to be "glad and rejoice for ever in that which I create: for, behold, I create Jerusalem a rejoicing, and her people a joy. And I will rejoice in Jerusalem, and joy in my people: and the voice of weeping shall be no more heard in her, nor the voice of crying" (65:18, 19). The psalmist wrote, "In thy presence is fulness of joy" (Psalm 16:11).

In heaven the saved will not exist in bodies like our present ones but will have new and glorious bodies. It is not known completely what these bodies will be like. But as mentioned earlier, "we shall be like him" (I John 3:2). There obviously will be a drastic change in our bodies since our present ones have been affected by sin, and our new ones shall be like His.

Paul drew a similar contrast between our present bodies and our heavenly ones. "As we have borne the image of the earthy, we shall also bear the image of the heavenly." The reason saints will bear a new image is that "flesh and blood cannot inherit the kingdom of God; neither doth corruption inherit incorruption" (I Corinthians 15:49, 50).

In I Corinthians 15 Paul established the doctrine of the resurrection. In doing so he answered the objections some might raise by questioning, "How are the dead raised up? and with what body do they come?" (v.35). In the answer he gave to these questions, we learn that our resurrected bodies will be different from our present bodies.

We see these differences illustrated in our present experiences. When a person plants a seed, the seed dies (ceases to be a seed) and sprouts into a new plant. That which is sown is "not that body that shall be, but bare grain.... But God giveth it a body as it hath pleased him, and to every seed his own body" (I Corinthians 15:37, 38). Just as each seed sprouts into its own form of life, this variety in bodies is found in other areas of our experiences. There is variety in animal life. "All flesh is not the same flesh" (v. 39). Men, beasts, fishes, and birds all have different kinds of bodies. There is also variety among heavenly and earthly bodies (vv. 40, 41).

"There is a natural body, and there is a spiritual body" (I Corinthians 15:44). The first comes from the first man, Adam. The second is brought about by the last Adam, Jesus Christ. He is the quickening Spirit, the One from whom Christians get their new spiritual bodies. "As we have borne the image of the earthy, we shall also bear the image of the heavenly" (v. 49). Our present bodies bear the marks of the first Adam, but the dead in Christ shall be raised in His image.

Jesus mentioned one important difference these new bodies will have. He said they shall "neither marry, nor [be] given in marriage; but [be] as the angels which are in heaven" (Mark 12:25; cf. Matthew 22:30; Luke 20:35). In heaven there will be no need for reproduction and child bearing; therefore sex and marriage will not be needed.

Christians will be rewarded for their obedience to God's will and service. Jesus said that Christians who are reviled, persecuted, and falsely spoken against will receive a "reward in heaven" (Matthew 5:12). He also said that those who give false alms will receive "no reward of your father" (6:1) and referred to a "righteous man's reward" (10:41) and to those who love their enemies and lend, that their "reward shall be great" (Luke 6:35).

When Is the Second Coming?

We have discussed the prophecies concerning the events leading to the second coming of Christ and judgment. After Jesus told His disciples of these events in the Olivet Discourse (see Matthew 24 and 25, Mark 13, and Luke 21), He spoke to them about the time of His coming and about the need to be ready for it.

Jesus bade the disciples to "learn a parable of the fig tree; When his branch is yet tender, and putteth forth leaves, ye know that summer is nigh; So likewise ye, when ye shall see all these things, know that it is near, even at the doors" (Matthew 24:32, 33; cf. Mark 13:28, 29; Luke 21:29-31). Man has learned to read natural signs. He can tell that summer is near when the fig tree sends its sap up through the branches, to soften them and cause them to send forth leaves. The disciple should also be ready to read the signs of the times. "When ye shall see all these things" (Matthew 24:33), Christ's disciples will know His second coming and the end are near.

Jesus goes on and clarifies the nearness of His coming to the appearance of the signs. "Verily I say unto you, This generation shall not pass, till all these things be fulfilled. Heaven and earth shall pass away, but my words shall not pass away" (Matthew 24:34, 35; cf. Mark 13:30, 31; Luke 21:32, 33). The generation that sees the things Jesus described in the Olivet Discourse will also see Jesus' return.

The coming will be that near to these events, within one generation, a period of thirty years.

The Day and Hour of His Coming

It is only natural for Christians to think beyond this general identification of the time of the second coming and wonder about the exact day and hour this will happen. These events point to the general time. Jesus knew many would want a specific date. Because of this Jesus went on to explain that no one knows the day and the hour of His coming. It will be sudden and unexpected, "for as the lightning cometh out of the east, and shineth even unto the west; so shall also the coming of the Son of man be" (Matthew 24:27; cf. Luke 17:24). "As the days of Noe [Noah] were, so shall also the coming of the Son of man be. For as in the days that were before the flood they were eating and drinking, marrying and giving in marriage, until the day that Noe entered the ark, and knew not until the flood came, and took them all away; so shall also the coming of the Son of man be" (Matthew 24:37-39; cf. Luke 17:26-30; see also Genesis 6:5; 7:6-23). The people in Noah's day heard Noah's message of a coming judgment but did not know the exact time. They did not prepare themselves for the coming judgment and let life go on as usual. This resulted in unexpected events overtaking them and all being lost (Genesis 7:21-23).

Be Prepared

Christians know that Jesus' coming will occur suddenly and unexpectedly. Jesus told us to keep this in mind. "Watch therefore: for ye know not what hour your Lord doth come. But know this, that if the goodman of the house had known in what watch the thief would come, he would have watched, and would not have suffered his house to be broken up. Therefore be ye also ready: for in such an hour as ye think not the Son of man cometh" (Matthew 24:42-44).

Following this admonition Jesus told His disciples three parables to warn them of the importance of being ready when He comes. The first one told them they should be as "the faithful and wise servant" (Matthew 25:45) who was put in charge of the household by his master. "Blessed is that servant, whom his Lord when he cometh shall find so doing" (v. 46). The faithful servant will be rewarded. But if he says in his heart, "My lord delayeth his coming" (v. 48) and is unfaithful, "The Lord of that servant shall come in a day when he looketh not for him, and in an hour that he is not aware of, and shall cut him asunder, and appoint him his portion with the hypocrites: there shall be weeping and gnashing of teeth" (vv. 50-51; see also Luke 12:39, 40; 21:34-36). This parable emphasizes that one should be ready for His coming at all times. Much is at stake. Because he does not know the hour Jesus is coming, the Christian should be motivated to be faithful at all times. He should not think he can indulge in sin for a time and repent just before his Master comes. When He comes, the time for repentance will be over. It will be a time for judgment.

The second of Jesus' three parables concerns the need to be watchful. This parable describes ten virgins who wait for a marriage festival. In first-century Jewish tradition, when two people were betrothed or engaged, they were considered man and wife, but they continued to live separately with their parents for a while. After a period of time, the bridegroom, accompanied by his friends, went to the bride's home and brought her with her maiden friends to their new home. Together they would observe a marriage festival.

Each of the bride's maiden friends had to have a lamp burning with oil when the group went to meet the bridegroom, if she was to enter the marriage festival with the bridegroom and bride. In this parable the bridegroom was delayed. "At midnight there was a cry made, Behold, the bridegroom cometh; go ye out to meet him" (Matthew 25:6). The maidens who were sleeping arose and trimmed their lamps. Five of the ten brought extra oil with them and filled their lamps. The other five, "the foolish [ones] said unto the wise, Give us of your oil; for our lamps are gone out" (v. 8). But the wise ones told them, "Not so, lest there be not enough for us and you: but go ye rather to them that sell, and buy for yourselves" (v. 9). The five foolish ones left and went to buy oil. While they were gone, "the bridegroom came; and they that were ready went in with him to the marriage: and the door was shut" (v.10). When the five foolish ones returned with their oil and were ready to enter, they cried to the bridegroom, "Lord, Lord, open to us" (v. 11). He did not open but told them, "Verily I say unto you, I know you not" (v. 12).

From this parable Jesus drew this lesson: "Watch therefore, for ye know neither the day nor the hour wherein the Son of man cometh"

(Matthew 25:13). The Christian must be prepared when Jesus returns. There will be no time to get ready for His coming at the last minute.

The third parable (Matthew 25:14-28) concerns a man who, just before he went on a journey, entrusted his possessions to his slaves. "And unto one he gave five talents, to another two, and to another one; to every man according to his several ability" (v. 15). The first two slaves put their possessions to work and doubled their worth. "But he that had received one went and digged in the earth, and hid his lord's money" (v. 18).

After a time the master returned and called in the slaves to settle the accounts. To the first two, who made a good gain, he said,

> Well done, thou good and faithful servant: thou has been faithful over a few things, I will make thee ruler over many things: enter thou into the joy of thy lord.... Then he which had received the one talent came and said, Lord, I knew thee that thou art an hard man, reaping where thou hast not sown, and gathering where thou hast not strawed: And I was afraid, and went and hid thy talent in the earth: lo, there thou hast that is thine. His lord answered and said unto him, Thou wicked and slothful servant, thou knewest that I reap where I sowed not, and gather where I have not strawed: Thou oughtest therefore to have put my money to the exchangers, and then at my coming I should have received mine own with usury. Take therefore the talent from him, and give it unto him which hath ten talents. Matthew 25:21-28

The lesson Jesus drew from this parable is, "For unto every one that hath shall be given, and he shall have abundance: but from him that hath not shall be taken away even that which he hath. And cast ye the unprofitable servant into outer darkness: there shall be weeping and gnashing of teeth" (Matthew 25:29, 30). The Christian must not neglect the gifts he has. He must put them to work to further the kingdom. He who does not will suffer loss and be punished.

This Message Told Elsewhere

The message Jesus gave above was told to others. Just before His ascension the disciples asked Jesus, "Lord, wilt thou at this time restore again the kingdom to Israel? And he said unto them, It is not for you to know the times or the seasons, which the Father hath put in his own power" (Acts 1:6, 7). The time of these further events is not for us to know.

Paul wrote to the Thessalonians,

> But of the times and the seasons, brethren, ye have no need that I write unto you. For yourselves know perfectly that the day of the Lord so cometh as a thief in the night. For when they shall say, Peace and safety; then sudden destruction cometh upon them, as travail upon a woman with child; and they shall not escape. But ye, brethren, are not in darkness, that that day should overtake you as a thief. Ye are all the children of light, and the children of the day: we are not of night, nor of darkness. Therefore let us not sleep, as do others; but let us watch and be sober. I Thessalonians 5:1-6

Christians are not to be in the dark about the second coming and the judgment. They know about it and have been admonished to stay alert and sober so they will not be destroyed with those in darkness.

Elsewhere Christians are told they are "waiting for the coming of our Lord Jesus Christ" (I Corinthians 1:7). Peter wrote,

> The Lord is not slack concerning his promise, as some men count slackness; but is longsuffering to us-ward, not willing that any should perish, but that all should come to repentance. But the day of the Lord will come as a thief in the night. . . . what manner of persons ought ye to be in all holy conversation [conduct] and godliness, looking for and hasting unto the coming of the day of God? . . . seeing that ye look for such things, be diligent that ye may be found of him in peace, without spot, and blameless. . . . Ye therefore, beloved, seeing ye know these things before, beware lest ye also, being led away with the error of the wicked, fall from your own steadfastness. But grow in grace, and in the knowledge of our Lord and Saviour Jesus Christ. II Peter 3:9-12, 14, 17, 18

The church at Sardis was told, "Remember therefore how thou hast received and heard, and hold fast, and repent. If therefore thou shalt not watch, I will come on thee as a thief, and thou shalt not know what hour I will come upon thee" (Revelation 3:3). Thus we see that the message Jesus gave on the Mount of Olives was repeated many times. It is an important one Christians must not forget.

Come

In the beginning God created man in His own image and gave him a perfect world to live in. "God saw every thing that he had made, and, behold, it was very good" (Genesis 1:31).

The Completion of Redemption

Man was placed in a garden. In this garden there were two special trees—"the tree of life" and "the tree of knowledge of good and evil" (Genesis 2:9). Man was told by God not to partake of the latter tree. By simple faith he could live in the presence of good alone and avoid knowing good and evil together. But man chose to disobey God's direction. He listened to Satan's advice and took of "the tree of knowledge of good and evil."

This act of disobedience placed a sin barrier between God and man. But God did not leave and forget man. He told Satan, "I will put enmity between thee and the woman . . . it shall bruise thy head, and thou shalt bruise his heel" (Genesis 3:15).

In this book we have shown how this promise was fulfilled. We have followed the path of events leading to redemption brought by Jesus Christ. We have traced God's actions throughout history in destroying the sin barrier and making it possible for man again to walk and talk with God.

We live in an age of fast-growing technology and knowledge of God's physical universe. But this does not change the simple truths revealed by God in His Word about the redemption brought by Jesus Christ. This knowledge of redemption is of prime importance to each of us.

The Spirit and the bride say, Come. And let him that heareth say, Come. And let him that is athirst come. And whosoever will, let him take the water of life freely. . . . The grace of our Lord Jesus Christ be with you all. Amen. Revelation 22:17, 21

Bibliography

Arndt, William F., and F. Wilbur Gingrich. *A Greek-English Lexicon of the New Testament*. Chicago: University of Chicago Press, 1979.

Clarke, Adam. *Clark's Commentary*. New York: Abingdon, n.d.

Edersheim, Alfred. *The Life and Times of Jesus The Messiah*. American Edition. Grand Rapids: Eerdmans, 1962.

Elwell, Walter A., ed. *Baker Encyclopedia of the Bible*. Grand Rapids: Baker Book House, 1988.

────────. *Evangelical Dictionary of Theology*. Grand Rapids: Baker Book House, 1984.

Greathouse, William M., Donald S. Metz, and Frank G. Carver. *Beacon Bible Commentary*. Kansas City: Beacon Hill, 1968.

Grider, J. Kenneth. *A Wesleyan-Holiness Theology*. Kansas City: Beacon Hill, 1994.

Hodge, A. A. *Outlines of Theology*. Reprint. Grand Rapids: Zondervan, 1879, 1972.

Lange, John Peter. *Commentary of the Holy Scriptures*. New ed. Grand Rapids: Zondervan, 1960.

Lehman, Chester K. *Biblical Theology*. Scottdale, Penn.: Herald Press, 1974.

Lenski, R. C. H. *Interpretation of . . .*, Columbus, Ohio: Wartburg Press, 1946.

MacArthur, John F., Jr. *Faith Works*. Dallas: Word, 1993.

Miley, John. *Systematic Theology*. New York: Eaton and Mains, 1892.

Morgan, G. Campbell. *The Gospel According to Matthew*. Old Tappan, N. J.: Fleming Revell, n.d.

Pope, William Burt. *A Compendium of Christian Theology*. 2nd ed. London: Beveridge, 1879.

Robertson, Archibald Thomas. *Word Pictures in the New Testament*. Grand Rapids: Baker Book House, 1933.

Smith, J. B. *A Revelation of Jesus Christ*. Scottdale, Penn.: Herald Press, 1961.

Stauffer, John L. *Studies in the Revelation of Jesus Christ*. Harrisonburg, Va.: Sword and Trumpet, 1956.

Shank, Robert. *Elect in the Son*. Springfield, Missouri: Westcott, 1970.

Sheldon, Henry C. *System of Christian Doctrine*. Cincinnati, Ohio: Jennings and Pye, 1903.

Strong, James. *Strong's Exhaustive Concordance of the Bible*. New York: Abingdon, 1890.

Thayer, Joseph Henry. *A Greek-English Lexicon of the New Testament*. Grand Rapids: Baker Book House, 1977.

Vincent, Marvin R. *Word Studies in the New Testament*. Peabody, Mass.: Hendrickson, n.d.

Wenger, John Christian. *Introduction to Theology*. Scottdale, Penn.: Herald Press, 1954.

——————. *Lay Guide to Romans*. Scottdale, Penn.: Herald Press, 1983.

——————. *The Way to a New Life*. Scottdale, Penn.: Herald Press, 1977.

Wiley, H. Orton. *Christian Theology*. Kansas City: Beacon Hill, 1943.

——————. *The Epistle To The Hebrews*, Kansas City: Beacon Hill, 1959.

Wiley, H. Orton, and Paul T. Culbertson. *Introduction to Theology*. Kansas City: Beacon Hill, 1946.

Whedon, D. D. *Whedon's Commentary*. revised ed. Harrisonburg, Va.: Christian Light Publications, 1981.

Index

Aaron, First high priest • 25
Abraham • 18, 29, 144, 146
   Faith • 19, 127, 146
   Works • 20, 142, 146, 155
Adam and Eve • 10
Antinomianism • 102
Arminius, James • 99
Ascension • 82, 83
Atonement • 27, 92
BABYLON THE GREAT • 206
Baptism • 133, 137
Believe • 11, 130
Bethlehem • 35, 40
Bible • 65
Binding and loosing • 64
Birth of Christ • 40
Blood • 27, 87, 89, 91
Born again • 47
Born of water • 133
Call on Lord • 136, 171
Canaan • 28
Carnal mind • 134, 154
Central truth of the Gospel • 48
Chief priests and elders • 69
Chosen people • 18, 23, 86, 139, 141, 144, 173, 174, 175
Christ • 84
   Abraham's Seed • 143
   authority challenged • 69
   baptized • 43
   burial • 79
   crucifixion • 76
   death of • 87
   destroy this temple • 47
   early life • 42
   establishes His kingdom • 199
   foretells His death and resurrection • 66
   gave life by own testimony • 74
   increasing opposition • 61
   Lamb • 195, 204, 208
   Lamb of God • 34, 43, 45, 82, 89
   mighty works • 58
   ministry • 46
   only way • 56
   resurrection of • 80, 170
   scripture • 62
   Seed of woman • 18, 39
   Son of God • 39, 40, 44, 46, 64, 65, 74, 76, 78, 105, 131, 136, 138, 179, 200, 219, 223
   Son of man • 48, 54, 63, 65, 72, 89, 131, 181, 190, 205, 209, 223, 233, 234
   suffering • 77, 79, 81, 84, 93
   Temple cleansed • 47, 69
   temptations • 44
   trial • 74
   union with • 176
Christian growth • 150, 177
Circumcision • 19, 145
Circumcision party • 143
Commandments, Keep God's • 138
Confession • 136
Creation of man • 9
Cross • 55
Crucifixion • 76
David • 31, 39
Day of Atonement • 25, 27, 91
Deny self • 55
Discipleship • 7, 54, 137
Divine nature • 105
Doctrine • 125
Egypt • 21
Election • 20, 70, 107, 166, 167, 172, 175
Eli, Eli, lama sabachthani • 77
Elisabeth • 39
Empty tomb • 80
Eternal punishment • 226
Eternal reward • 228
Ethics • 52
Evidence to know • 126
Expiation • 90
Faith • 121
   alone • 146
   and obedience • 149
   and works • 155
   appropriates grace • 122
   assurance • 126
   by hearing • 171
   Christian truth • 128
   due to grace • 123, 147
   intellectual assent • 129, 131, 155
   new birth, repentance • 135

real • 132
self-surrender • 128
several meanings • 125
trust • 125, 127
Faith chapter • 128
Fall • 11
Feet washing • 73
Flesh • 154, 159
Foreordained • 17
Forty years • 28
Free choice • 10
Fruit of the Spirit • 159
Fullness of time • 32, 36
Galatians-By Law or by Faith • 142
Garden of Eden • 85
Gentiles • 169, 173
Gentiles, Part of the chosen people • **175**
Gethsemane • 73
God
  attributes • 16
  hatred of sin • 16
  holiness • 11, 16, 26, 86
  love • 17, 86, 110, 119
God's will for Christians • 65, 157
Good works • 89, 109, 151, 152, 225
Governmental theory • 99
Grace • 108
  and the Holy Spirit • 51, 111, 136
  and truth • 107
  Divine influence • 108
  example of Paul's life • 112
  free from sin's power • 150
  free gift of • 113
  influence • 51, 103, 109, 111, 112, 132
  meaning of • 108

power in Christian's lives • 113
repentance and faith • 111
High priest • 161
Holiness and love • 16
Holy Spirit • 7, 60, 64, 137
  and grace • 51
  Counselor • 83
  Incarnation • 40, 170
Interpretation
  common-sense principle • 184
  of prophecy • 183
Isaac • 19
Isaiah • 33
Israel • 21
Israel's rejection • 171
Jacob • 20
James and Paul's emphasis • 156
Jerusalem • 67, 72
Jews
  Church outreach to • 140
  hypocrisy • 71
  Promised Land • 217
  rebellion • 28, 139
  return to the Promised Land • 185
  status of • 165
  stubbornness and blindness • 70
  stumbling • 165, 169, 172
John the Baptist • 38, 42, 60, 116
Joseph • 21
Joshua • 29
Judges • 30
Judgment, final • 222, 224
Justification • 109, 123, 147

and sanctification • 150
by faith • 123, 124, 144
by grace • 109
theme of Romans • 144
Keys • 64
King for Israel • 30
Kingdom
  future literal • 50
  of God • 48, 50, 70, 117, 132, 137
  spiritual • 51
  Two types • 52
Lamb • 22, 45
Lamb's book of life • 221
Latter-Day Events • 182
Law • 62, 123
  and Christians • 142, 144, 152, 160
  Christian dissension over • 141
  educational functions • 26
  given at Sinai • 23
  schoolmaster • 143
Lazarus • 68
Legalism • 62, 140
Lord's Supper • 72
Love • 157
Malachi • 35
Man
  all have sinned • 12
  created in God's image • 9
  likeness of God • 104
  natural • 12
  spiritual nature • 9, 48, 107, 133, 211, 231
Marriage Feast • 208
Melchisedec • 161
Mercy seat • 27, 91
Messiah • 84

Messianic prophecies • 32
Miracles • 59
Moses • 22, 23, 29
Mount of Olives • 73
Nations against Jerusalem • 212
Nazareth • 49
New birth • 51, 56, 132, 133, 137
New covenant • 91, 104, 107, 124
Nicodemus • 47, 132
Northern Kingdom • 32
Obedience • 18, 26, 29, 31, 41, 46, 52, 58, 72, 73, 94, 112, 132, 138, 139, 141, 143, 148, 149, 157, 161, 170, 179, 208, 232
  Is possible • 152, 154
Olivet Discourse • 182, 186
Only way • 56
Paschal Lamb • 79
Passover • 22, 47, 66, 68, 72
Pentecost sermon • 83
Peter • 83
  confession of • 64
Pharaoh • 22, 167
Pharisees • 61, 62, 70, 116, 117
Priesthood • 25
Promised Land • 28
Propitiation • 90
Punishment • 15
  degrees of • 14
Punishment Theory • 96
Ransom • 67, 89
  to whom paid • 90
Rapture • 188, 209, 212, 223
Rebirth, repentance, faith • 135

Reconciliation • 86, 103, 148
Redemption • 85, 88
  effects of • 104
Repent • 84
Repentance • 114
  change mind about God • 118
  faith, and rebirth • 135
  importance of • 117, 121
  removes sin • 116
  required for kingdom of God • 117
  sorrow • 120
  turning from sin • 118
Righteous by faith • 123
Sadducees • 71
Samaritan women • 49
Samuel • 30
Sanctification • 108, 150
Satan • 10, 44, 104
  destruction of his power • 15, 105, 177
  final defeat • 222
  influence of • 12
Saul • 30
Scapegoat • 27, 91
Scripture • 14, 62, 106, 158
Second Coming • 180
  be prepared • 233
  when • 232
Seed of woman • 18, 33, 39, 143
Sermon on the Mount • 52
Seven seals • 195
Sheol • 80
Sin • 11, 13, 26, 107
  revealed by the law • 14
Solomon • 31
Son of God • 103

Sons of God • 131
Southern Kingdom • 32
Substitutionary death • 93
Tabernacle • 24, 26
Temple • 68, 69
  cleansing of • 47, 69
  rebuilt • 194
  veil ripped • 78
Ten Commandments • 24
Thousand-year reign • 217
Transfiguration • 65
Tribulation • 188
  Daniel's • 191
  in Book of Revelation • 195
  preaching the gospel • 198
Triumphant entry • 68
Turn to God • 119
Twelve disciples • 59
Union of believers with Christ • 149, 176
Vicarious death • 93
Virgin birth • 39
Virgin Mary • 39
Warning • 132
Wars of the Beast • 201
Zacharias • 38

Genesis
1:26, 28 • 9
1:27 • 9
1:31 • 236
2:7 • 9
2:9 • 237
2:15-17 • 10
2:17 • 13
3:1 • 44
3:4-6 • 10
3:11-13 • 10
3:14, 15 • 11
3:15 • 15, 18, 33, 39, 105, 237
3:16, 19, 23 • 11
3:23, 24 • 12
4:7 • 11
5:3 • 9
6:5 • 233
6:5, 11-13 • 12
6:5-8 • 190
7:6-23 • 190, 233
9:6 • 9
12:1 • 128
12:1-3 • 18
12:1-3, 7 • 174
12:4-8 • 18
13:16 • 18, 174
15:5, 7, 18 • 18, 174
15:6 • 18, 142, 146
16 • 166
17:1-4 • 127
17:1-11 • 19
17:4ff. • 174
17:15-17 • 19
19 • 174
21:1-7 • 12, 19, 127
21:12 • 166, 174
22:2 • 156
22:2, 12 • 20, 127
22:13, 18 • 20
22:16ff. • 174
22:18 • 41
25:1, 2 • 166
25:29-34 • 20
26:3, 4 • 20, 174
26:23 • 20
27:7 • 20
27:30-45 • 20
28:4 • 21
28:13 • 174
32:28 • 21
35:10-12 • 21
35:12 • 174
37 • 21
41:16 • 21
46:3, 4 • 21

Exodus
1:7-22 • 21
1:15-22 • 22
2:23, 24 • 22
3-12 • 22
4:21 • 168
5:2 • 168
5:22–6:8 • 167
7:3 • 168
8:15; cf. 8:32 • 168
9:12 • 168
10:1, 20, 27 • 168
11:10 • 168
12:13, 14 • 23
12:32, 37, 40 • 23
12:46 • 79
13:2, 13 • 41
14:24 • 28
19:1 • 23
19:3-6 • 23
19:8 • 23
20:3-17 • 24
21-23 • 24
21:30 • 89
24:3, 7, 8 • 24
25-27 • 24
25:17-22 • 91
28-29 • 25
29 • 25
32 • 29
32:25-29 • 25
33:9, 10 • 28
33:19 • 167
34:6, 7 • 17
40:34, 35 • 28

Leviticus
1:4 • 26
4:20, 26, 31, 35 • 98
4:24 • 99
8 • 25
10:1-5 • 25
10:6-20 • 25
11:44 • 16
16 • 27
16:7, 8 • 91
16:11-17 • 25
16:13, 14 • 123
16:13, 14; 17:11 • 91
16:16 • 27
16:21 • 27
16:22 • 98
17:11 • 26, 27
18:4, 5 • 26, 86
18:5 • 170
19:2 • 16
19:18 • 157
24:8 • 27

Numbers
9:12 • 79
13:27-30 • 28
14:2, 3 • 28
14:18 • 17
18:15, 16 • 41
20 • 28
20:8 • 28
27:18-23 • 29

Deuteronomy
2:34 • 28
4 • 28
6:5 • 157
6:12, 13 • 28
6:13 • 45
7:2 • 28
7:6ff. • 175
7:13 • 17
8:1-3 • 44
9 • 29
9:6 • 29
10:8, 9 • 25
10:12, 13 • 157
10:15 • 175
11:26-28 • 26
19:15 • 74

21:23 • 79
23:5 • 17
30:11-14 • 170
32:21 • 171
33:3 • 17

Joshua
1:2, 5 • 29
2 • 156
6 • 29
7, 8 • 29
9, 10 • 29
11, 12 • 29
13-20 • 29
14:4 • 29
23, 24 • 30

Judges
2:11, 12 • 30
21:25 • 30

I Samuel
8:1-22 • 30
9:16, 17 • 30
12:12-15 • 31
13:13, 14 • 31
14:24, 27, 39 • 31
15:23 • 31

II Samuel
7 • 31
7:12-17 • 217
7:16 • 217

I Kings
2:3, 4 • 217
6 • 194
8:46 • 12
8:46-48 • 116
9:4-9 • 217
10:9 • 17

II Kings
17:14 • 32
19 • 32
20:17 • 32

I Chronicles
21:1 • 45
22:3 • 194

II Chronicles
2:11 • 17
3-5 • 194
6:37-39 • 116
9:8 • 17

Ezra
3-6 • 194

Nehemiah
9:2 • 32
9:17 • 17

Psalm
5:5 • 16
8:5 • 9
11:5 • 16
16:10 • 80
16:11 • 231
34:19-22 • 79
45:7 • 16
69:22, 23 • 172
89:35-37 • 217
91:11-12 • 45
97:10 • 17
99:9 • 16
102:25, 26 • 229
103:8 • 17
145:17 • 16
147:8 • 17

Proverbs
13:8 • 89
15:9 • 16

Ecclesiastes
7:20 • 12

Isaiah
1:16-18 • 116
2:2-4 • 220
7:14 • 33, 39
9:1, 2 • 33
9:6 • 33, 40
9:6ff. • 218

10:22, 23 • 169
11:6-9 • 220
14:12-15 • 10
24–28 • 195
24:23 • 218
25:8 • 231
27:9 • 174
28:16 • 170
29:10 • 172
29:13 • 140
32:1ff. • 218
35:1, 2 • 220
37:22 • 204
40:3 • 33, 38, 43, 116
42:4 • 218
48:14 • 17
52:7 • 171
53:1 • 171
53:3 • 72
53:3-12 • 34
53:4-6 • 93, 96
53:6 • 12
53:6, 11, 12 • 97
53:10 • 98
55:7 • 116
59:1, 2 • 16
59:2 • 11
59:20, 21 • 174
61:1 • 46, 49
62:2 • 34
63:3 • 206
65:1 • 171
65:2 • 171
65:15 • 34
65:17-19 • 229
65:18, 19 • 231
65:19, 20, 25 • 221
66:22 • 229

Jeremiah
13:13, 14 • 217
22:2-5, 17, 18, 24-30 • 217
23:5 • 218
25:30, 31 • 206
29:16-19 • 217
30:3 • 185
30:7 • 193, 194

30; 31; 33 • 221
31:4, 21 • 204
31:31-34 • 34, 163
31:33 • 104
31:33, 34 • 165
32:18 • 17
33:7-9 • 185
33:14-16 • 40
33:15ff. • 218
36:3-8 • 217

Lamentations
2:13 • 204

Ezekiel
14:6 • 116
18:4, 20 • 26
18:21-32 • 116
21:27 • 218
26-28 • 15
28:2 • 15
28:15-17 • 10
33:10 • 185
34:23 • 218
36 • 221
37:11, 12 • 185
37:15, 17 • 185
37:21-23 • 186
37:24 • 186
37:28 • 186
38:2-4 • 212
38:8, 9 • 213
38:13 • 213
38:14, 23 • 216
38:14-16 • 213
38:19-23 • 214
39:4, 9, 12, 17 • 216
39:6-8 • 216
39:13, 21, 22, 25 • 216
39:24 • 195
39:28, 29 • 216

Daniel
2:35, 44 • 184, 201
2:41ff. • 207
2:44 • 218
7:1-8 • 192
7:7, 24 • 207

7:17 • 192
7:21, 22 • 201
7:23-25 • 202
7:23-27 • 192
7:27 • 202, 218
8:23-25 • 192
9:24-27 • 193, 195
9:26 • 193
9:27 • 193, 194, 197, 198
11:31 • 194, 198
11:36-39 • 202
11:36-45 • 199
11:40-44 • 212
11:40ff. • 202
11:44 • 213
11:45 • 213
12:1 • 193, 194, 195
12:1-3 • 215
12:11 • 194, 195

Hosea
1:10 • 169
2:23 • 169
3:4, 5 • 218
11:1 • 42

Joel
2:28 • 35
2:28, 32 • 170
2:28-32 • 84
2:32 • 136

Amos
5:2 • 204

Jonah
3:8, 10 • 118
3:8-10 • 116
4:2 • 17

Micah
4, 5 • 221
5:2 • 35, 40

Habakkuk
1:12, 13 • 16
2:4 • 123, 143

Zechariah
3:8, 9 • 35
9:9 • 35, 67
9:9, 10 • 218
11:12 • 35
12-14 • 199
12 ff. • 195
12:1-3, 6 • 214
12:8, 9 • 214
12:10 • 35
12:10-11, 13:1 • 211
13:2-6 • 212
13:6 • 35
13:7 • 35
14 • 174
14:9 • 218
14:16 • 221
14:16, 17 • 221

Malachi
3:1 • 35, 43
3:1, 2 • 40
4:5, 6 • 35, 43

Matthew
1:16 • 40
1:18-22 • 63
1:20, 22, 23 • 39
1:21 • 87
1:23 • 33, 106
2 • 35
2:1 • 40
2:12-18 • 199
2:13-15 • 42
2:23 • 42
3 • 35
3:1-10 • 116
3:2 • 114
3:3 • 33, 43, 116
3:6 • 43
3:7, 10 • 116
3:8, 10 • 43
3:9 • 43
3:11 • 43
3:12 • 226
3:14-16 • 43
3:17 • 66

4:1-11 • 44	9:35 • 50, 59	16:8-10 • 129
4:3, 4 • 44	10:1, 7 • 59	16:13-20 • 63
4:5-7 • 45	10:15 • 228	16:21 • 93
4:8, 10 • 45	10:16-18 • 59	16:21, 23 • 66
4:11 • 45	10:16-25 • 56	16:24, 25 • 55, 138
4:15, 16 • 33	10:24-28 • 60	16:27 • 11, 13, 224
4:17 • 114, 117	10:32, 33 • 136	17:2, 3, 5 • 65
4:17, 23 • 50	10:33 • 225	17:9, 12, 13 • 65
4:23 • 50	10:34-39 • 55	17:12 • 93
4:23-25 • 49	10:36, 37 • 56	17:22, 23 • 66
5–7 • 52, 158	10:38, 39 • 137	18:1-6 • 134
5:6 • 117	10:41 • 232	18:3 • 51, 133
5:8 • 134	11:1 • 50	18:9 • 226
5:10 • 117	11:10 • 38	19:1-12 • 63
5:12 • 232	11:13-15 • 43	19:28ff. • 219
5:17-20 • 62	11:20-23 • 120	20:18, 19 • 66
5:18 • 182, 229	11:21, 22 • 14, 228	20:18ff. • 75
5:20 • 53, 117	11:28-30 • 56	20:25-28 • 67
5:22 • 226	12:1-8 • 62	20:27, 28 • 90
5:38-45 • 158	12:22-30 • 52	20:28 • 41, 87
5:46 • 11	12:28, 29 • 105	21:1-9 • 218
6:1 • 232	12:38 • 50	21:5, 7-11 • 67
6:1-34 • 53	12:41 • 118, 120	21:6, 7 • 187
6:30 • 129	13 • 171	21:12, 13 • 69
6:33 • 117	13:3-9 • 51	21:15, 16 • 68
6:9 • 16	13:15 • 119	21:18-22 • 130
7:1-12 • 53	13:16, 17 • 63	21:23-25 • 70
7:13, 14 • 53, 224	13:18-23 • 130	21:28–22:14 • 70
7:15ff. • 53	13:18-30 • 51	21:29 • 118
7:21 • 137	13:24-30, 36-43 • 190	21:32 • 118
7:21-27 • 53	13:31, 32 • 51	21:42, 43 • 70
7:22, 23 • 224	13:33 • 51	21:43 • 70
7:23 • 226	13:36-43 • 51	21:45, 46 • 70
7:29 • 50	13:38 • 12, 52, 158	22:8, 9 • 173
8:1-4 • 59	13:40-43, 49 • 223	22:13 • 15, 227
8:2-34 • 59	13:42 • 227	22:14 • 70
8:8-10 • 129	13:42, 50 • 15, 226	22:15-18, 21 • 70
8:12 • 15, 227	13:43 • 230	22:29-33 • 71
8:13 • 130	13:44-50 • 51	22:30 • 232
8:23-27 • 129	14:1-12 • 60	22:36-40 • 71, 157
9:1-34 • 59	14:5, 7 • 60	22:37, 39 • 134
9:2 • 129	14:13 • 61	22:42-45 • 71
9:8, 26, 31, 33 • 59	14:13-21 • 61	23:3, 4, 13, 24-27, 37-39 • 71
9:9-13 • 54	14:31 • 129	23:15 • 228
9:13 • 114, 117	15:1-9 • 140	23:37-39 • 66
9:14-17 • 62	15:3, 7-9 • 61	24 • 190, 195
9:20-22 • 129	15:11, 19 • 61	24, 25 • 72, 181, 186
9:28, 29 • 130	16:3, 4 • 62	

Redemption Realized through Christ 247

24:2 • 68, 182, 194
24:3 • 181, 182
24:4, 5 • 186
24:4, 5, 11-13 • 102
24:6, 7 • 196
24:6, 8 • 187
24:6-8 • 191
24:8 • 198
24:9 • 187
24:10 • 188
24:11-13 • 188
24:14 • 198
24:15 • 194
24:15, 16 • 198
24:21 • 193
24:27 • 233
24:29-31 • 190, 209
24:30 • 181
24:32, 33 • 232
24:33 • 232
24:34, 35 • 232
24:37 • 181
24:37-39 • 190, 233
24:42, 44 • 181
24:42-44 • 233
24:51 • 15, 227
25:1-12 • 234
25:1-13 • 204
25:6, 10 • 191
25:13 • 235
25:14-28 • 235
25:21-28 • 235
25:29, 30 • 235
25:30 • 227
25:31 • 181, 223
25:32, 33, 40 • 223
25:41 • 226
25:41, 46 • 226
25:45 • 233
25:48-51 • 233
26:1-5 • 72
26:26, 28, 36 • 40
26:26-28 • 73
26:28 • 90
26:30-35 • 73
26:31 • 35
26:39-46 • 73
26:47-56 • 74

26:59-61 • 74
26:63, 64 • 74
26:64 • 181
26:65-68 • 74
27:1, 2 • 75
27:3 • 35
27:18 • 75
27:22-25 • 76
27:27-37 • 76
27:29, 33 • 76
27:38-44 • 77
27:40-43 • 77
27:45, 46 • 77
27:46 • 77
27:51-53 • 78
27:54 • 78
27:57-61 • 79
27:64, 65 • 79
28:1-6 • 80
28:16, 17 • 81
28:18-20 • 83
28:19 • 140

Mark
1:12 • 44
1:12, 13 • 44
1:14, 15, 22 • 49
1:14, 38, 39 • 50
1:15 • 60, 114, 116, 122, 130, 158
2:5 • 122, 129
2:10 • 58
2:17 • 114, 117
2:18-28 • 62
2:23-28 • 62
3:12 • 59
4:1-20 • 51
4:13-20 • 130
4:30-32 • 51
4:36-41 • 129
5:25-34 • 129
5:35 • 50
5:43 • 59
6:11 • 115
6:12 • 114
6:14-29 • 60
6:31 • 61
6:32, 33 • 61

6:35-44 • 61
7:1-13 • 61, 140
7:14-23 • 61
7:36 • 59
8:10-12 • 62
8:22-26, 30 • 59
8:27-30 • 64
8:31 • 93
8:31-33 • 66
8:34, 35 • 138
8:34–9:1 • 55
8:38 • 225
9:2-13 • 65
9:9 • 59
9:43, 48 • 226
9:45, 46 • 227
10:13-16 • 134
10:32-34 • 66
10:42-45 • 67
10:45 • 87, 90
11:1-10 • 67
11:7-10 • 218
11:15-17 • 69
11:18 • 69
11:22- 24 • 130
11:27-33 • 70
12:1-11 • 70
12:12 • 70
12:13-17 • 71
12:18-27 • 71
12:25 • 232
12:28-34 • 71
12:35-37 • 71
12:38-40 • 72
13 • 186
13:12 • 188
13:13 • 188
13:14 • 198
13:19 • 193
13:2 • 68, 182, 194
13:4 • 181, 182
13:5, 6 • 186
13:7, 8 • 187
13:9, 11 • 59, 187
13:24-27 • 190
13:28, 29 • 232
13:30, 31 • 232
13:31 • 229

14:1, 2 • 72
14:22-25 • 73
14:24 • 90
14:26-31 • 73
14:27 • 35
14:32-42 • 73
14:43-50 • 74
14:53-65 • 75
15:1 • 75
15:7-15 • 76
15:16-26 • 76
15:29-32 • 77
15:33-35 • 77
15:38 • 78
15:39 • 78
15:42-47 • 79
16:1-6 • 80, 122
16:14 • 81
17:33 • 55

Luke
1:5, 6 • 38
1:9, 15-17 • 38
1:15 • 50
1:16, 17 • 119
1:27-35 • 39
1:32, 33 • 200, 219
1:68-75 • 219
1:80 • 42
2:1-7 • 40
2:5 • 122, 129
2:7-11 • 40
2:10 • 58
2:14 • 54
2:17 • 114, 117
2:18-28 • 62
2:23, 24 • 41
2:23-28 • 62
2:29-32 • 41
2:36-38 • 41
2:41-51 • 42
2:46, 47, 49 • 42
3:1-14 • 116
3:2-4 • 42
3:4 • 116
3:4-6 • 43
3:7, 8 • 116
3:12 • 59

3:23, 31 • 40
4:1-4 • 45
4:1-13 • 44
4:1-20 • 51
4:5-12 • 45
4:13 • 45
4:13-20 • 130
4:16-21, 24, 28, 29 • 49
4:18 • 46
4:21-30 • 49
4:30-32 • 51
4:36-41 • 129
4:44 • 50
5:20 • 122, 129
5:25-34 • 129
5:31, 32 • 117
5:32 • 114
5:33-38 • 62
5:35 • 50
5:43 • 59
6:1-5 • 62
6:11 • 115
6:12 • 114
6:14-29 • 60
6:31 • 61
6:32, 33 • 61
6:35 • 232
6:35-44 • 61
7:1-13 • 61, 140
7:7-9 • 129
7:14-23 • 61
7:27 • 38
7:36 • 59
7:36-50 • 62, 130
7:48 • 58
8:1 • 50
8:4-15 • 51
8:9-15 • 130
8:10-12 • 62
8:11-14 • 130
8:12 • 122
8:22-25 • 129
8:22-26, 30 • 59
8:27-30 • 64
8:31 • 93
8:31-33 • 66
8:34, 35 • 138
8:34–9:1 • 55

8:38 • 225
8:43-48 • 129
9:2-13 • 65
9:7-9 • 60
9:9 • 59
9:18-21 • 64
9:22 • 93
9:23, 24 • 137
9:23-27 • 55
9:26 • 225
9:28-36 • 65
9:43, 48 • 226
9:45, 46 • 227
9:57, 58 • 54
9:59-62 • 54
9:62 • 161
10:3 • 56, 60
10:13 • 120
10:13, 14 • 228
10:23, 24 • 63
10:27 • 134
10:27, 28 • 157
11:32 • 118, 120
12:8, 9 • 136
12:28 • 129
12:39, 40 • 234
12:47, 48 • 15, 228
12:51-53 • 55
13:3 • 114, 117
13:3, 5 • 120
13:27 • 224, 226
13:28 • 15, 227
13:33-35 • 66
14:26 • 55
14:27 • 55
14:27, 33 • 56
15:7, 10 • 117
16:23, 24 • 226
16:26 • 226
17, 21 • 186
17-21 • 181
17:1, 3 • 118
17:20, 21 • 52
17:24 • 233
17:25 • 93
17:26 • 181
17:26-30 • 190, 233
18:17 • 134

18:18 • 50	23:9, 11 • 75	3:2, 5, 6 • 47
18:31-33 • 66	23:13-25 • 76	3:3 • 52, 104, 133
19:10 • 103	23:14-16 • 75	3:3, 5 • 52
19:28-40 • 67	23:27-38 • 76	3:3-6 • 132
19:35-38 • 218	23:34 • 77	3:3-7 • 27, 51
19:39, 40 • 68	23:35-37 • 77	3:5, 6 • 137
19:41-44 • 68	23:44 • 77	3:6 • 134, 177
19:45, 46 • 69	23:46 • 40, 78	3:7, 8 • 133
20:1-8 • 70	23:47 • 78	3:9-15 • 48
20:9-18 • 70	23:48 • 78	3:10-15 • 48
20:19, 20 • 70	23:50-56 • 79	3:14, 15 • 131
20:21-26 • 71	24:1-7 • 80	3:15-18 • 122
20:27-40 • 71	24:11 • 80	3:16 • 17, 86, 103
20:35 • 232	24:14-27 • 80	3:16-18 • 131
20:41-44 • 71	24:27, 44ff • 63	3:16-21 • 48
20:45-47 • 72	24:31-39 • 81	3:17 • 67
21:5-19 • 56	24:39 • 40	3:18 • 102
21:6 • 182, 194	24:44-49 • 81	3:29 • 208
21:7 • 181, 182	24:46 • 81, 93	3:30-36 • 44
21:8 • 186	24:47 • 115, 117, 121, 140	4:21-24 • 49
21:9-11 • 187		5:1-18 • 62
21:11 • 187		5:17, 18 • 40
21:12-15 • 59	John	5:21 • 46
21:12-19 • 60	1:1, 14 • 39	5:22 • 215
21:15 • 187	1:1-3, 14 • 40	5:22, 27 • 205
21:16 • 188	1:10, 14 • 40	5:24 • 122, 131, 225
21:20, 21 • 198	1:12 • 103	5:25-29 • 119, 223
21:24 • 51, 174	1:12, 13 • 131	5:29 • 11, 13
21:25-28 • 190	1:14 • 40	6:2, 14 • 59
21:29-31 • 232	1:14-17 • 107	6:32-58 • 176
21:32, 33 • 232	1:18, 29 • 101	6:35, 40, 45-51 • 57
21:34-36 • 234	1:23 • 43, 116	6:37-44 • 190
21:36 • 181, 189	1:29 • 45, 78, 95, 98, 99, 101	6:39, 40 • 223
22:1 • 100	1:29-31, 34, 36 • 43	6:40 • 131
22:1, 2 • 72	1:29-34 • 43	6:44, 54 • 223
22:15 • 93	1:36, -37, 41 • 46	6:45 • 104
22:17-20 • 73	1:38 • 50	6:47 • 122
22:19 • 87	1:40-42 • 46	7:31 • 59
22:20 • 90	1:41 • 63	8:1-8 • 62
22:29, 30 • 219	1:43, 45, 49 • 46	8:12 • 57
22:31-38 • 73	2:1-11 • 47	8:29 • 46
22:32 • 119	2:4, 11 • 47	8:31, 32, 51 • 138
22:39-46 • 74	2:11, 23 • 59	8:31-36, 51 • 57
22:42 • 102	2:16 • 47	8:31-38 • 138
22:47-53 • 74	2:19 • 47	8:40 • 40
22:66-71 • 75	2:23 • 47	8:44 • 12, 52, 158
23:1 • 75	3:2 • 50, 59, 132	8:46 • 46
23:4, -5 • 75		8:56 • 63

8:58 • 40
9:5 • 57
9:16, 31-33 • 59
9:35 • 50
10:1-17 • 57
10:10-18 • 67
10:11, 15, 16 • 87
10:17, 18 • 78
10:25-28 • 122
10:27, 28 • 135
10:35 • 62
11:1 • 50
11:24 • 223
11:25, 26 • 57, 122
11:33 • 40
11:47-53 • 69
11:53 • 69
12:12-16 • 218
12:12-19 • 67
12:15 • 35
12:18 • 59, 68
12:19 • 69
12:28 • 66
12:31 • 12, 105
12:35, 36 • 57
12:36, 44, 46 • 122
12:37, 42-43 • 72
12:41 • 33, 93, 95
12:42, 43 • 72
12:46-48 • 215
12:47 • 67
12:47, 48 • 72
12:47-50 • 58
12:48 • 225
13:5, 15-17 • 73
13:13 • 50
14:1, 6 • 122
14:2, 3 • 181
14:3, 23 • 189
14:15 • 134, 157
14:15, 21 • 135
14:15, 21-24 • 58
14:15-24 • 135
14:16, 17 • 60
14:21-24 • 138
14:23 • 208
14:26 • 60, 65, 83
14:27 • 56

14:27, 28 • 181
15:1, 11 • 58
15:1-6 • 102
15:1-8 • 135
15:2-10 • 177
15:6 • 226
15:8 • 208
15:9, 10 • 138
15:10 • 179
15:19 • 52, 158
15:26, 27 • 60
16:13-15 • 60
16:33 • 56
17:5 • 40
17:6 • 158
17:6, 16 • 52
17:7, 8, 17, 20 • 60
17:11 • 16
17:14 • 52
17:14, 16 • 158
17:17, 19 • 100
17:22, 23 • 177
18:3-11 • 74
18:12-24 • 75
18:28 • 75
18:31 • 75
18:38–19:16 • 76
19:12 • 75
19:19-22 • 76
19:28 • 77
19:30 • 78, 81
19:31-42 • 79
19:36, 37 • 79
19:37 • 35
20:9 • 79
20:30 • 59
20:30, 31 • 47, 131

Acts
1:3 • 82, 180
1:6, 7 • 219, 235
1:8 • 60, 65, 83, 115, 140
1:8-11 • 82, 180
1:9 • 83
1:11 • 181
2 • 35
2:12 • 84

2:16-21 • 84
2:21 • 136, 170
2:22 • 40
2:27, 31 • 80
2:37, 38 • 115
2:37-39 • 84
2:38 • 137
2:41 • 137
2:46 • 78
3:15 • 84
3:18 • 93
3:19 • 115, 118
3:20, 21 • 219
3:21 • 230
4:10-12 • 84
4:33 • 112
5:20 • 115
5:30, 31 • 84
5:31 • 115, 120
6:7 • 128
8 • 141
8:22 • 115
8:32, 35 • 85
9:35 • 119
10:13-15 • 140
10:17-35 • 140
10:39, 40, 43 • 85
10:42 • 119
11:18 • 115, 120
11:19 • 141
11:21 • 119, 179
11:21, 23 • 111
11:23 • 102, 108
13:28 • 106
13:32-39 • 85
13:38, 39, 43 • 107
13:43 • 108
14:3 • 112
14:15 • 119
14:21, 22 • 102
14:26 15:40 • 112
15 • 64
15:1, 2 • 141
15:9-11 • 141
15:11 • 108, 109
15:19 • 119
15:20, 28, 29 • 141
15:40 • 108

17:2, 3 • 85
17:11 • 185
17:18 • 85
17:30 • 115
17:31 • 85, 119, 215
18:5, 6 • 173
18:27 • 109, 123
24:16 • 128
26:18 • 12, 105
20:21 • 115, 116, 118
20:21, 24 • 111
20:24 • 108
26:20 • 115, 118, 119, 121
26:22, 23 • 85, 93

Romans
1:4 • 80
1:5 • 112
1:16, 17 • 123, 144
1:18 • 13
1:18-31 • 144
1:18-32 • 13
1:20 • 14
1:24, 26, 28 • 144, 168
2:1 • 144
2:4 • 119
2:4-11 • 145
2:6 • 11
2:6-9 • 224
2:8, 9 • 13
2:12, 14 • 145
2:14, 15 • 14
2:20 • 26
2:25, 28 • 145
3:1, 2, 9-12 • 145
3:9 • 12
3:10-18 • 13
3:19-30 • 145
3:20 • 14, 26
3:20-22 • 123
3:21 • 91, 124
3:23 • 13
3:24 • 109, 113
3:24, 25 • 89, 124
3:24, 26 • 92
3:25 • 91, 92, 132
3:25, 26 • 123

3:26 • 123
3:28 • 155
4:1-5 • 146
4:3 • 142
4:5, 9-11 • 146
4:13-15 • 147
4:16 • 122, 124
4:16-21 • 147
4:24, 25 • 123, 147
4:25 • 80, 82, 95
5:1 • 123, 124
5:1-10 • 147
5:2 • 124
5:6, 8 • 95
5:6 • 95
5:6, 8 • 95
5:6-8 • 17
5:8 • 86
5:8, 10 • 103
5:8, 18 • 101
5:10, 11 • 104
5:11 • 92
5:12 • 12
5:15 • 40, 108, 148
5:15, 20, 21 • 114
5:18-21 • 148
5:19 • 12, 95
5:20, 21 • 110
6 • 155, 156
6:1 • 149
6:1, 2, 15 • 102
6:2 • 110
6:2-4 • 136
6:2-11 • 149
6:3, 4 • 137
6:4 • 178
6:4, 6 • 105
6:4, 8-12 • 178
6:5, 6 • 177
6:8, 11 • 178
6:10 • 78
6:12, 13 • 149
6:13, 16, 18, 19 • 208
6:14 • 107, 149
6:14, 15, 18 • 110
6:16-18 • 149
6:19, 20, 22 • 150
6:23 • 13

7:4, 6 • 152
7:5 • 134
7:7 • 14
7:7-12 • 152
7:8-12 • 153
7:14-20 • 153
7:18-25 • 153
8:2 • 46
8:3, 4 • 40, 41, 99
8:4-6 • 154
8:7 • 86
8:7, 8 • 134
8:7-13 • 154
8:9, 10, 16 • 132
8:9-11 • 177
8:11, 13 • 112
8:14 • 103, 154
8:14-17 • 155
8:17 • 56
8:21, 22 • 230
8:32 • 17, 87
8:33 • 190
8:34 • 87
9 • 167
9–11 • 166
9:4, 5 • 166
9:6-8 • 166
9:11-13 • 166
9:14 • 166
9:15, 16 • 167
9:17 • 167
9:18 • 168
9:19, 20, 23 • 168
9:25, 26 • 169
9:27, 29 • 169
9:30-32 • 169
9:30ff. • 173
10:1 • 169
10:2-4 • 169
10:4 • 124
10:5 • 170
10:6, 7 • 170
10:8-10 • 170
10:9, 10 • 124, 136
10:10 • 131, 136
10:11 • 170
10:13 • 136
10:15 • 171

10:16 • 171	11:23-26 • 73	2:16 • 124, 125, 142
10:18 • 171	11:26 • 181	2:20 • 125
10:19-21 • 171	12:13 • 137	2:21 • 108
10:21 • 171	13:12 • 230	3 • 127
11:1, 2 • 171	15:3 • 91	3:6-8, 10 • 142
11:3-6 • 172	15:9 • 9	3:12-14 • 143
11:5, 6 • 107	15:10 • 112	3:13 • 89
11:7 • 172	15:17 • 82	3:14 • 125
11:8-10 • 172	15:21 • 40	3:16, 17 • 143
11:11 • 172	15:21, 22 • 12	3:19-29 • 143
11:13, 14 • 173	15:22-24 • 210	3:27 • 137
11:15 • 173	15:23 • 181	3:28 • 176
11:16 • 173	15:35 • 231	4:4 • 38
11:17, 18 • 173	15:35-44 • 211	4:4, 5 • 36, 89
11:19-24 • 174	15:37-41 • 231	4:9 • 126
11:25 • 51	15:44, 49 • 231	4:9, 10 • 143
11:25, 26 • 174	15:45 • 46	4:19 • 105
11:28, 29 • 174	15:49, 50 • 231	5:3, 4 • 108
11:31-33, 36 • 175	15:50-53 • 211	5:4, 6 • 144
12–16 • 158	15:54-57 • 161	5:14 • 157
12:2 • 158	16:23 • 108	5:16, 21, 24 • 150
13:8-10 • 157		5:19-21 • 13
13:12 • 52	II Corinthians	5:22 • 56
14:8, 9 • 87	1:12 • 111	5:24 • 55, 105, 134, 178
14:10 • 119	3:18 • 105, 112	6:7, 8 • 224
14:15 • 87	4:4 • 12	6:10 • 128
14:17 • 56	5:10 • 11, 119, 224	6:14 • 178
15:15 • 112	5:14, 15 • 86, 101	6:15 • 134, 144
15:16 • 112	5:14, 15, 17, 21 • 150	6:18 • 108
15:16-19 • 150	5:15 • 100	
16:20, 24 • 108	5:17 • 27, 134	Ephesians
16:25, 26 • 18	5:17, 18 • 104	1:1, 7 • 125
	5:18, 19, 21 • 101	1:4 • 175
I Corinthians	5:21 • 46, 82, 96, 98, 100, 147	1:6, 7 • 114
1:2 • 137	7:9-11 • 120	1:7 • 103, 106
1:5 • 126	8:1 • 108, 113	1:7, 8 • 89
1:7 • 181, 236	9:14 • 108	1:17, 18 • 126
1:21 • 123	9:14, 15 • 114	2:1-5, 10 • 150
2:12, 13 • 112	9:8, 14 • 113	2:1-10 • 111
2:16 • 102	11:2 • 204	2:2 • 12, 52, 200
3:10 • 108, 112	11:3 • 10	2:3 • 12
4:5 • 119, 181		2:4, 5 • 17
6:20 • 89, 90	Galatians	2:5 • 109, 178
7:23 • 89, 90	1:4 • 87, 95	2:5, 6 • 175
8:11 • 87	1:6 • 108, 142	2:6, 7 • 179
9:25 • 121	1:11, 12 • 142	2:8 • 114, 123
9:27 • 128	1:15 • 113	2:8, 9 • 124
11:7 • 9		

2:11, 14, 16 • 175
2:11-22 • 175
2:13 • 87
2:16 • 104
2:19, 20 • 65
3:1, 6, 8 • 175
3:2, 7, 8 • 113
3:5, 6, 9 • 176
4:5, 13 • 128
4:17 • 175
4:22, 23 • 52
4:23, 24 • 106
4:24 • 9, 104
5:2 • 86, 99
5:25-27 • 208

Philippians
1:29, 30 • 56
2:5-8 • 55, 88
2:6-8 • 40
2:7 • 39
3:9 • 124
3:10 • 56, 126
3:10, 11 • 178
4:23 • 108

Colossians
1:2, 10, 13 • 125
1:2, 10, 13, 21, 22 • 151
1:5, 6, 10 • 111
1:13 • 12
1:13, 14 • 89
1:14 • 103
1:15-19 • 151
1:19 • 40
1:19, 20 • 104
1:21 • 12
1:23 • 102
2:4-8, 18, 19 • 102
2:7 • 128
2:11, 12, 14 • 151
2:12 • 137, 178
2:13 • 103, 178
2:16, 17 • 26
3:1 • 178
3:2 • 134
3:4 • 181

3:9, 10 • 52, 105
3:10 • 9
3:11 • 176
3:12 • 190
3:14 • 157
3:25 • 11, 13, 224
5:6 • 125

I Thessalonians
1:9 • 119
1:10 • 181
2:19 • 181
3:13 • 181
4:1, 3, 7 • 151
4:13-17 • 210
4:13-18 • 189
4:14 • 88
4:14-17 • 188
4:15-17 • 181
4:17 • 191
5:1-6 • 236
5:2 • 181
5:3, 9 • 189
5:28 • 109

II Thessalonians
1:7, 8 • 225
1:7, 10 • 181
1:8, 9 • 13
1:9 • 227
1:12 • 109
2:2, 8 • 181
2:3, 4 • 194
2:8-10 • 203
2:13 • 150
2:16 • 109, 114
3:18 • 109

I Timothy
1:5 • 134
1:13, 14 • 113
1:14 • 109
2:3, 4 • 126
2:4, 6 • 101
2:5 • 40, 46, 106
2:5, 6 • 88, 90
2:6 • 106
2:9 • 158

3:6 • 10
3:16 • 40
4:1 • 128
4:1, 16 • 102
4:10 • 101
5:8 • 128
6:10 • 128
6:14 • 181

II Timothy
1:9 • 17, 109, 114
1:12 • 126, 127
2:10 • 190
2:12 • 56
2:25 • 120
3:14 • 102
3:16 • 131
3:16, 17 • 158
4:3, 4 • 102
4:7 • 128

Titus
1:1 • 190
1:2 • 17
2:11 • 109
2:11, 12 • 109
2:11-14 • 151
2:13 • 181
2:13, 14 • 89
2:13,14 • 88
3:3-7 • 152
3:4, 5 • 86
3:4-7 • 108
3:5 • 27, 112, 137
3:5, 7 • 122
3:7 • 109

Philemon
25 • 109

Hebrews
1:2, 3 • 40
2:1, 3 • 160
2:1-3 • 102
2:8, 9 • 161
2:9 • 9, 95, 101, 108
2:9, 10 • 93
2:9, 10, 17 • 92

2:14 • 39
2:14, 15 • 105, 161
2:17 • 161
2:17, 18 • 45
3:1-14 • 102
3:7, 8, 12, 13 • 160
4:15 • 39, 45, 106
4:16 • 113
5:1, 6, 8-10 • 161
5:8, 9 • 94
5:8-10 • 161
6:1 • 118, 125
6:4-6 • 160
7:3 • 162
7:4, 6, 7, 9 • 162
7:11 • 162
7:16-19 • 162
7:22 • 104
7:24, 25 • 162
7:26, 27 • 163
7:26-28 • 78
8:1, 2, 5, 6 • 163
8:5 • 26
8:8-12 • 34
8:10 • 104
8:12 • 118
9:5 • 91
9:7 • 25
9:7, 12-14, 26, 28 • 91
9:9-14 • 163
9:12, 14 • 82
9:12, 14, 26 • 78
9:12, 15 • 89
9:14 • 45, 46
9:15 • 164
9:22 • 27
9:22, 26, 28 • 99
9:22-28 • 164
9:24, 26 • 80
9:26 • 96
9:28 • 97, 99
10 • 102
10:1 • 26
10:1-14 • 164
10:4, 12, 14 • 92
10:12 • 78, 88, 96
10:12, 14 • 99
10:16 • 104

10:16-17 • 165
10:17 • 118
10:19-23 • 165
10:20, 22 • 104
10:26, 27 • 161
10:32-39 • 165
10:37-39 • 125
11 • 126, 128
11:1, 3, 6 • 126
11:13, 40 • 63
12:1, 4 • 121
12:15 • 108
13:9 • 113
13:12 • 88

James
1:1 • 186
2:8 • 157
2:14-16 • 155
2:18 • 155
2:19 • 155
2:21, 22 • 128
2:22-24 • 156
2:24 • 155
2:25 • 156
2:26 • 156
3:9 • 9
4:6 • 114
5:7 • 181
5:19, 20 • 102

I Peter
1:2 • 150
1:10, 11 • 33, 63, 184
1:14-16 • 159
1:15, 16 • 16
1:17 • 11
1:18, 19 • 89, 90, 95
1:19 • 45, 97, 99, 106
1:20 • 17
1:23 • 52, 134
2:2 • 52
2:22 • 39, 45
2:22, 24 • 97
2:24 • 94, 147
3:3 • 158
3:18 • 94, 97, 106
3:21 • 137

4:12-14 • 56
5:4 • 181
5:10 • 56

II Peter
1:4 • 105
1:8-11 • 102
1:16 • 181
1:16-18 • 66
1:21 • 131
2:1 • 89
2:4, 17 • 227
2:20 • 111
3:4, 8-12 • 181
3:9 • 119
3:9-18 • 236
3:10-13 • 230
3:12 • 229
3:16 • 167
3:18, 20 • 111

I John
1:7 • 88
2:1, 2 • 92
2:2 • 91, 101, 106
2:3, 5 • 132
2:5 • 179
2:12 • 103
2:15-17 • 159
2:23-25 • 102
2:28 • 181, 231
3:1 • 103, 106
3:2, 3 • 230
3:2, 10 • 134
3:4 • 14, 86
3:6-10 • 147
3:8 • 12, 105
3:9 • 121
3:10, 14, 18, 19; 4:7
3:16 • 88
3:23, 24 • 179
3:24; 4: 13 • 132
4:2 • 40
4:7, 8, 11 • 134
4:8, 16 • 17
4:9 • 17
4:9, 10 • 86
4:10 • 91, 92

Redemption Realized through Christ 255

4:14 • 101
4:15 • 136
4:15, 16 • 179
4:19 • 86
5:1-5 • 138
5:2 • 132
5:2, 3 • 157
5:13 • 102
5:19 • 126

Jude
3 • 128
4 • 108
7 • 226
13 • 227
15 • 225

Revelation
1:1 • 183
1:7 • 181
1:13, 20 • 205
1:19 • 183, 195
1:20 • 184
2:4, 5 • 120
2:15, 16, 20 • 121
2:23 • 225
3:3 • 236
3:3, 15, 16, 19 • 121
3:10 • 189
3:12 • 228
4:1 • 195
5:1, 2, 9, 10, 12 • 195
5:9 • 88, 89
6–8 • 195
6:2-8 • 196
6:8 • 197
6:9-11 • 190, 196, 201, 217
6:11 • 209
6:16 • 196
7:1, 3, 4 • 196
7:1-4 • 189
7:4 • 204
7:9, 14 • 190, 196
8:7-12 • 197
9:1-19 • 197
9:4 • 190
9:4, 20 • 197

10:1-4 • 197
10:6, 11 • 197
11:1, 2 • 197
11:2 • 195
11:2, 3 • 193
11:7, 10, 11, 13 • 198
11:8 • 184
11:15, 17, 18 • 199
12:2-4 • 199
12:3 • 184
12:5 • 200
12:6 • 193, 200
12:7, 9 • 200
12:9 • 10
12:10, 12 • 200
12:13, 14, 17 • 201
12:17 • 190
12-19 • 199
13:1 • 201
13:1, 11 • 203
13:3, 4 • 203
13:5 • 193
13:5-7 • 203
13:7 • 190, 217
13:9-11 • 203
13:12, 13, 15 • 203
13:15 • 204
13:16-18 • 204
14:1-5 • 204
14:2-4 • 209
14:4, 5 • 204
14:7, 9, 10 • 205
14:9, 12 • 190
14:12, 13, 17 • 205
14:13 • 217
14:14, 15 • 205
14:18, 19 • 205
15:1 • 206
16 • 206
16:14, 16 • 206, 216
17 • 213
17:1, 2 • 206
17:3, 12 • 184
17:3, 5, 18 • 206
17:3, 5, 6 • 206
17:6 • 190, 217
17:7 • 206
17:8, 11 • 206

17:9 • 184
17:9, 10 • 184, 206
17:9-12 • 201
17:12 • 207
17:15 • 201, 203, 207
17:16, 17 • 207
18:4 • 190
18:4, 5, 8 • 207
18:9-11 • 207
18:17, 18 • 207
18:20 • 207
19 • 190, 194
19:1, 2 • 208
19:7 • 190, 209
19:7, 8 • 208
19:9 • 208
19:11, 14-16 • 215
19:11-20 • 206
19:11-21 • 189
19:11ff • 181
19:16 • 220
19:19 • 216
19:20, 21 • 216
20:2 • 10
20:2, 3 • 217
20:4 • 217, 220
20:4-6 • 190, 217
20:7, 8 • 222
20:9, 10 • 222
20:11 • 222
20:12, 13 • 222
20:12-15 • 13, 224
21 • 221
21:1 • 229
21:1, 2 • 221
21:1-3 • 228
21:3-5 • 229
21:4 • 230
21:6, 8 • 229
21:8 • 229
21:9, 24, 27 • 221
21:9-21 • 222
22:12, 20 • 181
22:17, 21 • 237
22:7 • 183